It's very good; wish I had read it forty years ago, even though I wasn't involved ...
church planting.

Mary Jane Faircloth - OMF retired

Cross-cultural church planting, especially among least-reached peoples, is not for the faint of heart. It is arguably the most challenging work in the world, requiring immense insight, tact, spiritual sensitivity, and perseverance. *Cross-Cultural Church Planting for Probies* helps to demystify this central core of our mission. It sounds a clarion call for serious practitioners and a thoughtful preparation and process, commensurate with the task. Roger and Jan Dixon steer clear of reductionist approaches, presenting instead a comprehensive yet hopeful picture of the church-planting journey that is forged in decades of scholarship and ministry to Muslims. This book is a gold mine of wisdom and guidance for any individual, team or church that is contemplating cross-cultural work.

Steve Richardson - President, Pioneers-USA

Roger and Jan Dixon have done the newest generations of church planters a great favor. Drawing on their own 50 year experience and study of church planting, and writing with new practitioners very much in mind, the Dixons have helped fill a crucial niche in equipping "probies," both young and old.

Gary R. Corwin, Missiologist with SIM International Leadership
and Services and Associate Editor of *EMQ*

This book is a remarkable blend of spiritual, social scientific, and leadership insights which every mission candidate and practitioner needs. Roger and Jan went to Indonesia about the same time as my wife and I. All of us were ministering in church planting and development, though with different people groups. Looking back over the struggles, successes, and disappointment we faced, I wish we'd had this book to help us with the many questions we experienced along the way. The book may seem heavy going in places. It may be best studied in a group of candidates or new missionaries.

Dr. Dale F. Walker, Affiliate Professor, Asbury Theological Seminary

Thank you so much for this labor of love. The book "Climbing Higher" was so valuable to our teams to read, yet we didn't know this book was on the way! During the past 5 years, your "Cross Cultural Training Manual," which you taught us in Thailand, was translated/ printed.

Our "unreached people" have begun to be "Sending their 70" like the baton Vision we passed them. Glory to God and thank you for your mentoring.

Thank you for being faithful shepherds to our teams/ feeding His sheep! This fodder is delicious, refreshing and nutritious to the Spirit!!

Anonymous Cross Cultural Leaders among the Muslims in Asia

Cross-Cultural Church Planting for Probies provides a firm and comprehensive foundation for newbies sent by the Great Initiator to engage UPGs. If church planters follow the simple (but not simplistic) steps laid out in this book written by two veterans, chances for holistic movements of multiplying churches will certainly increase.

Tom Steffen, Emeritus professor of intercultural Studies,
Cook School of Intercultural Studies, Biola University

Roger & Jan Dixon have written a primer for missionary candidates, giving wisdom to Christians, who wish to serve among the hardest unreached areas reaching Muslims with the gospel of Jesus Christ. With more than 40 years of experience in Indonesia, the largest Muslim Country, Roger Dixon is a major person we listen to in understanding what needs to be done, and what excesses (Insider Movements) need to be avoided. The book is practical, accessible and a valuable read for Christians called to finish the great commission among Muslims, which is, all of us.

Prof. Joshua Lingel, President i2 Ministries

Roger and Jan Dixon have written an incisive book toward helping rookie church planters engage their cross-cultural contexts with a proper biblical approach and excellent practical ways in doing contextualization.

This is a work of fine blend of biblical principles and workable cross-cultural presentations. It is a must read for beginners as well as those already mature doing missions among the unreached people. I recommend it enthusiastically!

Daniel Lucas Lukito, President, Southeast Asia Bible Seminary, Malang, Indonesia

When I joined a mission working in rural America twenty-plus years ago, I was introduced to the idea that rural church planting in the States is a cross-cultural experience for most of those planters, given that most of them are city people! While this book is geared toward those who are serving in mostly third-world countries, there are plenty of transferable principles to ministry right here in our own backyard, whether born and bred rural people or newly-arrived immigrants. An added bonus is the fact that it's not just a book on the mechanics of church planting, but also the spiritual life of the church planter.

Gary Roseboom - Associate Director- RHMA (Rural Home Missionary Association), Morton, Illinois

Roger and Jan Dixon have done an invaluable service in writing *Cross-Cultural Church Planting for Probies.* They bring years of experience and theoretical insight in cross-cultural church planting among Unevangelized People Groups. Their eight phases of church planting extensively covers from preparing to go into missions to the complex roles of mentoring/coaching, negotiating people/topics and leadership. The wisdom is based in reality giving ideal models to follow, pitfalls to avoid, but acknowledging that failures will happen. The potential thorny subject of contextualization is handled with sensitivity bringing clarity placing it in the context of the whole body of Christ. I highly recommend this excellent work.

Rev. Roy Oksnevad, PhD, Muslim Ministries, Billy Graham Center for Evangelism

Cross-Cultural Church Planting for Probies

A Learning Process Model

ENVISIONING AND FACILITATING HOLISTIC CHURCH
PLANTING AMONG UNREACHED PEOPLE GROUPS FROM
PREPARATION TO CLOSURE

Rev. 7:9-10 -
Roger Dixon
Jan Dixon

Roger L. Dixon Ph.D.

Jan B. Dixon M.Psy.

Bedford, VA

ABOUT THE MICE -

The mice represent what the simplicity and humility of the cross-cultural church planter should be and they perform a role like a Greek chorus in providing variety of background and summary information that helps lighten the heavy material in the book.

TABLE OF CONTENTS

DEDICATION

To all the friends who prayed for and supported us, to all the mentors, both Indonesian and other nationalities, who taught and encouraged us, we dedicate this with thanks and love.

That the Lord God might be glorified in the nations!

PREFACE

This manual is unique in that it contains explanations of mentoring, engagement, negotiation, and a case study of contextualization. These are woven together with other critical aspects that are necessary in a cross-cultural church plant. You will learn how important these skills are to your success. To paraphrase Harry Wong, the renowned teacher trainer, the difference between ineffective cross-cultural church planters and effective cross-cultural church planters is that the former do not do what the latter do. Learn what effective cross-cultural church planters do and follow their example.

These lessons apply to every cross-cultural vocation, particularly those in church work. We help you work effectively as we define the Cross-Cultural Church Planting project; i.e., to obtain clarity, fit, and agreement. You will find an outline of this process in Appendix 4 - Envisioning the Church Planting Project. A Learning Process model is fleshed out in this manual. Each chapter endeavors to explain in more detail the phases you will encounter. At the end of some chapters there are lists of End Results linked with the phase. These are the most important goals you will want to achieve in each phase of the CC CP Project. New workers learn cross-cultural church planting as they "put their hand to the plow" to process these key tasks and reach the end results.

We define CC CP in Chapter One. As we conceptualize it, CC CP has eight (8) phases. We use phases rather than stages because there is no clear boundary between them. The phases have progression but they cannot be compartmentalized. They describe an overlapping and integration of various experiences in the process of CC CP. Some of the so-called phases run on through most of the process while others are more limited. We describe the preparation you need and introduce the various major elements as you might encounter them. That is why the theology of church planting is introduced in chapter 4 but Contextualization in chapter 9. However, you can read them in whichever order you feel the need.

You will find some necessary repetition in the chapters due to information that is pertinent to several phases. Share constantly with your colleagues, friends, acquaintances, and even strangers. You never know when you will find that pearl of wisdom which opens your mind to understand an entirely new way of adjusting evangelism or Christian nurture and even infrastructure to a different culture and belief system.

Although this is not primarily a book about one's spiritual walk with God, that aspect of one's life is the main channel through which God works. The reader will be constantly reminded that CC CP is God's work. The condition of our spiritual lives is much more critical than our abilities and our skills. No matter how much we absorb, we will never be effective church planters unless the Holy Spirit is working through us with power.

Roger Dixon, Ph.D.
Jan Dixon, M. Psy.

GLOSSARY – How we use the terms

CC CP   - Cross-Cultural Church Planting

Coach   - a more controlled process than mentoring; it is guiding people through the process as opposed to mentoring which is explaining the process.

Contextualization - characteristics that emerge through the thought and actions of the focus people and are implemented by them in accordance with their cultural patterns. - defined in detail in Chapter Nine

Counter part   - a national or focus group co-worker of equal status

Expatriate   - all workers from countries foreign to the one where the church planting is being done – used in reference to foreign missionaries.

Focus group/people - the Unreached People Group that is the focus of the ministry

Indigenous   - commonly defined as emerging from the people; in reference to the church it usually means self governing, self-supporting, & self-propagating

Locals   - members of the focus group

Mentor   - a person who can give you information that will guide you in ministering to the focus group

Nationals   - citizens who are from other ethnic groups in the same country with the UPG/ focus group.

Patron-Client   - a type of social organization that is common in a UPG (see Appendix 6)

Tentmaker   - a term taken from Acts 18:3 to indicate that the church planter has a secular profession (actual or theoretical).

UPG   - stands for Unreached People Group; commonly described as an ethnic people with less than 2% Christian with a weak church planting outreach.

CHAPTER ONE

WHAT IS CROSS-CULTURAL CHURCH PLANTING?

Ephesians 3:10 - *"through the **church** the manifold wisdom of God might now be made known to the rulers and authorities in the heavenly places"*

I will never forget the meeting when a young missionary wife in a church planting team among an unreached people group (UPG) asked this question: "What is church planting?" Some of us were stunned that an intelligent, dedicated young woman with Bible training would wind up on the field without even knowing what she was supposed to be doing there. As time has passed, we have found that there are more than a few who are in the same situation as this worker.

Some agencies report as high as 47% of their personnel leave the field in the first 5 years (Taylor, 1997). Others stay longer but do not really succeed in planting churches. This is a tragic waste of outstanding and committed people. We cannot expect them to do a job they have never been trained to do. The new entrepreneurial mission model may be largely to blame for many of the weaknesses. This model is the result of a combination of factors too complicated to discuss here, but include excessive self-confidence, the raising of salary and funds by the individual candidate, and the lack of experienced leadership. Many modern missionaries see themselves as professionals who are already experts, having been allowed by their agencies to train themselves. Some are more mature individuals who have had successful careers, and perhaps the assumption is made that they automatically have the skills they need for church planting.

The worker needs supervision

Americans, like most other national groups, are primarily a supervised labor force. Entrepreneurs are an isolated few. Practically everyone in every country works under the supervision of a foreman, office manager, supervisor or some equivalent position. By its very nature, ministry among a UPG implies that a person be a self starter who can initiate, structure, and carry out work on his or her own. However, many people who come to such a ministry are not even able to structure their daily work schedule. Due to the nature of pioneer church planting, senior workers are seldom on their field to supervise them. In addition, they may not be willing to take supervision because they raise their own support and feel an independence from any authority. And yet, it has become clear to many of us in the past few years that truly learning CC CP must be done in the field.

While books can give guiding principles to elucidate various approaches, and classroom discussions can impart much wisdom, true CC CP has so much variety that it must be learned through experience. When you land in your focus group, you will be in a new laboratory where most of your experiences will be unique. You will have to find your own way by interacting with the phenomena of the new culture. This book attempts to enhance that process by outlining the phases through which you will inevitably go. As David A. Kolb has written, "... this learning process must be reimbued [sic] with the texture and feeling of human experiences shared and interpreted through dialogue with one another" (1983:2).

So much to learn

The Challenge

Very few if any jobs in Christian ministry can compete with cross-cultural church planting for sheer difficulty. In our opinion, no mono-cultural job can. It requires a second language and the complete relearning of one's cultural cues. The average cross-cultural church planter requires 4-5 years in training on the field before he or she can adequately cope with the intricacies of cross-cultural interaction. Even the commitment of many years does not guarantee that one is going to effectively negotiate all the pitfalls involved in the adjustment to another culture. You might have heard or read the phrase "15 years a missionary" as though that is the apex of the profession. In fact, it is probably just at the point of becoming really effective in church planting.

Make no mistake about it. There is no "silver bullet" in CC CP. A very few may have results after a short time but, for the vast majority, any success requires years of training and work. Cross-cultural church planting demands a total commitment of one's gifts, time, energy, and spiritual devotion. It is not a 40 hour week but rather a 24/7 commitment. It is a long journey and we describe phases of that journey in the following chapters.

Cross-cultural church planting is incredibly difficult

Cross-cultural Church Planting Defined

We explain CC CP as comprising three large functions of ministry. These are evangelism, Christian nurture, and church infrastructure. Evangelism is basically explaining the gospel in terms that people can understand as it relates to their own cultural/religious experience. The gospel does not change but there are aspects of it that are more relevant than others. For example, the message of the forgiveness of sin is not too powerful to some people in cultures where sin is not understood as separation from a holy God. This theological awareness and understanding will come later in a person's response to God. The Javanese culture illustrates this. They are more interested in the aspects of power and blessing and these features of the gospel speak to their worldview. It takes study, investigation, and experience to discover what parts of the gospel are most compelling in a given culture.

The models of evangelism are so numerous it is impossible even to list them here. In previous years, the Four Spiritual Facts were used. Then Campus Crusade developed the Four Spiritual Laws. In more recent time, the Church Planting Movement (CPM) has developed a pattern for reaching what they call the "Man of Peace." All of these evangelism tools can be used but you will most likely develop a new approach for your UPG that will relate better to their mindset and will answer their spiritual questions. To be most productive, an evangelism model must answer at least some of a culture's spiritual questions. If you don't speak to a person's spiritual questions you won't likely create any interest in what you are saying.

CC CP has 3 major facets

Christian Nurture

Christian nurture is the second large area of church planting. Stated simply it is mentoring a convert into a close relationship with Jesus. Normally, it is not difficult to nurture a convert in a Christianized culture because the ethics, mores, and rites of passage are influenced by the Bible to the point that a convert *recognizes* many aspects of the biblical faith which have been incorporated into the culture over many centuries. However, in a cross-cultural church plant, this is unlikely because the values and customs are usually quite different due to the influence of a different religion. Biblical theology and its relationship to worldview must be explained clearly or the convert will become a victim of syncretism; that is, biblical doctrine will be blended with the religion of the culture. This is understandable because the convert's entire being is permeated with the worldview of the local religion or belief system. This is what makes Christian nurture so necessary as well as so difficult in the cross-cultural church plant.

Beginning with Christ

Christian nurture begins when a person receives Christ. Most evangelism models incorporate a follow-up of some kind that involves counseling the convert in assurance of salvation. This may be done immediately or in a future meeting. If there is a congregation already formed, the convert will be incorporated into the congregation. However, in the early stages of church planting, the congregation may be very small and fluid with many dropouts due to family and community pressures. New converts should be given some type of catechism in which Christian doctrine and worldview is presented in a systematic way.

The CPM model has an innovative feature to draw the enquirer into a continuing relationship. This method, which they call the "Person of Peace," suggests the forming of a Discovery Bible Study (DBS) to gather the enquirer/family/group to discover God and His salvation. They don't call this catechism but their series of Bible studies functions as one. This method is not evangelism separated from ongoing nurture. Instead, both of these features are linked to the embryo of a congregation. This model incorporates Christian nurture in that it includes prayer, worship, and an accountability structure. Accountability is structured through a series of questions concerning what lessons were shared with others and what ways the lessons were applied during the week.

All Christian evangelism should lead to practices similar to the CPM model if it is to be effective. Different models can be used but the results should be similar. The important point here is that cross-cultural church planting should have some type of catechism integrated in its model because nurture should start immediately.

By using DBS, the CPM model begins Christian nurture very early. Some other evangelism models may not be as intentional in this respect. However, all effective evangelism models will flow into Christian nurture. The narrative theology of much of the Bible is a model for teaching worldview. The Holy Spirit led the writers to record stories that would teach lessons about the nature of God, man, sin, evil, and other aspects of life. There are worldview considerations in all the Bible stories. And these stories are about truth and how God reveals it to mankind. For example, the story of David's adultery is not just about adultery but it is a teaching about the abuse of power and the consequences of sin. David's story is not only in the narrative but is also found in Psalm 51 where David cries out to God to have mercy "according to your steadfast love" and to "create a clean heart" and "renew a right spirit." These and other statements relate important worldview factors concerning God and mankind. Syncretism is always a challenge but it is particularly dangerous when new believers are not taught that biblical worldview is vastly different from that of other religions.

Christian nurture is central

Christian Nurture in the New Testament

The gospels as well as the writings of Paul and the other authors of New Testament letters show a particular concern with the differences between the gospel and the non-biblical philosophies and cosmologies of their day. Since many of these non-biblical constructs are present in UPGs in one form or another, we must wrestle with them. Otherwise, a convert will not grow spiritually. The great themes of the Bible such as those of the Trinity, humanity, sin, and salvation are replete with worldview concepts that must be addressed in any responsible Christian nurture. Even practical functions such as Baptism and the Eucharist (the Lord's Supper) involve worldview factors that should be recognized, explained, and incorporated into the life of a believer.

Church Infrastructure

The third aspect of church planting is church infrastructure. When workers have not had any experience in how a church is organized and operated, they cannot envision what they are trying to accomplish among the UPG. Churches have structure. This includes theology, worship, liturgy, organization, polity (government), and education. Many of these functions involve infrastructure.

Organization involves leadership categories such as pastors, elders, deacons, treasurers, and trustees. Various job descriptions or responsibilities have to be developed. Polity involves constitutions, budgets, committees, requirements for leaders, and various rules that govern the functions of the church. These church organizations frequently follow historical models such as Episcopal, Presbyterian, or Congregational. These are just a few examples. They are all part of infrastructure that must be put in place as the church develops.

A church plant is not a fellowship where there is no significant infrastructure. In a fellowship, there may be no one with responsibility to train evangelists, pastors, or lay leaders. A fellowship does not develop its own publications, music, or youth camps. In order to have long-term success in church development, the church planting team must have an idea of the kind of congregations that will thrive in the UPG.

The church functions within infrastructure

The goal is not to plant a clone church of another culture but rather birth an indigenous church. The leader/pastor should understand the language of the focus people along with the social, political, and leadership models of the culture. This is critical because it is impossible to counsel converts well without using their heart language. The models of the culture will tend to guide the organizational arrangement of the church. Those who mentor the church plant must be able to understand these social models.

The cross-cultural church planter may be involved in one or more of these three cross-cultural church planting functions. Many workers are only involved in one and sometimes in a very specific way. However, all these functions are critical in the planting of a contextualized church. The church planting team must coordinate them so that each function is unified with others as the church matures.

Explaining the Phases

We can describe CC CP as having the three divisions of evangelism, nurture, and infrastructure, but we cannot structure the skills and experiences you will need to do CC CP. The development of your skills and church growth will be fluid and unending. The phases cannot be compartmentalized. In Chapter Two, we introduce Phase One which is Preparation for CC CP. This preparation will continue throughout your career. First, we touch on preparation in your home culture and then preparation in your mission field. But this preparation becomes a way of life as you prepare for such skills as mentoring, engagement, and negotiation.

In Phase Two that is about arrival in your CC CP field, you will read about types of culture and cultural models with which you will have to become familiar. But this learning only begins in the arrival phase. It continues all your life. Most of the important experiences of your arrival phase are introductions to a much broader challenge of learning. In Chapter Four where we write about the theology of church planting, we don't call it a phase even though it can be an evolving process in your mind. Theology of church planting is set in scripture. For that reason we don't call it a phase. However, your theology of church planting should be developing as you orient to the focus group.

Phase Three we describe in Chapter Five as the orientation to the focus group. This phase may actually begin when you are in your home country if you are studying the focus group before you leave. It will undoubtedly be accelerated during the arrival phase but you really won't have much time to study the focus group deeply during that phase. You will be involved in language study, adjustment to your community, to your team, and to your family in this new situation. Phase Three goes on as long as you are living with your focus group.

But it is particularly critical for you to learn as much as you can as fast as you can without putting too much stress on yourself. Enjoy your experience.

Phase Four explains the mentoring component of CC CP in Chapter Six. We feel this skill is one of the key factors in successful CC CP. As you are learning new aspects of the focus culture, you should learn how people mentor. Many, if not all, UPG have mentoring models that are quite different from those used in other cultures and in other ethnic groups in the same country. If you don't learn this skill, it is unlikely you will guide a church plant effectively.

In Chapter Seven, Phase Five outlines the major characteristics of engagement. Many workers on CC CP teams fail to engage the focus people on an intimate basis. They allow such aspects as social distance, ethnic barriers, and even nostalgia for their home culture to prevent them from interacting with the focus people on a profound basis. In order to plant a strong church, a worker must have a close relationship with the focus people as they define closeness.

Phase Six is in Chapter Eight. This phase is where you learn negotiating on a comprehensive plane. Negotiating is the key to sound CC CP. While you do begin to negotiate early on, it is only after you learn the negotiating models of the focus group that you can perform on an enlightened level. Negotiating is a major factor in successfully planting a church.

Having a review of contextualization principles delayed until Chapter Nine does not mean it comes late in your church plant. You must begin to think about it from the beginning of your ministry. However, it is only after you learn the skills of mentoring, engagement, and negotiating that you will truly appreciate the contextualizing process. In general, we use the word contextual to describe characteristics that emerge through the thought and actions of the focus people and are implemented by them. We do not use it to describe models or templates that are created or imposed by non-focus outsiders. However, the focus group may borrow models from other cultures and implement whatever suits them. A contextual church is something that the focus people develop.

Chapter Ten begins the discussion of the Development stage in church planting. We call this Phase Seven. Development may begin early on in your ministry but the critical period begins when you have focus people leading the process. In Part One of the development discussion, we present some ideas about leadership that vary from the contributions of other books.

Part Two about the development phase is in Chapter Eleven. It covers such subjects as advanced steps in guiding the congregation and the development of advanced evangelism and nurture models. At this juncture in the life of the Church, it is critical to cast vision for outreach. Team building takes on new dimensions as focus people learn to work together.

Chapter Twelve completes the phase on development. Church theology, leadership models, governing models and ministry models are all discussed. Other important subjects are factors that hinder growth and the challenges and dangers to a developing church.

In Chapter Thirteen, we discuss closure and ongoing involvement in the church plant. Although a church planter may leave his comrades to carry on alone, it does not mean that there should be no further contact between them. Closure for the church planter is an important transition and may evolve in many ways.

CHAPTER TWO

PHASE ONE - PREPARATION FOR CROSS-CULTURAL CHURCH PLANTING

Ecclesiastes. 1:18 - *"For in much wisdom is much vexation, and he who increases knowledge increases sorrow."*

Now what is first?

INTRODUCTION

This section covers the time when the cross-cultural candidate in his or her home is preparing for field service in a different culture. It is a critical phase for the future success of the cross-cultural church planter. Concentration on areas of preparation and competencies are necessary for success. Competencies in the areas of theology, church polity, linguistics, communication theory, and the like may seem to be tiresome in the classroom but they are invaluable in the field. The lack of these does not mean that the Holy Spirit cannot use a person. However, people with this basic preparation are likely to be used more effectively and more quickly when they reach their assignment. They are less likely to make critical mistakes.

MAJOR PROBLEM

The major problem that most cross-cultural church planters face is a lack of church planting experience. If a person has not done church planting in his/her home country, it will be difficult to do it in a foreign country. The reason is pretty simple and should be obvious. Pioneer church planting involves a complex series of competencies that are only truly understood through involvement. A naïve assumption that people will suddenly understand the complexities of church theology and organization when they go to another country often leads to immature outcomes.

Many people assume that the people in a third world country live a much simpler life than their own. They think this will enable them to adjust easily to the new culture. However, this is a total misunderstanding of the complexity of culture. Even though people in the focus culture may have a simple life style, they are still complex human beings with intricate social structures that affect their behavior.

The outsider only sees the tip of the culture and has difficulty learning what is not spoken but rather is transmitted through experience. Edgar Schein (1992:139) illustrates this by saying: "The final and, perhaps, most difficult aspect of the analysis of such a wide set of assumptions deals with the degree to which they come to be interlocked into paradigms or coherent patterns."

Expatriates are not the only church planters to face difficulties. Nationals also have problems crossing cultural boundaries to minister to people of other ethnic backgrounds. Although the nationals may come from a church background, they cannot automatically structure a church theology and polity for a different ethnic group. This exercise takes considerable time and experience. In the modern revival of outreach beginning in the 1960s to the Sundanese in West Java, most of the work done in the first 20 years by Indonesians of other ethnic groups collapsed and disappeared. This happened primarily because little effort was made to understand and engage Sundanese spiritual questions, social dependency, and leadership principles. Like the iceberg, a certain

Most of culture is unseen

amount of culture is obvious but the much larger part lies beneath the surface. The effective cross-cultural church planter discovers the part that is not seen.

Difficulty of Cross-cultural Ministry

Even before a person begins to fashion an approach to evangelism and church planting, it is important to adjust to a diverse cultural life. The teaching and learning models of education may be different from the ones that are familiar to the expatriate or the outsider. The field of ethics and other characteristics of spiritual and social relationships often vary drastically. For example, social distance is not the same in all cultures and this results in class relationships that are difficult to penetrate. An illustration of this is how the concept of Time takes on a distinctive meaning. Change may happen at a slower or faster pace. The way emotional stress is defined in seemingly incongruous ways makes personal and family relationships incomprehensible to the outsider. Personal relationships are impacted differently in important areas such as spiritual maturity, attitudes, dispositions, and language facility.

Lack of Mentors

All of these challenges are compounded in the Unreached People Group (UPG) by the lack of mentors who are experienced in guiding expatriates. Mission agencies usually have not had much experience in these new fields. Even mission executives frequently lack the experience necessary for counseling the field worker. Surprisingly, workers seldom consult mission bodies other than their own even when others have more experience. Thus, training models are often not adjusted to the UPG. Many reasons for this can be seen in the seminaries and Bible schools where workers are being trained. There are very few seminaries or Bible schools with a curriculum that is geared to training a person to cross cultural boundaries.

You must learn the church-planting competencies

Besides having an agency support system that is inexperienced, expatriates may not be able to find mentors in the focus group who know how to guide an expatriate. For an extensive discussion of indigenous mentors see Phase Four. There is often a problem of social distance that prevents the local mentor from correcting the expatriate. Variant concepts of role and status may also hinder a person from even attempting to communicate error or right action to an expatriate. Unless an expatriate learns how to identify and access the skill of mentors, he/she will have difficulty progressing.

Answering the Problem

Obstacles of many kinds can be overcome with preparation for cross-cultural church planting in a UPG. Such preparation takes time and cannot be gotten simply by taking a few summer courses and short-term mission trips. Oswald Chambers (1975:40) wrote the following. "Preparation is not something suddenly accomplished, but a process steadily maintained."

Roger's Suggested Reading List

During recent interviews with workers on a UPG field and with candidates for a UPG ministry, we found that only 20% of them had any work experience requiring regular attendance at a daily job. Also, fewer than that had any experience working on a church staff in any capacity. Most of them had taught a Sunday School class but had no role in policy making or other leadership functions. Their cross-cultural experience was not much better. Many of the workers that we have known have superior spiritual qualities and a commitment to plant churches. Unfortunately, most have not succeeded because they do not know how to set goals to achieve that purpose. They do not know because they have never gotten the skills or competencies needed to do effective CC CP.

STEPS TO SOLID PREPARATION

Whether you are presently on a field or are in your home country, if you are considering CC CP **it is important that you begin with preparation**. This preparation can be illustrated by the painting "Unsung." It is a canvas by James Dietz showing a four man crew working on a World War II airplane- the Douglas Scout Dive Bomber. The plane is located on a carrier's lower hangar deck. The four men who are working will never be noticed by anyone other than the pilot and their supervisor. But they know that the plane will not operate properly without their attention. They are necessary in order for the plane to complete its mission successfully. This is an example of unsung preparation.

Preparation at home

The cross-cultural church planter goes through a series of preparations before he or she can operate effectively in a cross-cultural situation. Some of this preparation should be done before leaving the home culture to go to the assignment. Few will notice as the candidate goes through this

"If you fail to prepare, prepare to fail."

lengthy training in schools or in an internship. It is something we have to do in virtual obscurity from all except those who experience it with us. This is the unsung preparation of cross-cultural church planting.

But the preparation done in a mono-cultural situation is never sufficient to prepare us for the encounters of a new culture. Once we settle in at a cross-cultural setting with a church planting job to do we begin to realize that we have not prepared enough. Once again, we must continue in preparation with only our family and our supervisor and a few close friends aware of what we are doing. This again is unsung preparation. This is what creates the effective church planter.

Making the decision to go

BEGINNING THE PROCESS

Once you have decided to take part in CC CP, the place to begin is with an examination of your own experience and skills. A critical part of this is a personal evaluation. Spiritual maturity and experience are the most important aspects of the successful church planter in cross-cultural venues. Your pastor and mentors and friends will be able to help you in evaluating your spiritual maturity.

TIP: Learn to <u>pray</u> and be patient for God's time <u>before</u> you leave home.

We believe God's time will come when we have enough knowledge and skill to learn how to operate in the cross-cultural church planting situation. The reader will notice that we wrote, "learn how to operate." This book is designed to elaborate on the way education and skills interact in that area. The effective church planter is always learning. But even before one arrives at the place of ministry, some groundwork should be laid.

Examine yourself

There are a number of instruments that mission agencies use to evaluate preparedness. But before we even get to an agency, there are checklists we can use to guide us. This Personal Data form will help you to begin.

PERSONAL DATA This section is designed to ascertain your personal status when you felt called to CC CP or before you trained for it. Your answers here should indicate to you important areas you need to assess. Spouses should fill this out together.

Name : _____

Age : _____

Marital status _____

Number & ages of Children _____

Educational level: _____

Religious Experience: _____

    How long had you been a born again Christian? Years____ Months_____

    Have you had a "call" or clear leading or command from God to go to an unreached people? _____

    Do you have a strong, personal relationship with Jesus Christ and a consistent, satisfying devotional life? _____

Job experience: _____

    How long have you worked in a permanent, full time job? _____ part time job _____

What permanent, full time jobs have you had?_____
-include military service   _____

Have you ever held a full time job on a church staff? _____
How long? _____ Part time job? _____ How long? _____

Have you ever held any position in a church (e.g., official board member, SS teacher, etc.)? What position? _____ How long? _____

Cross-cultural Experience: _____
Have you lived in a culture foreign to your own? Years_____
Months _____

In what capacity did you live there? _____
(e.g., held a job; parents lived there; summer visitor)

Did you learn the local language? _____ What language? ____

RESULTS OF POOR PREPARATION

Counting the Cost

In the book *Too Valuable to Lose*, William Taylor (1997:93) reports the five top reasons for missionary attrition. They are normal retirement, children, change of job, health problems, and problems with peers. An example of a major difficulty in CC CP is that it occurs in out of the way places where there are seldom schools and other accommodations for children. Many workers spend years preparing for cross-cultural church planting and then fail to carry it through because of the needs of their children. Generally speaking, workers who begin their assignment with no children or small children will have more time to succeed. Count the cost before leaving home.

There may be a huge loss of workers

Spiritual Pressure

People who feel they have a vague relationship with Jesus Christ and are uncertain of any call to enter the arduous work of CC CP are unlikely to complete such a difficult task. The spiritual pressure is enormous among a UPG and there are few support systems in place. We have known many workers who came for the "long haul" who did not do much more than learn the language before they left for another job. A dynamic sense of being personally appointed by the Lord to a specific UPG is the strongest motivation one can have both to begin and to stay.

Inability to Structure Work

Many people who come to a UPG without extensive work experience cannot structure their daily work schedule. As stated earlier, ministry among a UPG implies that a person be a self-starter. If a worker cannot initiate, structure, and carry out work on his or her own, he or she becomes a hindrance to others. As a team member, one should be accountable to carry part of the load and complete one's tasks without wasting other team member's time. If a worker cannot do this, he or she is a drag on the team. Such competence should be gained through work experience outside the UPG field.

Learning how to work

Lack of Experience

When a worker helps create a church, it is necessary to have a concept in mind toward which to work. A church is different from a fellowship or an agency or another kind of organization. If a church planting team does not have any idea of what kind of congregation it wants to have, long-term success is unlikely. Experience in the church gives the necessary perspective.

Many workers have difficulty understanding how the Church would form and function in a non-Christian culture. For example, in America the propaganda for separation of church and state makes many candidates for missions think of the church in terms of isolation from the state. Such a mono-cultural view can affect one's theology of the Church in a UPG that exists within a multicultural nation.

Inability to Adjust Culturally

Extensive cross-cultural experience is invaluable to successful cross-cultural church planting. That seems to be an axiom that is unnecessary to state. But, in fact, very few new workers among the UPG have any extensive cross-cultural experience. Some workers have transferred from other fields where they got their cross-cultural experience. But most workers start cold in the UPG or in an adjacent area to the UPG without much cross-cultural experience. The effective church planter seeks that experience.

Take leadership in a church

PREPARATION CHECK LIST ON CROSS-CULTURAL ADJUSTMENT

This checklist is a guide to the kind of cross-cultural training one should have before going to a UPG. Try to get some education in as many of these categories as possible. They all relate to CC CP. If you are presently working with an unreached people group, you can note the academic training that would be valuable for you at this time. Don't fail to be aware of and pursue the training you need. If you are new to these categories it would help to discuss them with an experienced worker and with your support group.

To be an effective cross-cultural church planter, study habits are critical. Don't be like Norman in the comic strip *Drabble*. Norman holds an open book and says, "Final exams are in one week. It's time to start studying." Then the book opens with a cracking noise. He sniffs the book and says, "I love the aroma of a book that has never been opened before."

> *The effective worker has good habits*

1. Personal devotional life _____ Personal holiness _____ Spiritual warfare and prayer _____ Understanding spiritual forces in an unreached people group _____

2. Theology of the Church _____ Theology of the Trinity _____ Theology of evangelism _____ Theology of Church Planting _____

3. Church government _____ Church administration _____ Church ministry or philosophy of ministry _____

4. Theology of mission _____ Principles of Church planting _____ Church planting in Islamic/other religious context _____ Islamic/other religious belief systems _____ (whatever religious category that agrees with that of your UPG)

5. Linguistics _____ Other language acquisition course _____

6. Communication theory _____ Cross-cultural communication _____ Evangelism _____ Cross-cultural evangelism _____ Cross-cultural Church Planting _____

7. Family concerns on the foreign field _____ Lifestyle issues in foreign service _____ If single, have investigated lifestyle issues in foreign cultures _____

8. Concepts, dynamics, or philosophy of team ministry _____ Principles and practices of team ministry _____

9. Philosophy and practices of tentmaker ministries _____ Role of the consultant _____ Community development _____ Other subjects related to secular work overseas _____ (please specify _____)

10. Any UPG history or social studies _____ Asian & other histories and/or social studies _____ Mission history _____ Any UPG mission history _____

11. Challenge of the unreached people groups _____ Culture stress/shock _____ Maintaining personal emotional health _____ Working with nationals _____ Dealing with security concerns _____ Maintaining personal ethical practices _____

12. Models of contextualization _____ Indigenous principles and/or movements _____ About any UPG contextualization style _____

13. Models of leadership ____ Cross-cultural leadership ____ Your focus group leadership style ____ Patron-client relations ____

14. Culture change ____ Anthropology ____ Sociology ____ Status & role of westerner in the regional societies around your UPG ____

15. Principles of social change ____ Barriers to change ____ Innovators and change agents ____

16. Teaching/learning models ____ Learning in a cross-cultural context ____ Your focus group world view ____ Asian WV ____ European WV___ Mid Eastern WV_____ , etc.

DEVELOPING AN OUTCOMES PROFILE

Jonathan Lewis and Robert Ferris (1995:23-41) have developed a profiling exercise that is fashioned to define outcome goals. This helps you to clarify what goals you hope to accomplish as you move into your focus group. It is not included here but you can go to the source referenced and find it. The authors describe how to identify the critical areas that relate to the missionary vocation. "When we define outcome goals, we describe the results that can be expected from carrying out a training programme" (p. 23).

To prepare oneself intelligently and adequately for cross-cultural church planting, one needs to "determine the desired outcomes and then build 'backwards'..." (Ibid.). This process develops an outcomes profile. This is important because it is an exercise in structuring your focus and activities to achieve your goals. This type of preparation influences success or failure. The outcomes profile suggested by Lewis and Ferris will identify the type of missionary you need to be for your field, the general areas of qualification and the specific qualities and competencies needed. You will identify both the character qualities and the skills you will need to acquire for the ministry you desire to fulfill.

BLAKE'S ACADEMIC ADMINISTRATOR GRID

When Blake's Academic Administrator Grid (Blake, 1982) is adjusted for cross-cultural church planting, it will resemble the chart below.

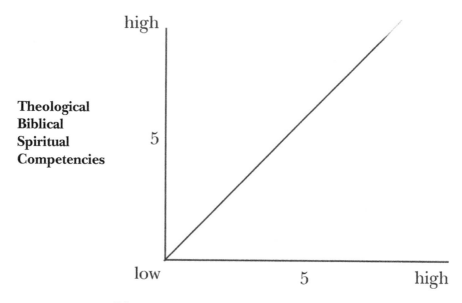

Management Competencies/ Skills

On the vertical side of the grid, we can rate theological, biblical, and spiritual competencies. The horizontal side is reserved for management competencies or skills. It is important to visualize each competency on the grid. Examples of the competencies can be found in "Missionaries' Competencies Profile: Argentina" (See Appendix 1).

For example, where would you rate yourself on such competencies as church relations, cultural anthropology, biblical knowledge, or linguistic acquisition? There are many more. On the management grid, rate yourself on leadership skills, bookkeeping, correspondence, and church polity. These are only a few of the competencies but they will enable you to visualize where you might fall on this grid. The competencies or skills one has in the low area are the ones that need to be addressed <u>before</u> one goes to the field. Don't assume that you will be able to ignore these in CC CP because your level of adequacy in them may determine whether you succeed or fail in the planting of a viable church.

Later, when you are able to plot on both arms of the grid all the competencies and skills listed in Appendix 1 you will see a relationship between the competencies on the vertical line with those on the horizontal line. This is done by plotting each score on a diagonal line from the left bottom corner that splits the grid into two parts. It may be that you are high in the religious categories but low in the organizational skills necessary for structuring a church. *This is an example of what you want to find out before you leave for your assignment.*

Seeking learning and experience

AREAS OF SOLID PREPARATION

The categories in the competencies profile mentioned above are areas of study that reflect solid preparation. You should endeavor to master or at least engage these before leaving for your assignment in the UPG. The picture above represents the frantic effort of the CC CP candidate trying to get in as much learning as possible. Do your best to get as much study in each area as you can. Set your mind to continue your study after you arrive in your assignment area. Effectiveness in UPG work frequently correlates to the amount of preparation one has done to meet the challenge of the UPG.

1. **Biblical Studies:** Formal and informal biblical studies are foremost. In previous generations, this was a given, and few candidates for cross-cultural ministry were selected if they did not have considerable Bible training. This has changed and many people are being accepted for UPG work who do not have sufficient Bible knowledge to train a new church. We will see the

Check your preparation

importance of Bible knowledge later when we discuss church theology, contextualization, discipleship, and other teaching models in the church.

2. **Spiritual Disciplines:** Maturity in personal spiritual disciplines. Spiritual maturity is the result of one's being discipled. Bible reading, prayer, fellowship, and evangelism are learned disciplines. Very few people can learn these on their own. They are acquired through discipleship. Discipleship is one of the critical models in the development of a new church. In many UPG areas, people are easily evangelized but still fall away due to poor or non-existent discipling. Workers who have not been discipled themselves generally have no idea of what it entails and thus cannot disciple others.

3. **Family Dynamics:** Family dynamics and personal spiritual growth are keys to maintaining a viable witness in a community. For those who are attempting to penetrate an unreached people group, the most important aspect is nurturing the central core to stay close to God. This central core is the nuclear cross-cultural church planting family. The central core is formed by the husband (father), wife (mother), and any children they may have. Or it may be composed of a family with a single worker or a team of single workers. We can expand this concept to include a number of families or single workers in a church planting team. The ministry will stand or fall on the integrity of the central core. (See: Appendix 2: Nurturing the Central Core)

4. **Team Building:** Team concepts and interpersonal dynamics comprise the core of the cross-cultural church planting effort. As we stated in #3, the family or the nuclear unit is the center of that core. But the CC CP team comprises the basic community of each family. Therefore, the activity of the team affects every member. Unless a member has some knowledge of team building and nurture, it is unlikely that he or she will contribute much to the CC CP effort. In fact, experience has shown that many teams spend more time wrestling with the problems of nurturing and training their own team members than they do in CC CP work. Not a few teams collapse because of this shortcoming. [See: **The Formation of a Team** in Chapter 3]

Theology is key

5. **Theology of the Church**: Everything we do rises or falls on the theology of the Church. This is an area that is poorly defined for

many UPG workers. Many people who have been raised in independent churches or educated in insular Bible schools or seminaries have little understanding of such concepts as the historic Church, a creedal tradition, a covenant theology, the centrality of the sacraments, and the biblical role of the Church in God's plan for the nations and for the principalities and powers. Understanding how to contextualize Christian theology in a non-Christian environment is perhaps even more important. This knowledge is critical not only in the formation of one's church plant but also for understanding and cooperation with any Christian denomination that may exist in one's area.

6. **Mission Theory & Practice**: The experience and practice of others enlightens our journey. It is not wise to assume that no one has ever tried to reach your focus group. Many may have tried but failed. The UPG are very hard to penetrate. This is why they are "unreached." We need to learn all we can about what others have done. Our investigation should begin in intercultural studies and include theological studies done in our UPG or in similar groups. This would include contextualization because it is closely linked to theology. The effective church planter continues to study as long as he/she is engaged in the UPG.

7. **Cross-cultural Adjustment**: This is more than just wearing certain clothes, eating anything offered, or sleeping in any kind of circumstances. Most modern young people are quite good at these kinds of adjustments. Culture shock/trauma comes in many forms. We will discuss more of this later. The critical aspect of cross-cultural adjustment for the cross-cultural church planter is one's attitude toward the focus people. While we can be realistic in discussing perceived flaws, we should also be compassionate. A lack of respect for the culture and religion of the focus people will be hard to conceal from them. For many of us respect for the culture is a struggle that continues until we realize the complexity and power of the focus culture.

Some people won't change

8. **Language Acquisition:** Language is the most important of the early challenges we face in CC CP. It is important for every person to acquire the skills involved in learning a language. Due to the existence of language acquisition programs, it is now possible for everyone to learn how to get a good foundation in language learning.

9. **Cross-cultural Communication:** Besides knowing the vocabulary and grammar of a language, it is important to know how the people of a focus group use their language. There are many different models of communication in use around the world. We can use the basic components of communication to analyze the model used by our focus group. It is difficult for us to discern differing thought categories and assumptions as well as body language if we do not have any basic skill in communication theory.

Learn face-to-face communication

10. **Comparative Religion:** It is folly to think that we will understand the spiritual questions of a focus group if we do not understand their formal and informal religious belief systems. Most large UPG in the world belong to a major or a world religion. However, most also have a set of beliefs that function as an informal religion. Normally, each of these religious systems has its own practitioners. For example, it is possible for a person to be both Islamic and animistic. Frequently, it is difficult to tell which worldview is functioning at any given time. Study and pray and the Holy Spirit will reveal it to you.

Learn how to study the thought of other religions

11. **Leadership Principles & Practice:** Leadership models vary for political, religious, and kinship groups. Each may describe statuses, roles, and relationships in different ways. In Phases 4, 5, & 6 these principles are discussed in detail. It is critical for church leaders to use a model that is familiar to focus people. This goal is made more difficult by the fact that biblical leadership models vary from practically all worldly models. It is seldom effective to impose the biblical model without any effort to demonstrate how it integrates with or is superior to the primary model of the focus group.

12. **Contextualization Theory & Practices:** This category deserves its own mention even though it relates to the theology of the church, to mission theory and practice, and to other areas of preparation already mentioned. The study of contextualization is critical to a worker in today's world because there are so many evangelism and Christian nurture models being used that are marginal by biblical standards. A startling example is the deviance from the norm in Bible translation by the changing of familial terms for God the Father and God the Son and the terms for Son of God and Lord. This aberration is a topic that is a major issue in today's mission discussions.

13. **Introduction to Team Philosophy/Principles:** If you know which team you are going to join in a focus group, it is never too early to study their philosophy and their principles and practice. Taylor in *Too Valuable to Lose* (1997:93) points out that problems with peers is one of the top 5 reasons for attrition. It is important to ascertain as early as possible whether you will be happy with your assigned team.

You will live in the study of contextualization and syncretism

NON-NEGOTIABLES FOR YOUR FIELD OF MINISTRY

Some people cannot cover all the Areas of Solid Preparation listed above before leaving for the field. However, it is important to nail down some non-negotiables that you need to have in as much depth as possible. It is imperative to prepare in these areas before leaving for your assignment. Failure to prepare in these areas has cost many a worker to fail in his or her ministry. The effective church planter will be prepared in the following non-negotiables.

Learning in your homeland

A. Personal spiritual experience

Everything stands or falls on this. Maturity in spiritual disciplines is the position that one needs to be in before leaving for the field. An active membership in a local church should be a given. It is difficult to understand how a person can think he will be successful in perhaps the hardest ministry in the church if he is not even active in ministry at home.

Are you ready spiritually?

The identification and resolution of personal problems is an aspect of maturity that results from a personal spiritual experience with the Lord. Many workers go to the UPG without doing this. On their field, they experience areas of vulnerability that cripple them in their lives. Matters such as the negative residue of childhood experience, the lack of family unity, and personal fears of various kinds all need to be dealt with at home. When this is not done, it frequently escalates into a "hostile" environment, and in addition, it unfortunately eats up the energy and time of the experienced members of the field team.

B. Orientation to your focus group

It is quite amazing how many people come to their focus people with very little understanding of them. Even though you will eventually learn volumes about your focus group, you should garner as much knowledge as possible before entering the culture. Some of the basic studies would include:

1. History and politics
2. Formal religion and informal belief systems
3. History of the church in the area (if there is any)
4. Culture
5. Leadership principles & practice

There are many new workers who arrive on their fields without this basic orientation and it causes a great deal of time and effort of other team members to bring them up to speed. Because of possible naivety or arrogance, many do not even read materials that are prepared for their orientation.

C. Work experience

Informal surveys that I have taken indicate that the majority of candidates for overseas ministry have never held any job in a church. Not more than five per cent have held any kind of job on a church staff. Although these surveys are not scientific, they indicate something about the lack of preparation of workers for the UPG.

Perhaps the major shortcoming of tentmakers is that they do not understand ministry. We believe that every person who desires to do CC CP overseas in any capacity should have at least one year of full time work experience in a spiritual ministry under a supervisor. This can be either salaried or volunteer. It should include supervision in evangelism, discipleship training, teaching, spiritual problem solving, planning for ministry, prayer, spiritual warfare and decision-making.

Professors have shared with us that candidates do not receive this kind of training in formal education. Few want to spend extra time in the home country to acquire it. However, there are two good reasons to insist on this instruction at home. One is the high attrition rate of new workers. The second is the drain on experienced workers who have to spend their time tutoring the unprepared tentmakers. These two reasons alone are sufficient to show that having work experience in the home country is necessary for efficient and effective ministry.

D. Complete candidate course of local church

If possible, complete a candidate course in your local church. Not many churches have these courses because they depend on the mission agency to train you. Even though agencies have extensive psychological testing, interviews, candidate weeks, and the like, they are not able to know you as you are known in your local church. Your close friends and family are best able to advise you concerning the weaknesses in your spiritual and social skills.

E. Support Group

Even if your church does not have a candidate course, it is imperative that you recruit and train a support group who will pray for you and monitor your welfare on the field. Neil Pirolo has written extensively about this and gives guidelines on developing support groups. An example is *Serving As Senders* (1991).

F. Bivocational role

If you are going to a UPG in a tentmaker role, it is important for you to define and have some understanding of issues you will face. As a tentmaker, you will be playing two roles. One is that of a business person, teacher, student, or some other vocation that enables you to obtain a visa to work among the UPG. Although you may not reveal it at first, the other role will be that of a church planter. This may require you to function at different times as an evangelist, pastor, or teacher. Many new workers are confused and sometimes conflicted by having to play these two roles. They feel dishonest in not revealing their true purpose for being among the UPG. Everyone should have experienced mentoring in this area before going to the UPG.

G. Health

Any health issue of a newcomer is a factor that may consume enormous amounts of the precious time of members of the field team who have to care for the new worker. It is expedient for new workers to be sure their health is good and generally stable before they leave for their assignment.

H. Finances

Most workers are able to adjust to the living conditions of the focus people if it is only for a short duration. However, few can sustain that level for long. Although we might have to live on a higher level than our neighbors, we should be willing and able to live as simply as possible. The temptation to associate

We're on our way!

Oh – I'll miss our little church home!

- with mixed feelings -

with expatriate business people in their life style will minimize our commitment to the focus group.

EVALUATION of END RESULTS - CHECK LIST - PHASE ONE

[ ] am an active member of local church
[ ] have completed formal biblical studies
[ ] have 1 year's work experience as formal staff of local church ministry
[ ] have completed study in "Areas of Solid Preparation"
[ ] have dealt with each category under "Non-Negotiables"
[ ] have spent time with spouse and mentor in defining issues that need further work
[ ] if single, have spent time with mentor in defining issues that need further work
[ ] have orientation to the people group to whom I am going
[ ] have completed candidate course in local church & have local church blessing
[ ] have been accepted by agency working in focus area
[ ] am regular in both personal & corporate prayer & worship
[ ] can define what my "call" is to the unreached people

Note: Roland Müller (2006) has excellent lists at the end of his chapters which he calls "Questions for Reflection or Discussion." These kinds of checklists help us to not miss critical areas of preparation and planning.

"Lead on, O King Eternal, The day of march has come;
Henceforth in fields of conquest Thy tents shall be our home.
Thro' days of preparation Thy grace has made us strong;
And now, O King Eternal, We lift our battle song."
Ernest W. Shurtleff

CHAPTER THREE

PHASE TWO - ARRIVAL

"A wise man scales the city of the mighty and brings down the stronghold in which they trust."   Proverbs 21:22

The early days in a new culture can be overwhelming but they are usually exhilarating also. It is important that you not let first impressions affect you too much. When my wife and I arrived at the port near Jakarta, one of the customs officers asked us how much money we had. When I answered that we had three dollars, he asked for one of them. At that time, Jakarta was a very poor city and public management was chaotic. Broken down buses or trucks would sit in the road-way for days while mechanics tried to fix them. Electricity was off frequently and sometimes for days. The canals flooded into our home and into near-by homes and huge mounds of garbage collected on the streets. Several years later, a new governor turned the city around. Our first impression was no longer valid.

Prepared for tribal ministry

The arrival phase is an intense internship that may cover from six months to a year or longer. Matters such as your health and language learning progress will affect the duration of this period. It depends on how much quality time you give to it. I have known workers who began investigating adoption of children as soon as they arrived on the field. This activity was so intense that it consumed most of the time they should have been giving to orientation and severely affected their long-term adjustment.

The average worker going to a UPG has the mentality of a teacher. It is good to have confidence in oneself but it can also be a hindrance. As newcomers it is best if we assume the attitude of the learner rather than that of the teacher. Our time to teach will come later but we will always be learners. Psychologically, this is difficult for highly educated people. We are resistant when it comes to learning from people who are below our educational level. Roland Müller writes, "When a Christian worker or church-planter arrives in a new culture he faces a credibility problem." "Why should anyone listen to him? He doesn't speak the language, doesn't know the culture and isn't aware of the issues that people face among whom he is hoping to develop a ministry or plant a church" (2006:13).

The newcomer can do nothing more important than learning from everyone in the culture. We learn about people by conversing with them about their lives. From her experience in South Africa, Christine Jeske writes: "…in real life we do not come to understand a culture by seeing only their best and worst- their superstars and tsunamis. We come to know a culture or an issue one person at a time, one interaction at a time" (Jeske, 2010:19).

ARRIVAL MEANS PREPARATION IN A NEW CULTURE

In Phase One, we surveyed preparation in the home country. Hopefully, experiences in preparation primed you for cross-cultural comparison. On arrival we first begin to observe the characteristics of the new culture. Basically, this is laying a foundation for further study. In a real sense, we are doing preparation all over again. Only this time it is in a situation foreign to us and much more difficult to accomplish.

The critical importance of preparation was brought home to me once when I saw the concrete slab of a new building project. All over that concrete foundation were tubes of pvc pipe sticking up at various heights. These were conduits for plumbing, water, and electricity. All of these pipes had to be put in at the right places before the concrete was poured. If they were not placed correctly, the networks would not be in the walls of the building but all over the floor area. Careful preparation is needed for any good work. This is the case with CC CP. Knowing where we are going before we start is a given. We need to learn what is necessary to complete our task of CC CP. This also is unsung preparation. Very few people even understand what it entails. You are not going to be praised for language learning, cultural sensitivity, endless hours of reading about the local customs, and repeated attendance at various cultural ceremonies. But this is the education you must have in order to become an effective cross-cultural church planter. David Kyle says, "The seeds of any project's success or failure are found at the very beginning" (1990). You will enjoy it more if you allow yourself time without pressure to "produce."

You must lay the foundation carefully

In Luke 17:7-10, Jesus gives the example of the servant who comes in from the field and serves his master at table. Jesus asked if the master thanks the servant "because he did what was commanded? So you also, when you have done all that you were commanded say, 'We are unworthy servants; we have only done what was our duty.'" Do not expect thanks for the study you have done about which no one knows. But be grateful for the harvest you may reap because of it.

MULTIPLE CULTURES

Multiple languages

Please don't be discouraged when you hear that you will probably have to learn multiple cultures in order to be effective in your UPG. In today's world, most UPG reside in countries that are controlled by other ethnic groups. For example,

* (May I introduce myself? My name is John..)

Indonesia has hundreds of ethnic groups but uses the Indonesian language in all education. This means that everyone who goes to school can understand Indonesian but many still live in cultural environments that are very different from each other. Indonesian is the status language and it is difficult to have credibility as a teacher if one cannot use the national language well. Thus, one should learn Indonesian as well as one's UPG language.

Three types of culture

The nature of the UPG means that in most countries there exist at least three types of cultural orientation that have great impact. The first is the national culture. This is usually modern, global, business and youth oriented. If one cannot function in this culture it is hard to gain recognition as a "valuable person to know." Another culture is the social organization of the UPG. Without the knowledge embedded in this culture, it is impossible to plant a contextual church.

A third culture is that of the religious systems operating among the UPG. If there is only one, you are fortunate. As was mentioned in Chapter One, there are generally multiple belief systems operating in correlation or in conflict with one another. For example, in S.E. Asia there are very few UPG that do not have both a formal religion and an informal belief system operating at the same time. The informal system is usually a set of traditional beliefs based on ancient religious practices. This informal religion may not have a name but it is a powerful influence in their lives. People integrate the various religious beliefs so that they seem compatible. They may not be able to explain contradictory beliefs rationally, but emotionally they flow with them.

Become familiar with the cultures

A fourth culture

A fourth culture that may be present is that of the Christian church. If there is a church in your area, do not assume that you automatically understand it. When we arrived in our UPG area the church that had been planted by a Dutch mission was not cooperative with a new group of evangelists outside their church. For several years we did not understand why they seemed so negative and so set against any kind of outreach to Muslims. The answer came in historical studies when we learned that this church had been brutally terrorized by radical Muslims for about eight years after the Second World War. This experience had traumatized the leaders so badly that they withdrew from all evangelistic outreach. They welcomed people who came to their churches but did not seek them out. This is the kind of information one needs to know about the local church. Never dismiss a church as irrelevant because it is not doing what you think it should do.

It is important to study the theology, polity, philosophy of ministry, church structure, and other aspects of a church in your UPG. It has likely become contextual in some ways. It may not represent what you might define as contextual but it is a model that has attracted members of the UPG. For that reason, it needs to be understood.

BONDING

The expatriate model

Bonding is a controversial subject that requires considerable attention by the new arrival. Hopefully, you will have some input from your team before you arrive on the field. In some cases, your team will require you to follow a certain pattern. Nevertheless, it behooves you to investigate the various forms of this learning model.

The traditional approach that dominated throughout most of the twentieth century was an expatriate community model that included missionaries as well as business people and foreign diplomats. The function of missionaries in their agencies was often considered more important than their adjustment to the local culture. An example of this is the way new workers were placed in houses in close proximity with other members of their agency. This enabled a senior member of their team to mentor them more easily in language and culture learning. Most questions about the local language or culture were answered by members of the expatriate team and not by nationals.

Various forms of bonding can be effective

In this model, the new workers were likely to spend much more time with their team colleagues and other members of the expatriate community than they did with nationals. They may have gone out into the local community to run errands and learn language, but generally they had relatively little social intercourse with local people. They did not eat with them in their homes, go on retreats and vacations together, or even visit with them extensively. Because of this, the new workers often did not learn how to ask the local people questions about the life and faith of the UPG. In most cases, they were not forbidden to fraternize with local people. It was just that learning cultural adjustment from nationals was not thought to be the most productive model. There was fear that the newcomer would make too many mistakes among the nationals, would not be indoctrinated into the team's philosophy of ministry, and would experience too much culture shock/stress.

Total Immersion

In 1976, E. Thomas Brewster and his wife, Elizabeth, published a book on language acquisition that has had enormous influence on the mission theory of bonding. Later, they published another book on bonding (1982). Stated simply, this second book propos-es that the new worker have direct and almost exclusive contact with the focus group during the early months in the UPG. According to their theory, all un-necessary social intercourse with non-UPG people must be eliminated during the early months. Exceptions may be made for necessary outside contact for such matters as visa and language learn-ing arrangements. But essentially there should be as little contact as possible with people outside the UPG.

At first, you are a novelty

To do this, the new workers are placed in a house with UPG people. This will enable them to learn the daily patterns of the family, the food they eat, the friends and visitors they have, their recreation habits, and all the observable aspects of their cultural lives. Some people who have followed this bonding model believe it is the best possible one. Others have had serious problems, such as poor health and difficulty with their children adjusting to the vastly different customs of the UPG.

It is important to remember that one can learn as much or more about family life living with a middle-income family as one can learn with a poor family. There is no reason to submit yourself deliberately to extremely unhealthy conditions on your arrival in the UPG. Many expatriate families who have immediately moved into lower economic class areas have suffered severe illnesses that prevented them from having the benefit of cultural learning. If a person's own physical or emotional load becomes too great, he or she can no longer absorb outside influences. Culture shock becomes overwhelming.

Alternative Models

There are many variations to the two major examples given here. Models will vary depending on whether a worker is single or married. People without children are usually able to adjust more easily. In some cases, single workers cannot stand the stress of total immersion bonding. We knew a male expatriate in Singapore who had to be removed from a UPG household because of illness and extreme loss of weight.

If the new workers are married, the nature of the family is important to consider. In the case of childless families, the husband and wife are free to move into any kind of conditions they desire. Although sanitary conditions are always important to consider, it becomes especially vital when one has children. In many, if not all, UPG homes there are germs, bacteria, and viruses that outsiders have never encountered. While the children of the local people can be immune or resistant to these diseases, newcomers are probably not.

Therefore, the model a new worker should choose (or have chosen for him or her) should depend on the condition of the family and the nature of the UPG culture. Many new workers do not have language acquisition skills and are not able to evaluate cultural experiences. For this reason, a common practice in some areas is to give the new worker six months to acclimate to the local culture and climate while learning language at a school. This allows the worker to adjust physically and health wise to the area and to learn how to use a language informant in a valuable way. In any case, a senior colleague should monitor new workers so that they will understand what is happening during the bonding experience and be able to stay on track.

Adjusting outside the CP area

Another variation to the adjustment model is having new workers live and learn during the first 6 months or so outside of the permanent area where they will be known. It is better to make mistakes with people who will not be your permanent community. This can be accomplished in another part of the city where you will be living or in a village different from the one in which you will be serving. Foreigners tend to make pretty bad cultural and diplomatic mistakes and it is useful not to have to live them down. For example, the frank American way is not polite in Indonesia and it is easy to gain a reputation for arrogance before you realize what is happening.

YOUR NEW HOME

Doing things the easy way

Finding a home

Finding a new home can sometimes be a traumatic experience. Because of this, many teams will house newcomers in temporary quarters just so they can get used to their new surroundings. Most workers who come to a UPG team have been traveling for months doing fund raising or other duties. They do not relish the idea of moving into temporary homes. They want to get unpacked. They want to get settled.

Appropriate communities

However, new people do not understand the local community and environment. Many newcomers have mistakenly moved into communities and housing that were unsuitable for them to learn language and engage in useful orientation to the culture. This can be complicated if rent has been paid in advance. In many places, rent has to be paid a year or two in advance. A mistake in renting can cause much trauma in the new worker's family because the rent money will likely not be reimbursed.

Learn about your community before you move there

Your choice of a new home will be influenced by the following:
1. bonding policy
2. language learning potential
3. appropriateness for children (education, etc.)
4. health conditions as good as possible (at least for the first 6 months)
5. the opportunity to establish yourself in the community as a neighbor and get involved in community activities
6. a simple life style that approximates that of your national co-workers (counterparts) in ministry
7. opportunity to live off the local market as much as possible

YOUR CHILDREN

Critical position

Under Family Dynamics in Phase One, we discussed the central core that is formed by the husband (father), wife (mother), and any children they may have. Maintaining the unity and strength of the family is second only to sustaining spiritual growth in one's relationship to God. The two are closely related. Our children may not be considered second to the "Lord's work" because they are entrusted to us ahead of anyone else. The father and mother may give as much time as they can to the work <u>after</u> they have given sufficient time to their children.

Monitor children

In many UPG societies children should be carefully monitored to prevent

Monitor your children

sexual and other abuse. Our own children were groped, burned with cigarettes, slapped, and abused in other ways. Much worse happened to other families we knew. It is impossible to watch over children every minute but it is our duty to protect them. They should be able to tell us when something does not seem right to them even when it involves other missionaries.

Guard and protect your children
Children are all different from one another. Even in the same family, one child might learn the local language well while others do not learn it at all. Some children are impervious to the pawing and pinching they endure from neighbors and strangers in some cultures. Others may dissolve in a paroxysm of rage. Most children require a lot of attention.

It is important that each family work this out for themselves but all should be aware that it is easier to neglect our children than it is to give them too much time. In all UPG ministry, the work load is beyond what a person can do. There is no end to the work. Therefore, the wise person learns to limit the load when it encroaches on the family. The lesser responsibility has to give way to the greater.

LANGUAGE STUDY

1. When to begin
Language study should begin as soon as possible. If one is studying at a school, it may be necessary to wait for the term to begin. If one is studying with a tutor or informant, it is possible to start at any time. Resettling in a tropical climate causes problems for some people. If you are in the tropics, it may take one or two weeks to get used to the heat before beginning any work schedule. Also, if you have jet lag it can be an aggravation for several weeks. However, many people begin their work schedules within a few days.

Some workers have language acquisition skills that enable them to begin learning the language on their own. It is not the purpose of this book to describe all these skills in detail but they are useful if acquired. However, most people do not have this ability even if they have gone through special courses in language acquisition. In the same way, most people do not have the ability to structure their language study or any other work they may undertake. In general, people are not trained to structure their own work days and thus very few missionaries are able to do so effectively. Mission Training International (MTI) in Palmer Lake, CO, is one example of a number of organizations that have programs relating to language learning and other life style skills for cross-cultural adjustment.

2. Aspects of language study

A tutor or informant is a high priority for effective language learning. That is why a good language school is the best way for most people to learn language. It is structured in such a way that people are guided in their study and do not have to organize the classes or material themselves. If one cannot go to an organized school, it is possible to learn from a good tutor who will guide the learner through the process. However, disciplining oneself to practice alone is hard for most people. Going out into the community and making contacts alone to practice language learning is also difficult for many people.

One should not depend entirely on information from expatriates or the average local people about language. You may find that local people have differing opinions about the language. For example, even noted experts in the Indonesian language disagree with one another about various aspects of grammar and vocabulary and argue about them in articles. However, as you learn through a tutor or through an immersion process you should not let certain irregularities in the language trouble you.

Use the most effective language learning model

"Let's state the obvious: We learn the language primarily from our interactions with *people* our friends, neighbors, and others around us. This is not primarily an endeavor in books, classrooms, vocabulary cards, and deskwork, though all of these have their place" (Sinclair, 2006:95). Pronunciation is the most important part of language learning in the early days and months for the following reason. If one has misunderstood the meaning of a word, it is relatively easy to relearn its definition. On the other hand, incorrect pronunciation of words is extremely difficult to correct if it has become an ingrained pattern. It is likely that the way women use language is different from the way men do. This is an important consideration. A new arrival's team mentor should help in areas like this to insure that the language learning process continues as efficiently as possible.

During the process of learning a language there should be an evaluation of a person's progress by an unbiased person. This is important because a good tutor will encourage learners with praise and sometimes mislead them into thinking they are doing better than they actually are. Some people tend to overrate their progress because they are unable to distinguish certain sounds or grasp sentence structure. They cannot tell what they are doing wrong without an honest evaluation by an outside language expert.

3. Multiple languages

In most UPG work, it is necessary to learn multiple languages. At a minimum, a worker should anticipate learning two languages. Frequently, these would be the national language used throughout the country as well as the ethnic language of the UPG. As in all the other areas of adjustment to UPG work, there are varying opinions about when to study which language.

It is worth repeating that when there are multiple languages operating in a country, one needs to understand the status position of each language. Which language is used in the educational institutions? Secondly, one needs to know which language is most necessary for the

Learning a new language can be painful

work among the UPG. At first glance, it would seem that it is always best to learn the UPG language first. But much depends on the number of other ethnic people involved in the ministry. It is likely that the expatriate worker will be used eventually in a teaching or infrastructure role. For example, one might be training people from other ethnic groups coming into the UPG. In such a case, the national language might be the most important to use. Either way, every worker will probably have to learn both languages.

4. Problems

Language learning is difficult for most people. We had a friend who was a college graduate who spent 3 months at our house when she first came to the field. She was supposed to be studying language but she admitted later that she spent most of the time reading novels and sleeping. It had been a vacation for her. Forcing oneself to learn language is very hard for many people.

When sleep is not helpful

TEAM RELATIONSHIPS

There are always new teams forming to engage UPG. However, most people who go to a UPG join a team that is already functioning. The following guidelines will apply to either.

Team Coach

1. Within the first few days you will meet with a coach from your team who will probably discuss an orientation packet with you and explain the role of team coach. This person will probably help you adjust to the conditions in your housing area and will help you understand the transportation system, the market, the postal system and other important infrastructure. This is practically always a fun time and most people really enjoy these early months on their field.

Your coach will discuss matters such as:
    a. team information
    b. spiritual & interpersonal dynamics
    c. format for business meetings
    d. home /office communication
    e. the role of sub teams, the administrative team, and Mentors
    f. the role and expectations for the new team member during his/her
       first year in relation to local churches, other team members, and
       ministries
    g. why language is a priority

Team philosophy

2. If you have not already done so, you should study your team's philosophy of ministry and other practices. These may vary widely with different teams in the same UPG. Since one of the five major problems missionaries experience is conflict with their peers, it is imperative that you be confident you will blend with your team and that you make a special effort to do so. In the early days, spend as much time as possible with your team members in prayer and fellowship. The time will soon come when you will be so busy that fellowship becomes another thing you have to schedule.

Adjustment to your team is critical

The Formation of a Team

3. Steve Richardson uses the model of Castles of Terrassa to illustrate various aspects of a functioning team. Look this up on the internet and see what team work can accomplish. Then think through Richardson's list below to consider some aspects of a team.

1) Lots of supporters
2) More team members = higher castle
3) Strongest hold the most weight
4) Some go first; others follow
5) Latecomers benefit from their predecessors
6) All team members reinforce one another
7) "Requires muscle, balance, & sheer determination"
8) Benefits from a long tradition and history
9) The right garb (tools) required
10) "Musicians" cheer the team on
11) Continually acquiring new young members
12) Team includes people from all backgrounds
13) Urgency: 2 minutes to build, 1 to unload
14) There is a point of "legitimacy": 5 tiers
15) "Unloading" is very important!

Building the Tower

Learn other ministry models

4. After a few months, branch out and learn all you can about what other teams in the UPG are thinking and doing. Lack of language might restrict this interaction to expatriates in the early months but soon you will be

46

able to communicate with the nationals. Read all the available literature in your language about ministry among your focus group. Don't limit your study to your ministry model alone. When you have the language, read all relevant histories and/or biographies about your focus group in whatever language you can. Study the other cultural groups living among your UPG. Find out what their statuses and roles are and what your status and role is so you will know how to relate to them. "When we know the behavior expected of us by our culture for each status we occupy and the behavior associated with the statuses of the people with whom we interact, we achieve a psychological security otherwise unattainable" (Foster, 1973:22).

Meet new people even if they are different from you

1. Within the First Six–Eight Weeks you should have made progress in the following areas:
   a. Have a meal with each team member and learn the role of that team member.
   b. Watch all team videos if there are any about the focus people. (This can be coordinated with other new members).
   c. Have your first language evaluation and a second meeting with your coach and Language Coordinator to discuss progress—with emphasis that language is priority one.
   d. Locate permanent housing (unless you are living in a bonding situation or have decided to use provided housing for 6 months).

2. Within the First Six Months it is best if you have done the following:
   a. Take at least ten days vacation.
   b. Listen to all the team videos for the second time. Your learning curve about culture will go on forever.
   c. Tour your team's ministry areas and meet all the national staff. Visit with them in their homes, if possible.
   d. Visit several churches (if there are any in the area). Learn all you can about them. Your focus group will tend to copy the systems of existing churches and you may want to selectively introduce something different.

3. Within the First 12–18 months your goals should be to achieve the following:
   a. Attain to level 3 or higher proficiency in your primary ministry language.
   b. Select or be assigned a specific job that you will do on the team or sub–team and attend their meetings,
   c. Select a local church in which to be involved and attend regularly in order to learn the Christian culture in your area. Try to choose a church that has the potential to be a sponsor for UPG church planting.

PERSONAL RELATIONSHIPS

1. Relationship with Christ

> *"Let my heart always think of him,*
> *Let my head always bow down to him,*
> *Let my lips always sing his praise,*
> *Let my hands always worship him,*
> *Let my body always serve him with love*
> *Jesus who is seated within my heart, fragrant like a flower."*
> H.A. Krishna Pillai, *Rakshanya Yātrikam*
> [Appasamy, (1966), p.65]

Put God first

   a. Your relationship with Jesus will determine all other relationships.
   b. Prioritize personal spiritual discipline.
   "Let us always remember: The missionary problem is a personal one. A passionate love to Jesus Christ, born out of his love, truly possessing each of us personally, will teach us to pray, to labor, and to suffer. Let us pray for such a love" (Murray, 1979:123).

   c. Be up front about your personal Christian belief while active in studying local culture (it is a mistake to pretend that you are not a Christian because when it is revealed, you will lose prestige with both those who are and those who are not). Remember that the disciples were known for being followers of Jesus. They were not incognito. However, this does not mean you have to reveal your long term CP purpose for being in the country.

d. Start verbal witnessing or sharing of your faith practices as soon as you can (if possible in English. If that is not possible, you will have to have some months of language learning).

e. Study local evangelism methods and models, if there are any, to find out how nationals are evangelizing your focus people. Don't assume that they don't know how just because they are not doing it.

f. Attend a local church (it is rarely good strategy to bypass the local Christians because your focus people are probably going to look to them for models of the Christian life and will need their spiritual support).

g. Be continually studying and practicing fruitful prayer. This is frequently referred to as spiritual warfare. There are many good books on this subject that will help you. The important thing is that you don't neglect to keep aware that you are in a spiritual combat and that it can affect your relationship with Christ and with your family.

2. **Relationships with Family or for Singles with housemates or friends**
   a. Set up the routine and discipline of your home as soon as possible (this will be very difficult while you bond with a local family).
   b. Give particular attention to spiritual formation for all family members.
   c. If single, give attention to spiritual formation of all house mates.
   d. Nurture a deepening relationship with your spouse. (Appendix 2: Nurturing The Central Core). For singles, this means a deepening relationship with an expatriate or national colleague who can nurture you.
   e. Envision how each family member or housemate fits into your ministry as a unity.
   f. Minister to your children's needs as well as those of your spouse.
   g. Be careful of your physical health and that of your family through family exercise and a balanced diet.
   h. Keep involved in family recreation or if single, in recreation with friends.

POTENTIAL PROBLEMS

1. Culture shock or cultural stress

> *Everyone has cultural shock or stress*

This is one of the early problems we face. Our understanding of culture shock is based on Kalervo Oberg's theory on culture shock. George Foster (1973:191-196) lists the stages as Incubation, Crisis, Recovery, Full or Near-full Recovery. There is disagreement about how long the process will last but it commonly begins around six months after a person arrives in a new culture and lasts for six or more months. It is not wise to take it lightly. In fact, many people never recover and it is one of the main reasons people leave the field. However, it is rarely listed as a reason because it exacerbates other weaknesses that then become the focus of a person's problem.

Everything is relative

Culture shock also happens to nationals who are working cross-culturally. However, the stress and subsequent problems it causes them may vary from those experienced by an expatriate. Myron Loss (1983:48-58) describes how culture shock is caused by real issues. One example is the change in social roles. In our own culture people may value our knowledge and skills. In a focus culture, our economic status may be most valued. This can be true even for national workers from another ethnic group.

The way we relate to the focus group is one example of how we may differ from nationals not of the focus group. We may not feel any loss of self-esteem while learning their language and culture. On the other hand, the ethnic nationals who are not from the focus group may feel a loss of both social status and self esteem if they identify themselves with the focus people. This is usual, especially if the focus people are considered a very low status group in the national society.

2. Change in language

A change in the use of language in the home can be severe if one's children are not able to understand conversation. Although family cultures vary, children tend to be included in group conversations. This will not be possible if they do not understand what is being said. One family we knew of used only the national language in conversing with their children. When they returned to their home country after six years, they switched to using their mother tongue. The children were emotionally confused coming and going by the sudden switch in the way their parents communicated with them.

3. Change in routine

The change in routine can be very drastic, depending on where one works. In Asian countries, people tend to rise much earlier in the morning than is normal for those from North America. If the Muslim faith is dominant, everyone rises for prayers about 4:30 a.m. This casts the daily routine on an entirely unfamiliar schedule for the expatriate. In Singapore, busy people tend to stay up late and phone calls after 11 p.m. are not unusual. In fact, many people will go out to eat about that time. It takes awhile to adjust to changes like this in one's routine.

4. Changes in interpersonal relationship formation

This is much more difficult than the preceding because it can be almost impossible to figure out. We discover that many aspects of friendship are defined differently by our focus culture. Acceptance and rejection, ways of asking for help and saying thank you, giving and receiving presents, encouraging others and showing appreciation for their accomplishments are a few of the many facets of social exchange which may be difficult to comprehend. We become aware that we can recognize who good friends are but not why they are friends. We observe some of the activities which friends do but we can't figure out how one goes about <u>becoming</u> a friend. Our approaches are often interpreted in other categories such as a patron-client relationship. When we inquire as to what it takes to be a friend, we may be met with a blank face. People expect us to know. They may not have ever had to consider this question and can't verbalize the answer. It can be very frustrating.

When I asked my national mentor why people would not answer my questions about culture, his response was: "If you need to ask, you don't need to know." So I asked him how anyone could ever find out any-thing. He advised me to start by showing awareness or knowledge of some aspect and asking someone to expand on that. In that way, a small bit of knowledge can grow into a significant foundation on which to build.

5. Health and illness

Practically everyone has illnesses from time to time that depress them. Illness can magnify any mental, emotional, or spiritual struggle one might be having. In the tropics, the climate alone is debilitating. One does not have to be ill to become depressed. A constant lack of energy might do it.

Health is a priority

Although there are many medicines to deal with all kinds of illnesses and conditions such as diarrhea, many doctors and experienced workers suggest trying to develop immunities to these common illnesses. Eventually, one will not succumb to them easily.

Emotional illnesses are much more difficult to overcome on the field. Many times, the worker should consider professional counseling. If that is not available, one can use the experienced counseling of a fellow worker. When the person involved does not understand the reason for feelings of insecurity, loneliness, and depression, it may take a lot of time for a counselor to help. It is wise to consider going back to one's home country for help rather than utilize the time of a busy field worker, unless that is their ministry.

Here again we must be aware of satanic attacks. You must always remember that you are attempting to "bind the strong man" and he will not stand still to let you do it. It is a tenet that emotional and physical health are the common areas of satanic op-pression. Learn to rebuke the devil in Jesus' name.

CULTURE SHOCK

6. Security- short term/long term

In today's world, security is one of the biggest challenges a new worker has to face. This is true of national workers as well as expatriates. Very few Christian families anywhere are happy about their adult children working in a UPG. But each person has to make that decision if the Lord calls. There is no guarantee of safety. Anyone can be kidnapped, injured, or killed for the sake of the gospel.

A serious issue in today's world is preparation for trauma. Every cross-cultural church planting model should have the experience of trauma or hostage training. Dr. Steve Sweatman of Mission Training International gives the following comment. "More and more of those we debrief have experienced some significant trauma related to bodily threat or damage. We have noticed that there are three distinct missionary eras:

The era when Western Expats and missionaries were considered TERRIFIC
The era when Western Expats and missionaries where TOLERATED
The era when Western Expats and missionaries are now TARGETED
For those we debrief, 50% are coming from countries in the TOLERATED era and the other half from countries where they are in the TARGETED era." (e-mail, Sept. 1, 2012).

7. Concern about revealing your purpose and strategy

Revealing your purpose and strategy is different from revealing your testimony and convictions. Every culture has spiritual practitioners who are known as such. If you desire to have people respect you as a person who has spiritual knowledge and spiritual power, you have to demonstrate that knowledge and power in some concrete way. However, this does not mean that you have to reveal your long-term purpose and strategy. See the article on GUIDELINES FOR TENTMAKERS in the Appendix 3.

ORIENTATION

A. Local Religion

In this orientation period you should spend as much time as possible finding out all you can about your focus people's religious beliefs. This will be a life-long learning process. Most UPG cultures have a formal religion such as Islam, Hinduism, or Buddhism. But they also have an informal religion such as

You must think outside the box to grasp new religions

53

shamanism, animism, or inner life spiritual disciplines. There are many variations to these belief systems and it takes a lot of work to discover and understand them.

The major reason an experienced church planter has such difficulty in envisioning CC CP work is that he or she has not yet appreciated the fact that almost everything one knows about church planting has to be reprocessed as one moves into another cultural situation. For example, in his book *Constructing Local Theologies*, Robert J. Schreiter points out that in the area of theology one has no "articulated philosophical foundation" that forms the basis for a systematic theology (p. 10). When a leader of a mosque center was interviewed about his belief in the placenta as a "friend" of the child being born, the CC CP worker had no basis on which to formulate theology in that area. This religious leader prays to his placenta when he has a problem because his Islamic religion is intertwined with another belief system so that the two operate in conjunction with one another. But the cross-cultural church planter has to learn the philosophical basis for that before he or she can speak to the belief.

Worshipping the spirit in the tree

B. Worldview

One will be able to learn how the worldview of the focus people differs from biblical worldview by identifying basic values in the society and comparing and contrasting beliefs. For example, these basic assumptions affect how one views the value of human life or the activity of supernatural forces in the affairs of humans. They exercise a strong influence on various spiritual understandings such as the nature of sin and salvation. When we bring our worldview into dialogue with other worldviews, there is a danger that even the biblical view of the character of God, himself, will be warped. This is why God has given us his own word as an unchanging guide.

Studying worldview is a long process that takes many years. We touch on this subject many times throughout this Manual. Worldview issues are basic to every phase of cross-cultural church planting and the effective cross-cultural church planter is a constant student of worldview.

> *A major goal is changing worldview*

C. **Work steadily, not frantically**

There is a lot to learn in the Arrival Phase of CC CP. It may seem overwhelming when one considers all the adjustments and learning areas involved. It is important to remember that it can only be taken a bit at a time. Break the areas of learning into small segments and process several at a time. "Perseverance is more prevailing than violence; and many things which cannot be overcome when they are together, yield themselves up when taken little by little" (Plutarch, *Lives. Sertorius*, p.688). Some people try frantically to race from one learning area to another thinking they are going to master all this information in a short time. That will not happen and they might collapse from the effort. It is best to work steadily so that day by day you make advances in some area of expertise such as various aspects of culture, history, or politics.

D. **Have some fun, enjoy the adventure**

Clay lies still, but blood's a rover;
Breath's a ware that will not keep.
Up, lad: when the journey's over
There'll be time enough to sleep.
Alfred Edward Housman, *A Stropshire Lad. II*

It will get better

EVALUATION of END RESULTS - CHECK LIST - PHASE TWO

[ ] have experienced bonding as it is reflected in the philosophy and practice of my church planting team
[ ] family is settled, stable, and happy
[ ] am eating from local market without difficulty

[ ] health is adequate

[ ] life style (housing/clothing/transportation, etc.) approximates that of national co-workers in ministry

[ ] language study is consistent and progressing

[ ] am maintaining personal spiritual disciplines in daily Bible reading and study, prayer, and devotional reading

[ ] am giving consistent attention to family spiritual formation including family devotions, etc.

[ ] if single, am giving consistent attention to spiritual formation including any co- workers, housemates, devotions, etc.

[ ] if married, relationships with spouse are deepening

[ ] am guarding against relationships with the opposite sex

[ ] am spending both quality and quantity time with children

[ ] if single, am spending quality time with a trusted friend or family

[ ] am spending time each day to develop good relationships in community

[ ] have begun witnessing in community

[ ] am spending a lot of time visiting with persons from the focus group

[ ] have cultivated a good relationship with a church

[ ] am reading frequently about focus group and other local cultures

[ ] am beginning to compare and contrast local religion with Biblical faith

Tips: 1. LEARN TO PRAY!

2. "Go slow to go fast" (David Kyle) - First 3 mos. – acclimatize/adjust (pace yourself). Second 3 mos.– increase activity up to full speed (will probably take less time for nationals in their home countries).

3. If one's period of adaptation is away from the CP area, one's mistakes will have less impact.

4. FIRST, YOU ARE HERE TO LEARN, NOT TO TEACH!

5. **Build credibility as a spiritual leader with the focus group.**

6. **Keep going deeper– don't let anything discourage you *long term*. There will certainly be short term discouragements.**

7. **CC CP is a <u>Long Hard Journey</u> (others will help you but they cannot carry you).**

CHAPTER FOUR

THEOLOGY OF CHURCH PLANTING

*"For which of you desiring to build a tower, does not first sit down
and count the cost, whether he has enough to complete it? ... Or what
king, going out to encounter another king in war, will not sit down
first and deliberate..."*
Luke 14:28, 31

As a church planter continues to process the focus culture's religious beliefs, he/she should be involved in contemplating an overall theology of church planting that will blend with the character of the people group to produce a church with a biblical worldview. Many workers come to their field with their biblical theology already set in stone and they do not realize that we grow as we see the depth of God's word. For example, in our theology of the church we can reproduce Episcopal, Presbyterian, Congregational or some other style churches. However, it is critical to understand the culture of our focus group in order to decide what form of church government will fit that culture. We may think that our theology of the Holy Spirit is set in stone but He teaches us continually. The biblical theology we present should speak to the worldview of the people. On one hand, it should correct any faulty worldview and on the other it will enhance the salutary parts. We should not assume that implementing a biblical theology for our focus group is merely translating our own culture's theology into the local language.

CROSS-CULTURAL THEOLOGY

In Chapter Three, orientation to the local religion and worldview was mentioned. As you consider how to formulate a theology of church planting these features become more and more

*A theology
of CC CP is
paramount*

important. If you have not previously developed a theology of cross-cultural church planting, this is the time for study. Very few seminaries and Bible schools teach this kind of theological model. Their primary purpose is to train workers for their own culture and they emphasize a theology that will fit their culture. This is true in Asia as well as in Europe and the Americas. Unless you attended a unique missionary training school that taught this subject, you probably would not know much about it.

Most cross-cultural church planters have been taught the church theology of their particular tradition such as Armenian or Calvinist. When the Dutch missionaries planted churches in Indonesia, they simply translated their Bible, hymnbook, liturgy, and doctrines into the local language. Indigenous people were taught biblical theology from a Dutch Reformed point of view. The ceremonies for birth, dedication, marriage, and death were all taken from the Dutch Reformed tradition and, as such, did not speak to many of the spiritual questions of the indigenous people about unseen beings, evil spirits, the nature of the soul after death, ghosts, and other matters. Because of this, many aspects of the indigenous theology submerged under the Christian theology and continued to function in the lives of the people. Syncretism resulted in many cases. When we do not utilize biblical teachings that speak to the nature of being and the cosmology of new believers, their worldview is not likely to change to a biblical one.

Theology is essential

It is critical to understand that theology covers every phase of cross-cultural church planting and we need to have a biblical basis for everything we do. One young American worker created a model of churches called the C1-C6 Spectrum that illustrated a "practical tool for defining six types of 'Christ-centered communities'" (Travis, 1998) but he did not base it on a biblical theology. This model has gained wide acceptance by young missionaries even though it was described as a "simple chart...to graphically portray these different expressions of faith by MBBs" (Travis, 2000). [MBB = Muslim Background Believer]. Unfortunately, the C1-C6 Spectrum deals with only a few aspects of a contextualized church. Many other aspects are described in Chapter Nine of this book. There is great danger of falling into simplistic explanations of cultural phenomenon and formulating one's approach based on these assumptions. It is important that we understand that no "simple chart" is going to give us the information we need to select a biblical theology which will speak to the focus group. It may be a starting point but it is only that. Understanding the complicated worldview of a focus group and formulating a biblical theology to answer their spiritual questions is an enormous undertaking that requires years to work out.

Present biblical theology that answers spiritual questions

KINGDOM OF GOD THEOLOGY

While teaching at the Fuller Theological Seminary School of World Mission, Dr. Arthur F. Glasser illuminated a theology of mission based on the rubric of the Kingdom of God. This biblical theme has long been of interest to theologians who have applied it to every aspect of the church's life. By gleaning the thought of many theologians, Glasser traces this theme through the entire Bible and applies it to cross-cultural church planting.

You are in one of two kingdoms

The Kingdom of God is anticipated in the Old Testament and is inaugurated, extended, and contextualized in the New Testament. Of course, these are only relative descriptions because the Kingdom of God is both fully active and partially completed in every period of biblical history up to today. Every people group who come into the Kingdom of God will experience it both in ways similar to our experience and also in different ways. One of the surprising experiences I had was to find that Indonesian believers have had the same experience with Jesus that I have had yet there are significant variations due to religious belief systems and worldview. One young Muslim lady had a dream of meeting Jesus and what was most impressive to her was that Jesus spoke to her in her own language. I have never heard of an American Christian who was awed by the fact that Jesus spoke in English to them in their dreams.

Two Mandates in Theology

Glasser highlights the two mandates of the Kingdom of God. One is the evangelistic or redemptive mandate and the other is the cultural mandate. Dr. I.W. Mastra of the Christian Protestant Church in Bali (*GKPB*), who was converted from the Hindu religion, discovered that the missionaries who had started his church promoted a theology of poverty among the members. According to their understanding of scripture, it was better to be poor than rich because it is very difficult for a rich man to enter heaven and the poor enter heaven before the rich. Mastra says, "First of all, that theology had to be changed so that the church does not emphasize that being poor is good. We had to erase that theology first so that the believers would work hard to improve their situation" (Dixon, 2009a). Before Mastra reformulated this aspect of theology for the Bali church, the people understood the evangelistic mandate but not the cultural mandate. Now, their ministry to the Balinese people has changed and they are fulfilling both mandates.

A theology of blessing is an example of contextual theology

Dr. Mastra took Genesis 12 as his theological basis and expounded it in reference to the cultural situation in Bali. Since the covenant of God is for Abraham and his seed to bless the nations, Mastra applied that to the Bali Church as Abraham's spiritual children. The Indonesian word for blessing is *berkat* and this is similar to the Hebrew *barakah*. It was not difficult for many in the church to understand the import of Mastra's theological orientation, and most appropriated it for their own. This aspect of his biblical theology could not only be accepted intellectually but it had power to change the church.

THEOLOGICAL HERMENEUTICS

Mastra's reformulation of theology from one of poverty to one of blessing is an example of hermeneutics. The biblical text must be allowed to speak fully to the context of the church. A narrow hermeneutic stressing poverty prevented believers from seeing their full potential, while a theology of blessing released them to achieve whatever they were capable of doing. The church had existed for 30 years when Mastra first began to instruct the church in a biblical theology that did not insist on poverty. This freed them to use God-given abilities and talents to reach their potential in society and today the believers are thriving members of their communities.

Hermeneutics is a process

There are a variety of theologies of mission but all of them should emerge from the biblical text. Biblical hermeneutics can begin at various points but a theology for cross-cultural church planting should include God's plan for the unreached people groups. As cross-cultural church planters, we begin with our theology of mission and start to form a church from a body of believers. However, success depends on involving the believers within a short time in biblical study to see what the text is saying to them about their church life. As Dr. Mastra puts it, new believers "must become the subject, not the object. At first, the mistake was made in making us [Bali Church] only the object. If there was hunger, we were given food and clothing. We became dependent on outsiders" (Dixon, 2009a). It is imperative that the indigenous believers be involved in contextualizing theology for their church and implementing it in their daily lives.

Another example of hermeneutics was given by a Sundanese convert concerning wearing a hat while praying. The Sundanese frequently wear head coverings in their prayers and he noticed that Christians did not. So he began reading the New Testament from cover to cover to see what it said about head coverings. When he came to the passage in 1 Corinthians 11:4 where Paul writes that "every man who prays or prophesies with his head covered dishonors his head," he took that passage as his answer. However, other Sundanese believers were not sure that this verse meant the same thing so they interacted about it. Since then, the question has not been fully resolved and the hermeneutical discussion goes on.

> *Involve the indigenous people in biblical theology*

THEOLOGY IN CONTEXT

Since every cross-cultural church planter brings a theology of missions to the task, it is critical to compare and contrast his/her biblical model with the focus culture's religious model. This is necessary because there are aspects of their religious model, which answer some of the spiritual questions and felt needs of the focus group. They are following their present religious model for specific reasons and we need to understand what those reasons are. In this way, we can present aspects of the gospel that are most pertinent to their context. This is important in both a positive and a negative way.

Learn the theology of the focus culture

First, we want the gospel to reinforce the positive aspects of their culture but not the negative. We do not want to contextualize in such a way that we reinforce mistaken or wrong theological concepts such as earning one's way to heaven through doing good works, or praying five times a day to achieve perfection in prayer. Every belief system has non-biblical theologies and we do not want to endorse them. In the same way, every belief system has biblically acceptable theologies such as proper relationships between men and women and we do not want to weaken those positive beliefs or cultural patterns.

The Holy Spirit inspires faith

Theology is based in a worldview

Throughout Asia the dominant philosophy of religion is represented by two models. One is the *Tao* and it is structured by the second model which is the *Yin* and *Yang* concept. Even if you do not work in Asia, the religion of your focus group may be based on a variation of this worldview. Even if it is not, the study of this worldview will give you a different insight from that of a western worldview. Although these are very developed concepts that cannot be fully explained here, they basically support the view that reality is dualistic. The *tao* is the "vital principle" or basic energy or force present in all of nature. It is the substance of all life. Humans have no special place within the *tao* because they are simply one of many manifestations of it. The *tao* is the unknown and complex way that nature is ordered.

According to the *Yin* and *Yang* model, all existence is shaped or determined by a contrasting character. Every being or condition in creation can be described as having two sides: that is, a nature that is in opposition to itself. The ideal state for this dual nature is to be in balance. When this happens, each side has relatively equal influence and there is no conflict. But because of its oppositional nature, this dualism is often thrown out of balance or is put into a state of conflict. Thus, there is no ultimate right and wrong but rather an effort to maintain balance in one's life. In multiple variations, the formal religions, belief systems, and spirit beliefs of Asian people reflect these models.

THEOLOGICAL MODELS

All theological models should be drawn from Scripture, but in actual practice secular models are also used. We can see this in the contrasts between various theological models that are being used in church plants. The list below gives us some examples.

Sharing in a biblical model

dominance	vs.	servant
individualist	vs.	corporate
compartmental	vs.	holistic
micro	vs.	macro
rigid	vs.	flexible
isolationist	vs.	sociable
low identity	vs.	high identity
confrontational	vs.	indirect (or circuitous)

Dominance models

It is easier to implement church models that are dominant in the focus culture but it will mean a very difficult shift later if these models are not biblical. For example, in a culture that is oriented around a dominance model, new believers will accept a theological model of dominance even though it is contrary to the servant model taught in scripture. Since the dominance model is counter-productive to the Lord's will in many aspects of our lives, the spiritual growth of the church will suffer.

Don't implement a non-biblical church model

Individualistic models

Many western missionaries have imposed an individualistic model on their church plants rather than the corporate or communal one common to the culture. This has created a dichotomy between the believers' church and their public lives, and has created non-contextual relationships between the believers and their community. Many young indigenous leaders who have been sent to foreign countries for theological study have experienced a re-culturalization that divorced them from their native cultures. A young seminary classmate of mine in the United States who was a Singaporean Chinese was an example of this. He asked me how he could minister to his congregation in Singapore about spirit beliefs when he neither believed in them nor understood why others did.

Theological models are extensive

Be careful about drawing theological models from the culture. Theological models drawn from the culture have form and meaning. For example, Hindu people may wash in the river Ganges frequently but sometimes it has a special religious meaning for them. Muslims may face toward Mecca at any time but there are special religious times when its meaning is unique. When we draw theological models from the local culture, we have to understand what they mean to the local people. They are not based on a biblical worldview and therefore are unlikely to contain biblical truth. We need to find out if they are compatible with a biblical worldview.

Know their creation stories!

For example, we can bring *sholat*-type prayers into a church service but that does not mean Muslim converts will understand the use of them. The form of the *sholat* prayers is part of the meaning of the prayers whereas the movements one makes in church prayers has little to do with the meaning of the prayers. While it is true some leaders ask the believers to bow their heads and close their eyes during prayer, most people do not consider it to be necessary. However, many Muslims believe that the *sholat* is not valid if the body movements are incorrectly made.

These are just a few examples of the many theological models present in any given society. Every cross-cultural church planter should identify these types of models and teach new believers biblical theology that relates to them. New converts will struggle with these theological issues to discern the nature of their new life in Christ.

THEOLOGY OF THE CHURCH

Unfortunately, many missionary evangelists do not really consider matters such as a theology of the church because their primary goal is to win souls. Many para-church organizations also do not have a developed theology of the church because their goal is to gather new believers into small groups and disciple them. Workers such as these do not have a developed theology for a church that will transform its society. They are doing good work but their approaches do not encompass all that it takes to establish a strong church.

Elements of a complete theology

Tom Steffen (1993) develops one feature of church theology in *Passing The Baton: Church Planting That Empowers*. He describes a strong Evangelistic-Discipleship Model that includes a segment about the function of the New Testament church. His extensive description about training church leaders is oriented to his intent to present a "comprehensive, phase-out oriented model." This model represents one important aspect of church theology. Although it is valuable, it is not intended to be a complete model of church theology. In today's world of "tentmakers" and other freelance workers, there are many partial models being implemented. We need to consider how every approach to church planting should be intentional in founding a church in an all-embracing biblical theology. While it is good that we describe all kinds of models for various aspects of ministry, the ultimate goal of all our efforts should be a church with an exhaustive biblical theology. It does not matter that it might take twenty or more years to accomplish that. It should be the goal of every worker.

Don't get stuck in a partial model

Church and para-church

In *The New Testament Order for Church and Missionary*, A.R. Hay describes church structure and church order that are based on theological precepts. He believes that the New Testament apostles took the synagogue as the general pattern and instituted certain new features as "the new spiritual order made necessary" (1947:133). A mission agency is not a church either by its methods or its organization and the confusion of the two is what has created difficulties in many areas for transformational ministries in societies. It is important for us to plant churches and not evangelistic bands or mission agencies. They will emerge but it is critical that we first focus on establishing a New Testament church.

The doctrine (or theology) of the Church is something that has been blurred in many areas of so-called "church planting." I propose that without a theology of the Church, it is impossible to plant a New Testament Church. We can introduce many aspects of church life but the fullness of God's intent will not be there. Theology elucidates important spiritual mysteries such as the meaning of the body of Christ, the gifts of the Spirit, and the divine mission to preach the gospel.

A.R. Hay points out that Paul's exposition in his letter to the Ephesians is concerned with the theology of the Church as a whole and not just with a local congregation. "It gives the structure of the Church and states the great spiritual principles that govern this structure, relating the whole to the fundamental purpose of God for man" (Ibid., 147). It is this theology that every church planter needs to imbibe for without it we are only doing part of the work that God has laid on our hearts. This is a call for every church planter to study and incorporate the theology of the Church into his or her church plant.

THEOLOGY OF A CHURCH PLANT

Comprehensive Theology

A comprehensive theology of church planting needs to cover the whole range of church planting, beginning with evangelism. For many, evangelism simply means the sharing of the gospel with individuals so that they come to faith. For others, it also includes discipling converts according to Matthew 28:18 but not necessarily reaching their entire family web. **A theology of evangelism should include not only reaching through converts to share with their family web but also moving past the family to impact their entire community with the gospel.** For many years, this understanding of evangelism was not generally taught in Indonesia. Bible schools and seminaries taught that our responsibility as believers was simply to share the gospel with others. However, an understanding of evangelism that included a convert's entire community has resulted in more and stronger church plants.

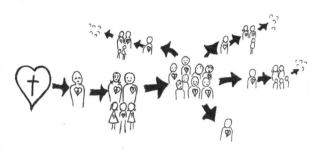

The gospel moves from one to another

Evangelistic models

An indigenous evangelistic model is also very important because imported models from the west such as "The Four Spiritual Laws" may not resonate with the indigenous people. Rodger Lewis gives an example of how Balinese evangelists

Create a model to impact all of society

illustrated the necessity of the new birth. This was used by one of the early evangelists. "It is like an egg. An egg must be born twice before it can become a chicken. If it is born once, it ends up being fried and eaten. If it is born twice, it becomes a life. If you are born only once, the devil will fry you in Hell. If you are born twice, you become a Christian" (1999:37-38).

Sundanese evangelists have many ways of explaining how God has revealed the cross in West Java. Some of these are strange to our western thought but Sundanese seem to enjoy them. They would say that God has used the cross in many ways to emphasize the cross of Christ. It is seen where roads cross each other. It is seen in the door where a mullion runs up the center of the door to form a cross with the parallel rails that strengthen the door. It can also be seen in the end of the house where a beam runs up the center of the wall to the roof ridge crossing the top plate of the wall.

Some of their theological explanations are also unique and while not always exactly correct, they blur worldview concepts so that the listeners are forced to consider a different worldview. Once when Kardi bin Karta had been called by the leading Muslim clerics (*Majelis Ulama-MU*) and asked what he worshipped, he answered, "Whether you say God's name in Arabic or Greek, the meaning is the same. In Arabic, you say *'Illahi Robbi, subhana wata Allah,'* but in Greek, you say, 'Yesus Kristus,' which means the same thing: that God is the Most High. The Greeks mean the same with Yesus Kristus. It's just a difference in languages." (Dixon, 1980). After that the MU did not call him again.

> *Implementing theology is a continual process*

Contextual Theology

The process of contextualizing the theology of a church plant takes place over a long period of time because essentially the converts should do it, and it takes time for them to learn the Word of God. Imposing a theology of the church by an outsider leads to the danger of not speaking to the spiritual questions of the new believers. Sadrach was a great Javanese Christian leader who has been used as an example of an insider and contextual giant. He was responsible for much of the Javanese mindset that contributed to the unprecedented turning of Muslims to Christ in Java. However, most people do not realize that Sadrach worked closely with non-Javanese Christians during the first 25 years of his ministry. Beginning in 1870 until he joined the Apostolic Church in 1899, Sadrach did not baptize believers. In the early years, he invited various ministers of the Dutch mission to baptize. Later, he asked J. Wilhelm of the Dutch Reformed Mission Organization (NGZV) to be the minister of his churches and from 1883 until 1892 Wilhelm taught Sadrach's followers from the Bible. After he became an ordained "apostle," Sadrach continued to invite Dutch missionaries to teach his congregations. In this way, Sadrach and his followers were guided in the formative years of their churches by experienced Bible teachers. Through discussions about a biblical expression of the gospel for their culture, the Javanese church grew strong.

A contextual theology in church planting compares and contrasts cultural worldview structures with biblical worldview. Many young workers fail to discern this complicated procedure, and implement non-biblical worldview from the indigenous religion without realizing its ultimate effect on the faith of new converts. Some workers have taken the Muslim form of prayer five times a day and revised it to use Christian prayers five times a day without realizing that the former is based on a non-biblical worldview and the latter on something they made up, thus validating a legalistic worldview.

In like manner, Christians do not face a particular direction during their prayers in church because the biblical worldview sees God as omnipresent and not limited in time or space. The direction in which one prays is not specified in the biblical worldview so it really does not matter which direction is used. However, by requiring that prayers be made in a specific direction, a non-biblical worldview is reinforced.

These simple examples can be multiplied numerous times because worldviews permeate a culture and affect all of the culture's structures. When our Sundanese church planting team began to study Sundanese music in 1985, they were influenced by a newly converted Sundanese musician to use the *gamelan* instruments for worship. However, after a few months of study, they learned that those instruments were associated with spirit worship and other non-biblical messages. They were told that another set of instruments called *degung* was more suitable for wor-

The gospel through indigenous music

ship, for honoring people, and for dedications of various sorts. Although these instruments were similar, they did not have an anti-biblical orientation. So they switched to the new instruments and learned to play them. Something relatively simple like this was not known to the young Sundanese evangelists and church planters. It took a process to lead them to the correct music.

Specific theologies

The role of women is an example of the specific theologies with which we need to wrestle in our church planting. Paul's first letter to the Corinthians highlights many aspects of the way women were viewed in the Greek culture. He writes not only about marriage but also about virgins, the unmarried, widows, and divorcees. In other letters, Paul writes about the relationship between husband and wife and the meaning of marriage in God's eyes.

In many cultures where there are no churches the physical and spiritual abuse of women is rampant. Women are not considered equal members of society and are excluded from many aspects of indigenous religion. Even in developed churches, on-going biblical contextualization is needed. In an interview, dr. Luh Debora Murthey said the following: "Yes, certainly the Bali church is thick with Bali culture that is very patriarchal. In the Bali culture women are not raised as people who have an active right to make a decision even though they have education and have become a doctor, a teacher, or a business person. However, when they are in the process of making a decision, they feel that they are not sufficiently competent to do so because they have not been trained from youth to be involved in decision making." "I feel that the Bali Church must make greater efforts to break through this culture and encourage families to give an equal role to both boys and girls" (Dixon, 2009b).

Conclusion

We can write a conclusion to this chapter but the reader will understand that the struggle for a biblical theology of the church is unending. It is most difficult in the cross-cultural situation and requires all the gifts God has given the church planter and his/her team. As we see in the Bali Church that has existed for nearly 80 years, wrestling with a biblical theology of the Church is the hallmark of contextualization. Though you may not have arrived at your focus group or only recently have arrived, it is not too early to start studying and learning how to understand the relationship between the indigenous theology and biblical theology.

EVALUATION of END RESULTS - CHECK LIST - CHAPTER FOUR

[ ] am continuing intensive study of New Testament theology
[ ] am studying the theology of the local religion and comparing it to biblical theology
[ ] have begun to identify aspects of the local worldview that compare and contrast to biblical worldview
[ ] am observing critical aspects of the focus culture that require understanding; such as spirit beliefs, dependency issues, feelings of inferiority, fear, and the like
[ ] am reading the myths of my focus group to learn about their worldview

[ ] am studying various theologies of mission that provide answers to the spiritual questions in the focus culture

[ ] am crafting a theology of mission as a servant model that empowers the individual as well as the community

[ ] am incorporating evangelism, nurture, and infrastructure models that will support the church planting goal

CHAPTER FIVE

PHASE THREE - ORIENTATION TO THE FOCUS GROUP

"The wise man also may hear and increase in learning and the man of understanding in skill." Proverbs 1:5

In one of his Peanuts comic strips, Charles Shultz has his character Lucy pretending to give psychiatric help. Lucy says the following to the dog, Snoopy. "It used to be that a person could live isolated from the world's problems.... Then it got to be that we all knew everything that was going on.... The problem now is that we know everything about everything except what's going on. That's why you feel so nervous...five cents, please!"

Worshipping graves makes me nervous

In the UPG, everyone except the outsider knows what's going on. As expatriates we may know everything about everything in the world at large but we don't know what is going on around us in the UPG. That is the challenge for the cross-cultural church planter. Our first task is to orient ourselves to the focus group. This is a responsibility that really never ends if we are going to be effective in CC CP. This familiarization has many levels and it can be described as superficial or as extremely complex. In this section we are talking about adjustment that would be necessary to begin your church planting model. This orientation can be described as late internship and it is moving into the complex arena. The intensive period may cover one to two years or longer.

SELF EVALUATION

Evaluate your experience

> *Seek the meaning behind the actions*

Just as you evaluated yourself in Phase One concerning your training for going to a UPG, in the same way, it is helpful to evaluate your experience on entering the focus group. An evaluation of this kind reveals areas in our lives that relate to those of our focus group. If you have few of these relational fields, it should motivate you to work on developing in those spheres. For example, if you have previously worked in a UPG there will many experiences that you will be able to transfer to this new UPG.

On the other hand, not every experience you had in another UPG will be useful in this new one. One of my colleagues was an example of this. He had worked for many years in a South American country before he came to our S.E. Asian country to work. He had adjusted beautifully in South America and had learned the language fluently. But culture was different in this new country and he could not feel his way. He was used to speaking frankly and bringing issues out into the open. He treated people the way he treated South Americans and there were many hurt feelings because of his bluntness. As time passed, he learned a new way to relate to people that was much more effective. He needed to adjust his previous learning experience to fit a new situation.

Survey

The following short survey is intended to help you note your areas of experience. It is important that you answer as honestly as possible. Pretending you are someone you are not will not help you adjust to a focus people. However, when you state frankly what your situation truly is, the Lord can guide you in strengthening the weak areas.

Phase Three - Orientation To The Focus Group

1. If this UPG was not your first assignment in foreign service, please indicate what was. _____

2. Before coming to your first assignment, how long did you live in a culture foreign to your own? Years_____ Months _____

3. In what capacity did you live there? _____ e.g., held a job; lived with parents; was a summer visitor.

4. Did you learn the local language? _____ What language? ____

5. Before coming to your first assignment, how long did you work in a permanent, full time job? _____ part time job? _____

6. What permanent, full time jobs have you had?_____in-clude military service _____

7. What was your level of education when you first came to an unreached people? _____

8. How old were you when you first came to an unreached people?_____

9. Were you married? _____ No. of children _____

10. How long had you been a born again Christian? Years____ Months_____

11. Did you have a "call" or clear leading or command from God to go to an unreached people?

12. Had you ever held a full time job on a church staff? ____ How long? ____ Part time job on a church staff? _____ How long? _____

13. Had you ever held any position in a church (e.g., SS teacher, etc.)? What position? _____ How long? _____

14. Did you have a strong, personal relationship with Jesus Christ and a consistent, satisfying devotional life? _____

Survey Debrief

Numbers 1-4

The following comments are intended to help you think through a few issues.

If Numbers 1-4 apply to you, then you bring a great deal of experience to your present challenge. The person who has actually lived in a culture foreign to his or her own, and especially if they have worked in it, begins with a great advantage. This is particularly true if one has learned a language other than one's mother tongue. Usually, second or third languages are easier for such persons.

Numbers 5-6 reveal our experience in actually doing a job on a regular basis. Many workers who come to a UPG have never held a full time job. The disadvantages of this are discussed briefly in the section on Phase One. Most of the adults you meet in a UPG will have responsibilities that keep them busy during the day. The men may work away from the home while the women work in the home. Many people will ask you about your work. This is true for national workers as well as expatriates. National workers have shared that one of the most confusing times for them has been when focus people asked them about their livelihood. In much of the church planting in the past, many of the evangelists did not have any job other than talking to people. It became apparent early on that being an evangelist among a UPG was not a profession valued by the focus people.

Number 7 relates to your level of education. If there is great variance between your educational level and that of your focus group, you may find difficulty communicating. Although language facility may be part of the problem, different ways of thinking are a much more serious issue. Research has found that all people do not learn the same way. In an article on cognitive styles, John Berry reviews some of the different approaches in understanding culture and cognition. In particular, he illustrates the field dependent-independent theory. "If one accepts uncritically the notion of 'general intelligence', then serious problems arise when we work cross-culturally" (1983:195). These different ways of learning confuse the inexperienced worker who only knows how to process information in the way he or she has been taught. Since people in the UPG have no idea of other ways to learn, it behooves the church planter to learn their ways. This can be an onerous task.

Numbers 8-9

Your age and/or marriage status as reflected in Numbers 8-9 have serious implications for your ability to relate to people in your UPG. Status and role generally have defined categories among most UPG. For example, youth rarely has influence upward. People who have never been married will likely have very little sway on those who are married. In some

Age & status will affect your influence

cultures, people who have never been married are not considered adults. During recent years, there has been significant change in some UPG due to the impact of education on the society. Youth with high education and important jobs may be imbued with prestige that overcomes the cultural prejudice against youth.

Numbers 10-11

Your spiritual maturity as indicated in Numbers 10-11 is critical to your success in the UPG. As was mentioned in Phase One, spiritual maturity and experience are the most important aspects of the effective church planter in cross-cultural venues. If the church planter's spiritual disciplines have been poorly developed or neglected due to the pressures of work or education, it is important that he or she give them primary attention at the outset of orientation to the UPG. At first, there may not seem to be much spiritual opposition to your presence in the UPG. But as soon as you begin to make some inroads in friendship and gospel sharing, you will encounter the spiritual forces latent in every locality and in every family. Begin with yourself and your family in building a strong spiritual relationship with the Lord. Every worker should have someone who is a spiritual mentor who can serve as a reminder of the importance of working at this most critical relationship.

Numbers 12-13 have to do with your experience in church work. This is different from Numbers 5-6 that have to do with secular work. Your experience in the church will impact how well you understand what it means to plant a church. It is apparent that the cross-cultural church planter has to know the structure and function of a church. We cannot expect to plant if we do not know what we are planting. Already in Phases One and Two, the importance of church theology, polity, structure and infrastructure have been mentioned. In a UPG, these various characteristics of a church may change from those of our native culture. However, there will always be similarities. The more deeply one has mastered the organization and theology of the church in one's own culture, the more easily one will be able to understand the development of an indigenous church in the focus group. If you do not have experience and knowledge in this area, it is imperative you prioritize it. Keep in mind, however, that the goal is not to plant western church clones.

Seek to know Jesus more

Number 14

The last item has to do with your personal relationship with Jesus in a stressful situation. If you have never had a secular or church job, then you have not had the opportunity of testing your faith in those circumstances. In that case, your new experiences in the UPG will bring new challenges in your relationship with Jesus. This is where your personal team mentor should be able to help you work through any issues that may develop. On the other hand, if you have had stress in a previous job, it is likely that the challenge of the UPG will cause this stress to show up again. As Paul tells us, it is common to have weaknesses that crop up over and over (2 Corinthians 13:4). You may need help from your personal mentor to avoid depression or discouragement in these areas.

SPIRITUAL MATURITY

The main key

Prioritize your personal relationship with God

This leads us into the <u>main key</u> to your fruitfulness in an unreached field. It is the continual effort you make to mature in your personal walk with God. In Matthew 16:24, Jesus tells us to deny ourselves and take up our cross and follow him. The denying of oneself has to be a daily experience in the UPG. If it is not, then we cannot hope to achieve much. One of the greatest barriers in cross-cultural church planting is adjusting to one's new self. When we are in our own culture and in our chosen career slot, we feel at home with ourselves. This all changes when we go cross-cultural. Adjusting to a different way of life is very difficult but adjusting to the fact that we are no longer our old self is even harder. Preparing ourselves for new identities is crucial for we will be given a series of new identities by the culture in which we work. In our own culture, we may have never been a patron, a healer, a teacher, or a spiritual advisor. But in our CC CP work we may become all of those. Jesus will call us to be what he wants us to be in order to communicate the gospel with a UPG.

Embrace your new identity

In Chapter Five, Luke describes the day that Jesus called Peter to accompany him full time. He said to Peter, "Do not be afraid; from now on you will be catching men." With those words, Jesus took away Peter's identity as a professional fisherman and called him to something he did not understand. Peter could have refused or he could have negotiated with Jesus to find out what he would be doing. Instead, he "left everything and followed him." He was willing to do whatever job Jesus needed done. That is the attitude the effective cross-cultural church planter will have. Many workers refuse to do the jobs that need to be done because they do not feel comfortable doing something that they did not learn in school. However, in CC CP we will often be doing something we did not learn in a school or something we do not "enjoy." It is necessary to be open to do whatever the Lord puts in our way.

1. **Personal prayer life & spiritual disciplines revisited**

In Colossian 4:2 Paul tells us to be watchful in prayer. The indication here is that even though we may be steadfast in prayer, it is possible to not give strict attention to it. Have you ever read your Bible and then couldn't remember what you just read? Have you ever prayed for a period and then could not remember what you were praying for? A busy church planter can unintentionally fall into this habit. It is possible to be praying a lot but not being "watchful." When the busyness of CC CP really hits you it will be easy to skip through spiritual disciplines to get on to the multiple tasks that need to be done. We must avoid this satanic trap.

Keep family & friends focused on the Lord

2. Family spiritual health

Just as you have to maintain your own spiritual disciplines, so it is imperative that you protect your family spiritually. The devil strikes at the weakest link and young children are vulnerable to various attacks. Our children as well as the children of friends were often beset with bad dreams that woke them in the night. At one period, our child woke up at midnight for night after night screaming in terror. After we rebuked the devil in Jesus' name, the terrors stopped and never returned. Children need to have the confidence that Jesus is our protector in all situations.

3. Expatriate Team

At this early period in your orientation, you should spend time deepening your relationships and friendships with fellow team members. You will spend a lot of time in the work place with them but you should also spend time in prayer and recreation getting to know and understand them. Your expatriate team members will likely be the only people in your area who can really understand you. Although you will eventually develop close friendships with nationals, it is unlikely that any will be able to comfort and support you in your early years as much as someone who has shared your experience. But beware of this becoming a safe "island" where you spend most of your time.

In an excellent article about preventing discouragement, David A. Diaso (2010:84) reports on a survey of 180 church planters. He highlights four components: a clear definition of the criteria for success; a clear description of tasks required to plant a church; training, coaching, and mentoring in tangible church-planting principles; and consistent encouragement and feedback from the mission agency and team leader/supervisor. Make sure these are clear on your team.

4. Claiming the unsaved for Christ

When Hudson Taylor became burdened for China, he claimed it for Christ. Even today, some workers might think it is foolish to claim a large

UPG for Christ when there is no chance of seeing them come to Christ in one's lifetime. However, that is the shortsighted view of those who do not understand CC CP. As Paul tells us in 1 Corinthians 3, one plants, another waters, and God gives the growth. We plant churches for the future because the kingdom of God grows like a mustard seed. In our lifetime, the church in the UPG may only be a small number of people but if we know how to plant, that small church will eventually impact an entire culture.

5. Continuing spiritual warfare prayer

Spiritual warfare as represented in 2 Cor.10:3-4 is different from your own spiritual health and your family's spiritual well being that are mentioned above. In order to reach the hearts of people in the UPG, it is important to bind the strong man and break through powerful forces that are enfolding them. In most UPG you will discover an underlying belief system that appeases spirit powers. It is common to discover that commitment to these spirit powers has bound the focus people for centuries. Overcoming their fears and getting them to truly listen to the gospel message is no easy task.

Evangelism is not a simple matter of getting people to agree with you that the gospel is a blessed hope. Your ministry must have the supernatural power of the Holy Spirit who will convict and convince people to turn to the Lord. We know many who said, "Your religion is better, but I cannot change."

6. Praying through your family's physical illnesses

The early years in the UPG are usually times of physical adjustment to the health dangers. Our bodies have to adjust to new germs and bacteria. Often, our children seem to have more problems with this. We need to learn to pray through all the family ailments and trust the Lord for healing and progressively stronger health as time goes by.

FAMILY RELATIONSHIPS

1. The second main key

While your personal walk with God is the main key in your being fruitful in an unreached field, the <u>second</u> main key is to give adequate attention to relationships with spouse and children. In many cases one is able to learn language, do a great deal of work, and contact many people in the UPG while not giving much attention to one's family. However, in the long run this will be a poor model for the developing congregation. If Christian people do not know how to model their faith as a family in their society, the presentation of the gospel will be warped. It is imperative that the church planter be that initial model of how a Christian family lives. The church among the Javanese Muslims took root and grew because the early leaders gave their attention to all the people and not just to the men.

Model a Christian family & Christian relationships

Single workers face more of a challenge in structuring personal relationships. Frequently, they can connect with another single worker or with a family. However, more often it is difficult to form close relationships. Interviewing a prospective friend and negotiating a spiritual relationship is something the Lord helps us do. Friends model biblical relationships in the give and take of a culture hostile to the word of God. Many UPG have little concept of what a biblical friendship would be like. Seeing this kind of experience gives a powerful testimony to the UPG culture.

Keep the family central

2. Unify the family model in love and discipline

It is important to be consistent in parenting but also contextual in your behavior as responsible parents. During our first year on the field, we took our new-born to church before he was 40 days old. We did not know that this was a serious breach of parental responsibility. In that culture, it was considered dangerous to the child's health to take it out earlier than 40 days. There were also some other spirit beliefs connected with this custom that we should have known. As we demonstrate the virtues of the Christian family, we also should try to learn the virtues of the family life of the focus group. (And yes, our child did get very ill).

3. Relationships outside the family

Avoid outside emotional liaisons that put stress on the family. In many UPG, men should not counsel with women and women should not counsel with men. Even corporate prayer can cause a problem if men lay their hands on women or vice versa. The common practice in many western countries of men and women holding hands and praying is not appropriate in many of the UPG areas. These intimate contacts can create emotional reactions in the unsuspecting. It is not uncommon for married or single missionaries of either sex to be attracted to nationals and fall into sin.

Be aware of Satan's desire to split your family. There are many missionary families that have been split by various unimportant as well as important differences of opinion. Nothing is too small or insignificant for Satan to use in driving a wedge between spouses.

4. Seek outside help

Don't be afraid of seeking outside help if you find that your family situation is deteriorating. If your team leader is mature, he or she will realize that you are going through something similar to that experienced by many before you. In the event your team leader does not understand your situation, there are many trained counselors now who can help you. Usually, your agency will know of some. There are also organizations such as Link Care in Fresno, CA that can give you advice and counseling.

Seek help for family problems

5. Family as a team

While it is not always possible for a family to participate in all aspects of the church planting effort, it should be functioning as a team in ministry. It is most desirable for the family to be seen and heard as unified in its purposes and goals. All negative issues in the family should be settled before leaving for the field. Husbands and wives who are not unified should not go to a UPG and burden a field team with their adjustment problems. There will be sufficient difficulties without adding unresolved marriage contentions to the list. One couple admitted that they thought becoming missionaries would solve their marriage problems. They are now divorced.

6. Relationship problems

Problems of all kinds should be addressed with expediency rather than postponing them. While this is the ideal, there are some expatriate cultures that prefer to ignore problems until they go away. Some of these consider it highly offensive to confront issues between workers. Therefore, it may be difficult on some teams to resolve differences between workers. This can also be true of disputes with people of the focus group. It is important to know how they settle differences. Some UPG do not have sound problem-solving methods. In some focus groups a person will never admit fault. The matter may fester until there is a blow up or people give it benign neglect until it fades in importance. This can be very stressful to some expatriate workers.

Address your problems

ENVISIONING YOUR STRATEGY AND METHODS FOR CHURCH PLANTING

1. Envisioning your church plant

The preparation for envisioning a church plant that you made during your arrival phase should now be extended to another level. Although it is difficult to envision how a church plant is going to develop before you actually do one, you should expend great effort to do so. To paraphrase David Kyles's advice, the seeds of any ministry's success or failure are found at its very beginning. The effective church planter learns to envision the contextual church he seeks to establish.

Continue to envision the church plant

There are many examples of workers who came to their focus group with a preconceived model of church planting that they intended to implement. **If I were to select the top five important subjects in this book, one would be to develop your model after you have been in your field of work, have learned the language, and have studied the culture enough to understand something about their social organization, leadership models, and how they define a spiritual practitioner.** These items will be discussed more thoroughly in Phases Four, Five, and Six.

2. Define the ministry in detail

There are many available tools we can use that will help us structure the strategy and methods we need for planting a church. One example already mentioned is Envisioning the CP Project (Appendix 4). This model is taken from a business environment and it gives us some guidelines in planning our ministry goals. David Kyle advises us to <u>define the project in detail</u>. Although you are not ready to do this as well as you would like, it is important to begin the process while you are in the orientation stage. Defining the church planting task is how you clarify the steps you need to take in order to create a contextual model. You begin this in Phase Three and finish as you move through Phase Six. This could take quite a few years.

3. Planning closure

Planning closure for your church planting team will need to be done during the early envisioning process. From the outset, it is important to decide what your requirements are for the handoff point to indigenous leadership. This is discussed in detail in Chapter Thirteen. It is frequently detrimental to the church planting task to postpone this decision until the missionary team feels that it is time. Church planters tend to take owner-ship of the church planting project and find multiple reasons why the project has to be continued. Many mission agencies have been literally forced by nationals to relinquish control of the distribution of personnel and resources because they had not decided on the indicators for closure. If you have the mentors who can help you, decide this issue from the outset.

Define your church plant

4. Appraise the environment

When you define the church planting in detail, you begin by appraising the environment in which the organization is to be developed. All churches are organizations of people and unless you create world-view changes, they will tend to operate in the way the focus

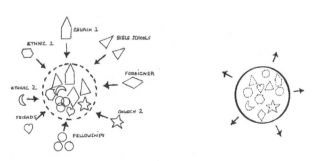

Multiple environments become unified

people function in all their organizations. The environment is broad and there are many aspects that have to be noted. You will study this in more detail when you implement the steps described in Appendix 4.

5. Define the magnitude of effort

The sketch above shows some of the many facets involved in a church plant. There are ethnic groups, friends, fellowships, Bible schools, and churches that may all play a part in your church plant. The challenge is bringing them into your circle because they are all individual entities with their own agendas. The second circle shows how they are working together for outreach. When each contribution is in harmony the church will move out into the community.

You will need to define the magnitude of effort before implementation. That is, you should strive to get some sense of the job/tasks involved, the number of evangelists you need, finances required, discipleship training, Christian life materials, and many other aspects of church life. This is critical for church planting. If you are only doing evangelism and/or fellowship groups, the task is fairly simple but it will not likely result in a mature church.

6. Develop an organization strategy

Finally, you should develop an organization strategy, i.e., a coherent set of tasks. You may have a strategy for your expatriate team but do you have one for the new team (or teams) that will be formed when you win focus people and disciple them to be evangelists? In Appendix 4, there are guidelines to help you think through these issues. When you follow well-developed guidelines, you can move ahead, experiment, and learn by doing with confidence that you are building a cohesive church planting strategy.

* In Chapter Eight on Negotiating, more information is given concerning starting a church plant.

Different ways to create a strategy

RECRUITING A NATIONAL TEAM

It is not always possible to recruit a national team during your late orientation period and it is not necessarily a good thing to do. Everything depends on your readiness to learn from the nationals and be continually mentored as you move forward. We will discuss mentoring in detail in the Phase Four section of this book (Chapter Six).

> *Aim for a national team or a focus group team*

1. Establish local context before recruiting a focus group team

It is usually not advantageous to recruit a team before a context has been created for you in which the team can thrive. Depending on the nature of the focus group, you may need to have a formal relationship with a national church or para-church organization that will form a network for your purposes. An example of this is a country like Indonesia where all religious groups are required to be registered with the Department of Religion. However, in some countries such as China unregistered groups abound despite the laws. It is best to know your context before you recruit others to face the difficulties of church planting in the UPG.

2. Youth learn more swiftly

When you are recruiting team members from nationals or from your focus group, it is well to remember that youth learn more easily than older people. Often, it is difficult for older persons to adjust to a new philosophy of ministry, a new strategy, or a new model of evangelism or Christian nurture. However, young people usually lack the experience, church relationship, or skills needed to deal with cultural matters. When we worked with a group of young evangelists, we learned that their parents did everything for them before they were married. They had not gotten a driver's license or any other document on their own. As a result, their knowledge of the culture was minimal and they had to minister for many years before they learned how to pastor a congregation.

3. Older people have more wisdom

On the other hand, the advantage of older people is they know the culture and they can mentor us so that we make fewer mistakes. Even though they may not respond to learning new models of ministry, they can help us to understand the culture in which we want to create new models.

When one of the national evangelists on our church planting team was planning to marry a girl from the focus group, the local custom required him to spend the night at the village of the bride. An old man who was living with the team warned them to send someone to accompany him. The prospective bridegroom was unconcerned and the other evangelists did not press him to take any of them along. The result was that the father of the bride and his pastor changed all the agreements about the wedding ceremony and ruined this young man's wedding day. The old man knew what we did not know but no one listened to him.

4. Recruiting for the UPG is difficult

Recruiting workers for the UPG among the other ethnic groups in the country is usually not an easy job. Christians are often living in ghetto cultures or are psychologically separated from the other religious traditions. In one of our training courses in Indonesia, we had two graduates from a leading seminary who did not know what the *Bismillah* meant. Although they had been raised in a predominantly Muslim society, they were unfamiliar with one of the most cardinal of Muslim formulae.

Pray for good workers

If one is recruiting evangelists for the UPG the most likely sources are the Bible schools. In many cases, their educational level may be low but their spiritual training and commitment to the Lord's work is usually higher than one finds in the local churches. Our experience in Indonesia has shown us that students like this may take five or more years to become accomplished evangelists and pastors in a UPG. If you are in a focus group where few believers can be recruited, expect a long-term adjustment and training period for non-focus people who join your team.

5. Accountability structure

An accountability structure is very important for your team. This is a set of guidelines that enables the sponsoring church or organization to have true oversight of the ministry. In some situations, the church planting team may exercise this oversight. When a church plant has been made, the church leaders will eventually assume this responsibility. Whether the evangelists are under the authority of the church planting team or the church, they should report to a supervisor each morning to verify their assignments for the day. At times, some of these workers might be constructing their own ministry schedule. However, even if that is so, someone should monitor their plans and ensure debriefing at the end of the day. Workers should not be left to fend for themselves in any area of ministry. Like workers everywhere in the world, a qualified and authorized supervisor should lead them.

6. **Difficulties of CCCP**

The cross-cultural church planter must always remember that it is usually extremely difficult to start a church among a UPG. Many UPG are not unreached because no one has ever tried to reach them. They are unreached because their faith system is extremely strong. They have been that way for hundreds or even thousands of years. There have been cross-cultural church planters who went confidently to a new people group with the stated goal of completing their mission in a few years, and found that they were unable to even befriend people in that length of time. It is not impossible for the church planting process to happen quickly. But we have to be prepared for the alternative.

UPG are unreached because they are closed communities

7. **National evangelists**

In the early years, national evangelists may have a difficult time incorporating a new strategy. If they come from Christian backgrounds, they already have ingrained models that are hard to reconstruct. If they come from the focus group, they have a low level of Bible knowledge and a non-biblical worldview that may confuse their presentation of the gospel. Misunderstandings of all kinds are common at these early stages of church planting and the church planting team can become discouraged and quit. Discouragement is a personal problem and it has to be dealt with on a personal level, in communion with God.

W.H. Burleigh has written these words in *Still Will We Trust.*
"Let us press on, in patient self denial,
Accept the hardship, shrink not from the loss:
Our portion lies beyond the hour of trial,
Our crown beyond the cross."

TEAM BUILDING

1. Cross-cultural teams

Cross-cultural teams are unique

There is a great deal in print about team building in general. The purpose of this section is to stimulate thinking about team building where it requires cross-cultural relationships. While we are in school, we usually develop skills to relate to others of our worldview and thought patterns. However, in CC CP you may experience three new kinds of team dynamics. One is the cross-cultural expatriate team where there are members from several different countries. The second might be a team composed of expatriates and nationals of various ethnic backgrounds. A third team that you may experience would be one formed by evangelists from the focus group. You would be less likely to have deep involvement with this third team after you have trained it because this team should operate from a contextual focus group model.

However, the basic cross-cultural church planting team in a focus group might be composed of expatriates from different countries, nationals from different ethnic groups, and members from the focus group. These very different people work together for a church plant. They may have to deal with multiple languages with many possibilities of misunderstandings and they have to deal with other cultural adjustments not found in mono-cultural teams.

2. Special skills

Involvement with these kinds of teams requires special skills. First, you must know the language well enough to communicate in prayer as well as in conversation. Prayer with a national team should be in their own language and not in that of an expatriate. In the same way, intergroup relations must be predicated on the local cultural conditions. In many countries, the youth are being educated in the national language and acculturated into the modern global culture. These are the areas of adjustment the outsider church planter must make to keep them in their highest learning curve. They will learn spiritual lessons and church planting models faster and more effectively if their trainers are operating in their cultural environment.

3. Leadership models

Another important area in cross-cultural team building is leadership models. While we may know a lot about leadership principles, it will be necessary to reevaluate them in light of the cross-cultural situation. Leadership that is not conceptualized following contextual forms will not be easily understood. The article on leadership in Appendix 5 follows the theory of Sherwood Lingenfelter on political leadership. His theory helps us examine the form of leadership used by our focus group. Most church planters do not understand contextual leadership until they have been in a culture for many years. However, if a church planter understands that this is something that needs to be studied, gifted mentors can minimize this shortcoming.

Don't dominate, serve

Lianne Roembke has multiple references in her book about leadership in multicultural teams. In her section on Leadership Styles, Authority, and Decision-Making, she writes: "The host culture should play the most significant role in forming the leadership style of the team. In practice, however, this is not always self-evident" (2000:153). She goes on to point out the difficulties created by the cultural make-up of a team. If most of the members are from a culture different from the host culture, they will tend to resist a foreign leadership style. Her book is an important resource for multicultural teams.

4. Partner for cross-cultural teams

Recruiting a national team should be done with a national co-worker. This is a given for cross-cultural workers but it is often ignored. Many expatriate workers have a false sense of their abilities, skills, and wisdom in making decisions concerning their national colleagues. In cross-cultural work, there should always be a system of checks and balances to ensure that the expatriate is not overriding the wisdom of the national. This is a sensitive and often

Partner with a national or focus group person to recruit a team

neglected area since much of the funding for work among the UPG comes from expatriate sources. It is good to study the mistakes of former missionary agencies in this regard so that we can avoid the kinds of embarrassment they endured.

5. Partner in developing a philosophy of ministry

In the same light, a philosophy of ministry for an approach to the focus people should be hammered out with national as well as expatriate colleagues. It is always regretful to observe teams that simply transfer foreign concepts when they are implementing a philosophy of ministry. In your early years you will naturally think about a philosophy of ministry from your own cultural view. After a number of years in the culture, you should begin to think about it in ways that are more related to the focus culture. Interacting with your national colleagues will help you process many aspects of the culture that you need to know in order to employ a philosophy of ministry that will be most appropriate and effective.

6. Partner in strategy and tactics

Strategy and tactics that we use to initiate an approach to the focus people are the products of a good philosophy of ministry (see: Appendix 8) and should be formulated with national workers. These would include the macro approaches that encompass the entire focus group and the micro ministries to individuals or small groups. Media and church music are examples of the former and evangelism and discipleship models are examples of the latter.

7. Status and role

Age, sex, status, education, & maturity affect a team

When a team is working cross-culturally, it needs to evaluate the status and role of all members. For example, singles are missionaries who have been through the same process as couples in joining the team. They are to be treated as mature, independent professionals, with the same expectations made of them as of any other missionary. However, in a cross-cultural situation, their status and role in ministry is likely going to be different from that of married couples. Status and role has to be informed by the expectations

I feel DIFFERENT in this !

of the focus culture. Interaction between the sexes, the attitudes one expresses, and even the clothes one wears should all be conditioned by the cultural mores of the focus group.

8. Five Dysfunctions of a Team

Patrick Lencioni (2002) has written a book about the five dysfunctions of a team. These are absence of trust, fear of conflict, lack of commitment, avoidance of accountability, and inattention to results. There is little doubt that you will encounter all five of these issues on your CC CP team whether it is an expatriate or a national team. Lencioni's insights are indeed difficult to instill and nurture in most teams but you should get this book and strive to implement its lessons. We have seen one or more of these dysfunctions on every team we have observed. Endeavor to strengthen every weak link in your team.

LEARNING CULTURE

1. Four categories

Learning a foreign culture is a vast and complicated process that is part of the anthropology discipline. However, for the purposes of the cross-cultural church planter, Paul Hiebert describes a systematic enquiry that can be undertaken in stages (1976). Of the many aspects of culture that must be considered by a cross-cultural church planter, I believe there are four categories that are essential.

Be sure you know the critical cultural structures

The first category contains four cultural orientations that we should master. These were discussed in the section on Phase 2 under MULTIPLE CULTURES. They are the national culture, the social culture of the UPG, the religious cultures operating in the UPG, and the Christian church culture if there is one. Most of the UPG have more than one religious culture and most countries have some type of Christian church culture.

The second category concerns the political and religious leadership principles and practice that operate in the focus group. When you gather a congregation, these principles and practice will come into play. If you are linking your church plant to a Christian denomination in the country, the leadership model will be critical to your success. See Appendix 5 for a type of leadership model.

The third category of culture is that of the dominant social organization model. In most Asian and African countries, it is some form of the Patron/Client model. See Appendix 6 for a description of the patron/client model.

The final key category is the culture of the religious specialists. Most cultures have both a formal and informal belief system. The formal religions have their priests, teachers, gurus, and holy men. The informal belief systems have practitioners such as shamen, prophets, diviners, seers, mediums, witches, sorcerers, and magicians. See: Turner, 1989.

I	1. National culture 2. Social culture 3. Religious culture 4. Christian church culture	
II	Political and religious leadership principles and practice	
III	Dominant social organization model	

IV	Religious specialists
	  Formal
	  Informal	

V	Communication models (teaching/learning)	

Categories of culture

2. A fifth category

Another category of culture that has come to the fore in recent years is that of communication models. See: Dissanayake, 1988, and Kraft, 1983. Communication includes teaching/learning methods that apply to evangelism as well as Christian nurture. The models and modes of communication vary widely between the oriental and the occidental.

3. Contextual strategy

A relatively deep knowledge of the local religion is necessary for developing a contextual strategy. Many expatriates come to the focus group with little or no understanding of their religious orientation. Unfortunately, many so-called contextual models are imposed on focus people before the CC CP team understands their spiritual questions. When spiritual questions are not answered, people may follow the evangelists for benefits such as

Learn the spiritual questions first

jobs, education, and health. Models that do not answer spiritual questions are not contextualized to the focus group but rather are imported models.

4. Status and role in culture

Status and role perceptions are another area of culture that is important to understand as early as possible. The importance of this was mentioned under the section on Team Building. In many societies, status and role are ascribed rather than achieved. This is why it is so difficult for the pastor of an initial church plant to gain respect in the village. If there has never been a church in that village, the cultural history does not have any assigned status for a Christian evangelist or pastor and no prescribed roles for them. Therefore, the evangelists or pastors have to achieve recognition before they are valued. However, if all status and roles are assigned in that culture, there may be few, if any, ways for Christian workers to achieve them. See Hiebert, 1976.

With this in mind, it should go without saying that from the very beginning of your church planting team you should be trying to gain status and role recognition in the focus community. In most countries the status and role system is changing so that those who are highly educated or who can contribute some special service to the community can achieve status. One of your tasks will be to discover how status and role can be acquired. Whatever your statuses and roles are, you must be able to reproduce them in the church plant.

HINDRANCES IN THE FOCUS GROUP

1. Show respect for those who hinder

In discussing the hindrances we face in cross-cultural church planting, there is no intention to criticize or insult the focus group. They have a culture that has existed for hundreds or maybe thousands of years and it is natural that they will be reluctant to accept outsiders who bring a new message that will change their lives.

Respect for all people is an absolute

2. Anti-Christian bias

The anti-Christian feeling among many UPG is the result of historical and theological differences and even conflicts between their formal religion and Christian elements. Even though we may not accept their interpretation of their religion's confrontation with Christianity, we have to deal with the consequences in our focus group. This anti-Christian mindset often causes an anti-foreign response also. When a foreigner or person from another ethnic group brings a new religious teaching, this anti-foreign emotion is easily excited.

3. Resentment

General resentment within the focus group can take many forms. If you are an expatriate you alone may suffer. Other types of ill will can be experienced by national colleagues or by converts from the focus group. While some of these are merely insults and contempt, others can take the form of abuse toward children such as groping them, hitting them, or burning them with chili peppers. This can be very difficult to endure and may lessen your desire to evangelize.

4. Isolation

The focus group may isolate your family in the community. In one place we lived, my wife had good response from youth who wanted to learn English. However, after they voluntarily attended a Christmas presentation where they had an opportunity to learn about Jesus, their parents isolated us from them. If you are not openly rejected, national co-workers may be. There are usually some leaders who will attempt to hinder free movement among the people by the evangelists.

5. Perceived deception

Be honest, be wise

Resentment can be especially strong against tentmakers who are perceived to be evangelists hiding behind their occupational skills. It is important for you to ascertain the general attitude toward a Christian witness in the workplace. Many tentmakers are openly accused of being missionaries in disguise and this is perceived as deceit. If we want to make a dynamic witness to the focus group, people will soon know who we are. In 2 Corinthians 4:2, Paul says: "We have renounced disgraceful, underhanded ways. We refuse to practice cunning or to tamper with God's word, but by the open statement of the truth we would commend ourselves to everyone's conscience in the sight of God."

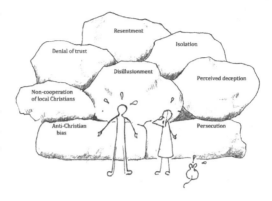

Hindrances are many

6. Denial of trust

Cross-cultural church planting begins with building relationships of trust so that differences in worldview can be overcome. However, establishing a trust bond is not an easy matter. Marvin Mayers (1987:4) states the prior question of trust: "*Is what I am doing, thinking, or saying building or undermining trust?*" People listen to the good news when they have confidence in us. When people believe we have their best interests at heart, they will respond to whatever we share with them. But a trust bond takes time. People have been conned too often by too many people to quickly put trust in a total stranger.

Remember the Trust Bond

7. Disillusionment

It is important to avoid disillusionment by your focus people. Many times the newcomer projects an unrealistic scenario to the people he or she wants to help. In many UPG, an outsider is seen as a potential patron and people will seek help from such a person. Our national team in Indonesia learned to not promise anything concerning the request of the focus person other than to listen and to pray with them. They even discovered that offering to "pray about it" might be taken as a promise to take action on their behalf. When nothing is done or given, people may become disappointed or angry and react against the church planter.

8. Non-cooperation by local Christians

A final hindrance we will most likely face is a lack of cooperation by local Christians. UPG are unreached because there is little or no vision among national Christians to reach them. While national Christians are strategically placed to reach out, they often fail to do so. However, one needs to discover the reasons why they fail and try to alleviate the situation. This requires much wisdom and patience and sometimes takes years. However, the support of the national church bodes well for long-term results.

KNOW YOUR FIELD

1. Know your environment

From some of the descriptions above, you will have deduced that one of the major tasks in this late orientation period is to learn everything possible about the situation in your UPG community. First of all, visit every person and every church and parachurch organization ministering in your focus group to find out what they are doing. In today's world, some of the church planting teams are reluctant to give information to someone outside their agency. As best you can, try to learn the philosophy of ministry/strategy of every church, group, and individual working in your UPG.

Spread your net wide

2. Do prayer walking in your focus communities

Walking around your community is not only helpful in identifying people and places to lift up in prayer, but it often gives us a chance to meet people that we would not otherwise see. This is not the same as mapping the community where you would identify the strategic areas of activity where social, political, and spiritual power operate. In prayer walking, the goal is to call on God's Spirit to move in the hearts of people. Since our focus area was so large, we often drove around with a car full of evangelists and prayed through parts of it. I guess this would be called Prayer Driving.

3. Identify key innovators

Identify key innovators in the areas you find interesting. These are the people who will be most valuable to you when you have to decide what your role will be in church planting. Pick their brains to discover all you can about the expertise you need to play a particular role and do a special job. Most church planters have to specialize.

4. Acquire broad knowledge

You won't be able to do everything there is to do in CC CP but you should know about everything there is to do. Many workers fail in this area and they make poor co-workers because they do not see the big picture and do not understand how their work fits into it. The effective worker learns as much as possible about every aspect of CC CP so the maximum contribution can be made.

5. Investigate failed models

Many expatriates are lazy in field research and thus waste time and energy in various ways. Some develop strategies that already have been proven unproductive. Others do work that is being done by someone else. This is not to say that you may not be able to do a better job than others. However, it makes sense to see if it is productive to rework a failed model or copy what others are doing.

6. Study history and tradition

Read everything you can find about your focus people and about ministries among them. Study history and tradition so that you can integrate all this information when you envision your ministry. Some of this information will be in languages that you do not yet know. Buy the books so that you may have them when you do know the language. Read the local newspapers. Watch national and local TV.

7. Double-check everything you hear

Evaluate and ponder everything you see and hear: everything you learn and implement. Don't count on expatriates or nationals to be correct in all their observations or assumptions. They may be right and they may not be right. Check out everything you hear. Talk to focus people about what you are learning. Try to get them to reflect on everything. Don't assume that anything is unimportant to you.

8. Keep your plans to yourself while identifying potential sponsors

During this period, you can let people know you are interested in ministry without revealing any specific plans you have. In the beginning, you should not really have any specific plans but, even if you do, it is not necessary to reveal them. Be open to those whose response may indicate that they are a potential sponsor for you. They may be able to recommend you to others who have a similar calling or even introduce you to focus people who will partner with you.

If you have read this far, you must surely be asking yourself how you are going to be able to learn all these things.

Phase 4 holds the answer. You will learn through **mentoring**. Keep your mind open to all kinds of mentors. They can be language teachers, team members, neighbors, friends, merchants, children, beggars, and all kinds of people. Some mentors may be books, newspapers, articles, poetry, or myths. Some mentors are temporary while others may last throughout your ministry. The secret is to utilize every opportunity to let others mentor you in their worldview and daily activities. Now, let us look at MENTORING.

EVALUATION of END RESULTS - CHECK LIST - PHASE THREE

[ ] am maintaining daily personal & family prayer life & Bible reading

[ ] am engaging in serious spiritual warfare for the focus group

[ ] can cite specific ways in which I am working for good relationships with spouse and children (see Family Dynamics in Phase 1)

[ ] am dealing with family relationship problems rather than postponing them (can name 5 we have dealt with this year)

[ ] am continuing to prioritize language learning

[ ] can name specific ways in which I am active in the community

[ ] have investigated ways to recruit a national team

[ ] have made efforts in understanding how local ministry teams function

[ ] am implementing Team philosophy of ministry and strategy in local relationships (name two ways)

[ ] have spent time studying church culture, national culture, and focus group culture

[ ] have made special effort to investigate leadership principles and practice (name 2 of those efforts)

[ ] am learning to deal with rejection and/or persecution

[ ] Describe in writing how you feel at this time about being in the unreached people group. Send this paper to your spiritual mentor.

Tips: 1. The spiritual challenge is enormous. An unreached people may have been engaged but never been penetrated.

2. Prayer is the spiritual weapon you will have most trouble using effectively.

3. There will be little vision among Christians—maybe none.

4. Overcome as many adjustment difficulties as you can during this period of Orientation.

5. Remember that your ultimate mission is to glorify God in the nations. We do that by loving him, being faithful to his call to love others and sharing the gospel.

6. Measure your success & self esteem by the level of your faithfulness. The CP assignments and/or accomplishments may not generate enough results to make you feel good about yourself.

7. Seek to emulate the best examples you can find but if you fall short, don't despair, keep trying.

CHAPTER SIX

PHASE FOUR - MENTORING

*"The fear of the Lord is the beginning of knowledge; fools
despise wisdom and instruction."*
Proverbs 1:7

*"How I hated discipline, and my heart despised reproof!
I did not listen to the voice of my teachers or incline my ear to my instructors."*
Proverbs 5:12-13

In a Dilbert comic strip, the boss comes to a worker and says, "Asok, I'm putting you on our special self-mentoring program. If you have any questions whatsoever, feel free to talk to yourself." Those of us in cross-cultural work can laugh at that because we know that many of us try to mentor ourselves in cross-cultural adjustment.

My first missionary ministry was in a large Indonesian speaking Chinese church in Jakarta. Shortly after I arrived, I met Freddy Tjan. He was a middle age man who had recently been converted and was on fire for Jesus. He accompanied me to meetings of the youth and I went with him on visitation evangelism. Whenever I would explain something to people in my poor Indonesian, Freddy would say the following, "What Rev. Dixon is trying to say is this." Then he would give a summary of what I had said. This experience had many benefits for me. First of all, it helped me understand the way I should

*Mentors
determine
success*

use the Indonesian language. Secondly, he empowered me as someone who should be respected. But most important of all, he made me realize the critical importance of mentors. Fortunately for me, that is a lesson that guided me through many a pitfall in church planting as I moved into my UPG.

While Phase 3 is considered late internship, mentoring is advanced or complex orientation. This mentoring is not something you do. Rather, it is something that happens to you. It may begin with your initial orientation to the focus group but should intensify as you move into your church planting mode. Mentoring takes place primarily in relationships but one can be mentored to a lesser degree by books, films, and other print and visual media. Whenever I teach or write I can say with confidence, *your mentors will make the critical difference in your effectiveness in cross-cultural church planting.*

SOME DEFINITIONS OF MENTOR

The word mentor comes from the name of a friend of Ulysses. This man named Mentor taught Telemachus, who was Ulysses' son. Mentor was so important that Athena the Greek goddess of wisdom sometimes appeared in the form of Mentor in order to advise Ulysses. (You can read about this in Homer's *Odyssey*.)

Mentors give insight

Reg Hamilton reports that a 1992 conference of educators "spent a good deal of time debating and disagreeing about what kind of people mentors were and what they should or should not do" (1993:2). Some thought that mentors were non-judgmental friends. Others thought they would advise or assess a trainee. But for the purposes of CC CP, we describe mentors as anyone who can give you insight concerning a cultural practice, ceremony, relationship, or situation.

Most of the material on mentoring describes it as having a formal structure though there are also examples of informal mentoring. Usually, mentoring relationships are set up when senior people take an interest in and promote the cause of a subordinate. This model might function within your team or perhaps in coordination with other teams or resource persons in your field of work. In such cases, mentors would be assigned to new workers to guide them through the rigors of adjustment to the field.

Non-focus group mentors can be misleading

However, when we consider cross-cultural mentoring, it is important to remember the dangers of misunderstanding that may occur when one is mentored into a second culture by someone who is not from that culture. This is true not only of the expatriate team member but also of the national who is from another ethnic group. The outsider who mentors other outsiders into the theology and social organization of the contextual church may create barriers that hinder them from seeing and hearing the models of the focus people.

People everywhere have prejudices about those from other cultures. Therefore, you must be careful to verify everything you hear about aspects of culture. This means that a second or third party should check all information you receive before you consider it as reality. In Indonesia, Chinese people generally believe that Sundanese are lazy. This is because their work ethic is not the same. However, Sundanese do not work as hard as Chinese because they do not believe that having money or a higher life style is worth working that hard. They value different aspects of life.

If you listen to the stereotypes about your focus group you will miss some important information you need to be a good church planter. On the other hand, store the stereotypes in your memory bank as insight and information about interactions among different ethnic groups in the country. This can be invaluable if you see it for what it is.

The mentor is powerful

Mentors teach you how to act

A mentor is a role model. Reg Hamilton (1993:17) says that "the nature of the relationship ensures this, even if it is not a planned part of the scheme." The mentor cannot give information to the learner without imparting the influence of his own attitudes, values, and general approaches to the task. By having a wide cross section of mentors you are able to gain broad knowledge of the various kinds of people and worldviews there are in the culture. In addition, a focus person will seek to mentor you in the same way he/ she would mentor another focus person. This is invaluable for the church planter who must envision the discipleship process for new believers.

A DEFINITION OF MENTOR FOR THE CROSS-CULTURAL CHURCH PLANTER

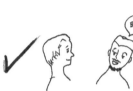

Cross-cultural mentoring is different

1. It is important that you do not confuse the nature of cross-cultural mentors with how mentors might be defined in education, business, or even those on your team. The pri-

Rather than talking, learn to listen

mary purpose of mentoring in secular organizations is to help you in the process of integration into the organization or into your role in that organization. This kind of mentor is an experienced person who functions like a coach. You may have mentors from your team who operate in this capacity but they cannot mentor you in the culture. They can only guide you in ways to study the culture much in the same way this book is doing. They can give you examples and encourage you to study certain areas of the culture and, in some cases, they can verify as true what you are learning. But after all is said and done, you must check your cultural clues with a mentor from the focus group.

The CC CP and general church planting books do not say much about mentoring. You have to go to books on leadership to find that. However, mentoring in those books is generally about the process of mentoring using the classic mentor/protégé model. For example, Robert Clinton has some excellent passages about mentoring in his *The Making of a Leader* (1988, Singapore: The Navigators/NavPress). Such examples are helpful but they do not strike at the unintentional mentoring relationships so valuable for the cross-cultural worker.

Average and superior mentors

2. A mentor can be anyone who will give you information about the culture and they can operate at any given time or place. Most mentors are unintentional and do not realize that they are mentoring you. An average mentor will disclose information about everyday life in the culture. A good mentor will reveal the important meaning about something you can see but do not understand. The French anthropologist Levi-Strauss calls this deep structure. It holds the cultural explanation for underlying observable behavior or events. A superior mentor will give you information you need without waiting for you to ask for it. Normally, you will not be able to tell if an average or good mentor is a superior one until you are given some revelation that sets him or her apart. It may be that a person will function as an average mentor for years before moving to another level.

Mentors differ in value

We had a Muslim landlord who was a former military officer. He had many experiences to share about Indonesia in the days of President Soekarno. These included insightful stories about how the president believed that magic would keep him from being killed. But our landlord's advice became personal when he told us not to move to a certain area of town because its residents were primarily anti-Christian. A superior mentor will give you guidance even when you have not asked for it.

Mentors come from all social levels

Formal and informal mentors

3. Mentors can be people whose social status is far above you or far below you. However, they will function in different ways. Some will be formal mentors while others will be informal. We feel that formal mentors are people who are conscious that they are mentoring you, while informal mentors will never be aware of that relationship.

A young expatriate went to the Department of Education to get permission to enroll in a university. Such permission was not easy to procure and the expatriate did not know anyone who could sponsor him. A senior official noticed him standing in the hall and asked him who he was. When he discovered that the expatriate was from Michigan, he invited him into his office. This official had studied at the University of Michigan and became interested in helping the young man. The expatriate was obviously young so the official created a father/son relationship and began calling him "Danny Boy" as a term of affection. He eventually succeeded in getting him a visa to study at the university. This is an example of formal mentoring.

Status and role affects mentoring

4. In most UPG, formal mentoring requires status recognition. Social relationships in most UPG are structured according to classes. In India, the caste system has an even stronger influence. In normal circumstances, you will be expected to operate within these boundaries. However, since cultures are changing at a rapid pace in many countries, your focus people may relate to you in more modern ways. The official mentioned above at the Department of Education created his own mentoring model which was beneficial to the expatriate. However, sometimes models can shift on you suddenly and inexplicably.

It is probable that a person of your status or higher will be willing or able to advise you concerning many aspects of the culture. People who are below your status will have to be recruited in a roundabout way. Some cultures ascribe or assign status while others recognize achieved status. Most European and North American cultures practice achieved status. In those cultures, it is possible to move between various social and economic groups based on your achievements. However, most UPG do not follow that model. They tend to practice ascribed status. Children who are born in the higher economic group or leadership group are respected because of that alone. They do not have to accomplish anything to obtain their status. However, higher education in many countries is changing some of these values.

Mentoring models vary

5. Good mentors can come from all status levels but the mentoring model will vary from person to person because they may not know that they are mentors. They are just sharing information with you. There are mentors who like to talk and they will give you information, unaware that it is buried in their rambling talk. Many people will spin stories that you need to remember even though you have no idea of their value at the time. It is best to keep journals and record this information as carefully as you can. We have interviewed people with a set of survey questions. Some would give brief answers while others would launch out into an answer that

lasted fifteen minutes or more. Some informants cannot be kept to the point. However, that does not mean they are useless. In many cases, they reveal brilliant insights but it takes patience to wait and sort it out.

Mentors are primarily transitory

6. Both formal and informal mentors can be temporary or permanent. Many are temporary and only a few are permanent. Focus group mentors can be anyone who can give you accurate information. While all focus people can be mentors in some areas, few can be mentors in every area. You may never meet such a person. You must seek focus people who can mentor you in specific areas. That is why cross-cultural mentors are transitory. Someone may mentor you for a few hours or a few days or a few weeks. Long-term mentors are rare because few people understand the breadth and depth of information that the church planter needs to know.

A transitory informal mentor can be someone who is old or young. Even a ditch digger knows more about the culture than the outsider church planter. Children can teach you things about the way children relate to one another and to adults. The church planter needs this knowledge. Being mentored means learning the indigenous patterns/models from insiders who are in the know. Although mentoring should start as soon as you arrive in the focus group, it should also continue as long as you are there. Remember, one never learns so much that mentors can be safely ignored.

Typical types of short term– long term mentors
1. servants/other workers in your household
2. neighbors
3. friends
4. counterparts in ministry
5. colleagues
6. counterparts in business if you are a tentmaker
7. church members
8. student friends or even one's own students
9. benefactors (patrons)
10. clients

Recruit all kinds of mentors from the focus group

7. It is important for you to recruit mentors from all levels of society. This will require wisdom as you move out of your status category. In some cases, you may be able to recruit a formal mentor from the top level of society. But those who perceive themselves as belonging to a lower status will be reluctant to advise you on anything. You must garner their wisdom indirectly through casual conversation. Frequently, this can be done while they are working or traveling.

Learn from the focus person

You must make opportunities to glean their experiences because many of those who come to know Christ will come from lower status groups.

THE MENTORING RELATIONSHIP

Learn to be mentored before you try to mentor!

You must learn how to mentor the focus group way

One of the most counter-productive things a new worker can do is to try to be a mentor to the focus people before one knows the "rules of the game" (by "rules" we mean key models of the culture such as teaching/learning styles, philosophy and values). It is counter-productive because it almost always leads to failure and you do not want your approaches to fail. People notice expatriates who launch projects that fail just as they notice the ones who succeed. Taking small steps that are successful is a major principle of church planting because it shows leadership and charisma. The effective church planter will learn how to be mentored before trying to mentor others. A team of nationals in our area started an agricultural project that was envisioned to enhance the harvest of a certain crop. Their system of planting was different from that used by the local farmers and they were told that it would not work because of the soil conditions. However, they forged ahead and the result was they had a poorer crop than the local farmers. Their goal was good but their execution was flawed. After this failure, the local people would not listen to their advice even though they had important knowledge about many subjects.

This is a common error for expatriates because they feel that they have come to the UPG to teach, not to learn. When the local people see that we want to change their lives and that we make mistake after mistake trying to do it with no effort to ask for advice or correction, they will likely decide that we are not a person who deserves a hearing. Before long, we will find ourselves isolated within a small circle of people who believe that we may be useful to them in some way. This is particularly probable if we begin by hiring workers to help us in church planting. Hired hands rarely correct their bosses.

Initiating the mentoring relationship

1. No one in the UPG will really be able to understand you, any more than you can comprehend what makes them tick. They will assume that you know a good deal about their culture. This will be especially so after you gain some facility in their language. It is not likely that they will take the initiative in mentoring you. A few people might, but you cannot afford to wait for that to happen. You know that there are great gaps in your cultural knowledge and you must take action to fill them.

2. When you recruit someone to mentor you, it means a teacher/pupil model is functioning. The mentor is the teacher and you are the student. However, it is unlikely that the mentor will think of himself or herself as a teacher. In addition, he or she will not know what you need to learn. Your role will be to ask questions in such a way that you can probe the mentor's experience. Recruiting a mentor does not mean that you set up a negotiated agreement to study under the mentor. That may happen from time to time. My son-in-law set up such a mentoring relationship with a Muslim teacher. However, under normal conditions the mentors will not even recognize that they are being mentors. It might just be a friendly relationship in which the mentor learns something from you and you, in turn, learn from him or her.

You must guide the mentor

3. The effective church planter will have a continual series of mentors from the local culture, lasting various periods of time and helping in numerous areas. When you begin your study in the area of politics, you should look for one or more mentors in that field. The same is true for education, economics,

Learn to probe the mentor's knowledge

leadership, and all areas of culture. You should be learning from mentors the entire time you are in the UPG, but especially for the first 10-15 years. Do not assume that your mentors are telling you everything you need to know. In the first place, it is unlikely they know what is needed to plant a church cross-culturally. They may mean well but you are going to have to ferret out the information you need.

This is not an easy job. It is hard work and you will have to read, study, discuss, investigate and pray so that you can build a biblically based church. A.C. Kruyt was a famous Dutch missionary who became an internationally renowned scholar on the life of the Toraja people of the Central Celebes (Sulawesi) in Indonesia. Although he lived among the Toraja people for 40 years, he was never aware that the baptized Christians were secretly following their spiritist tradition of burial after they had completed the Christian ceremony. You can't imagine how this non-biblical practice influenced the theology of death and resurrection in those churches.

Patiently accumulate knowledge

4. As you move into the experience of intense mentoring, you will begin to accumulate an incredible amount of information about the culture. But you will not necessarily understand the implications of this knowledge in church planting. That will come gradually over a period of time. Waiting for maturity in the culture is a very difficult experience. Many workers begin their evangelism, discipleship training, and church activities before they have processed enough information to be effective. The work in West Java in the 70s was very good in the area of evangelism but very poor in the area of Christian nurturing or pastoring. More than 60 home churches were started by a small group of national evangelists but all failed except a few. Failure was due to their lack of cultural understanding of the focus group.

Their main problem was the absence of a church planting model fashioned for the local Sundanese. The evangelists worked in the context of an evangelistic model combined with a discipleship model that functioned like a para-church. Their theology of evangelism was essentially individualistic whereas Sundanese society was strongly communal and closed. This led to weak leadership accountability. For example, evangelism, teaching, and worship were conducted mostly by non-Sundanese using the

Indonesian language. This meant that the Sundanese had to abandon important cultural and religious folkways in order to become Christian without fully understanding the rationale for it.

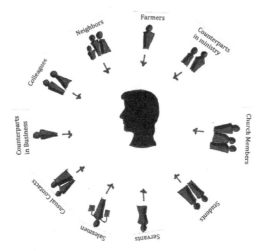

Various types of mentors

Seek mentoring in the areas of church planting

5. It will not be easy finding mentors who can guide you in areas relating to church planting. You will have to break down the various areas of the task. This will mean that you will have to find mentors who know about organizations and leadership, teaching and learning models, worldview, belief systems, and many other areas that impact the forming of a church. The wheel chart above indicates some of the multiple mentoring situations that may arise. Mentors can help you in these areas even though they will not understand how you are going to integrate this knowledge into a church planting model. Some of these areas are discussed below. Further examination is given in Phase 7 on Development.

6. If a mentor does not answer your questions, it does not mean that he or she does not know the answer. It may be that such inside information is not shared with outsiders. You have to probe continually and find something to pursue. When people see that you have some information, they will likely reveal a little more. Getting to the center of the truth can be a long process.

FINDING MENTORS

Everyone is a potential mentor

1. The effective church planter sees everyone as a potential mentor. (See the definition above.) As an outsider, we can learn from practically anyone. When we first came to the UPG, we found that many potential mentors came to our door. We had house help. There were merchants selling their goods through the community. Beggars came by almost daily.

Pedicab drivers were the transportation that would pick us up and return us to our door. Various workers fixed things in the house and in the yard. We did not even need to leave the house to meet numerous people. These were all our daily mentors because they knew things about the culture we did not. We learned from them.

The kerosene seller diluted his goods with water. The house help were afraid to do anything new without being told to do it. The gardener chopped up the edges of our lawn even though we told him not to do it, and completely tore out a cherished bed of mint (which is usually hard to do). Some beggars wanted money and distained the offer of food. The salesmen insisted on our buying something even though we did not want it. The repairmen insisted on fixing something their way rather than the way we wanted it fixed. It took time to process these experiences but they were all valuable. We learned something from all of them that helped us later in teaching new believers. We also learned a lot about ourselves.

Be open to all potential mentors

2. For many workers, the major problem is not <u>finding</u> mentors but rather <u>accepting</u> them when they cross one's path. If you do not feel you need to learn, you will miss opportunities. In our UPG, some agencies want their workers to use public transportation for at least 6 months after arriving. People of many different classes ride public transportation and it is an opportunity to meet new mentors. However, we knew workers who said they had learned all they needed after a few weeks. The agony of riding public transportation was too much for them.

At first, it is more comfortable to seek mentors from your own peer group. People of the same general age and gender tend to relate more easily. Since our sphere of influence tends to be greater in our own peer group, it makes sense to prioritize them. Many tentmakers teach English, study in a school, or work with small companies. In these kinds of sponsorships, it is easy to make friends. When you move around your neighborhood, you might find that people older than you are not as open to meaningful conversation.

Don't be concerned that you bond more closely with some mentors than with others. Your purpose is to learn what you can from a wide variety of mentors and not everyone wants to continue the relationship. They might be looking for some advantage in knowing you and if that does not materialize they may move on. Don't be upset by their leaving you unless you have offended them in some way. If you have offended, you may need another mentor to tell you how to make it right.

Learn from mentors

3. Before we teach, we must be willing to learn! This is very hard for most expatriates. We will admit we need to learn some things such as the language. But many do not realize that they need to learn an incredible variety of cultural models if they are going to understand and communicate with the focus people. We need mentors in order to learn those models. If we are convinced that what we know is better than what the focus people know, we will want to teach, not learn. New workers often do not realize that they do not have command of the teaching/learning models used by the focus group. They teach but they do not connect with the people and the people do not necessarily learn because they are not being taught in their learning style.

A doctor friend of ours in the Advent Hospital said this phrase to every patient, "Do not drink coffee, do not drink tea." One day I sat in the office and heard him give this advice to a sick old man. The man simply looked at him without replying so the doctor said it again to his wife who was standing beside him. "Okay, doctor," she replied, "only a little." "No, no," said the doctor, "Don't drink coffee and don't drink tea." "Okay," she replied, "only a little." The doctor knew only one way to give his advice, and because it did not make sense to the patient, it was not received.

4. It is critical to find mentors in each area of your concern. First, identify the areas of church planting. Some of these are theology, polity, and leadership. When you have identified these areas and comprehend how they are used in your own cultural church and in the local Christian church, you will be able to probe mentors as to how these social systems operate in the focus group. Although there may not be a church in the focus group, their organizations will function in a similar manner. As you come to understand them and the worldview behind them, you should try to envision how those systems would work

"A man is always better than a book"- Charles Copeland

in the church you will be planting. Changing the worldview of the focus people to a biblical worldview is no easy task. How you process your mentors' knowledge will determine how well you do this.

Inanimate mentors

5. As we mentioned before, mentors are not always people. We can learn from books, movies, television, and other media. But we must verify these messages by confirming them with real people. When my son was teaching a group of professional people, they commented on how wild and dangerous the American culture was. He asked them if they had encountered that. When they answered in the negative, he asked them how they knew that the American culture was dangerous. They replied that they saw it in the movies. To enlighten them, he gave an illustration of various things he had supposedly learned about them from their movies. They were horrified at his examples and explained that those movies were not true to real life. His teaching point was simply to tell them that many American movies were no more true to American life than their movies were to their lives.

There is not a lot of anthropological or sociological research for many UPG. Certain ethnic groups in the world seem to attract most of the attention of anthropologists. You must make every effort to read everything you can about your focus group. Search through bookstores. Go to second hand bookstores and stalls and ask the owners for books

Watch local language television

about your focus group. Visit libraries in the major cities to see what they have. Ask at university libraries to see if any research has been done among your focus group. Frequently, you will find theses written by students that will be helpful. If your country of choice was previously colonized, there might be a wealth of information in the libraries of the colonizing nation.

Watch television; study the way news is reported and the way a weather report is given. You will discover that they are often given in ways different from your cultural patterns. Ask mentors why things are presented as they are. There are many reasons why news is reported in a certain way.

About 30 years ago, a number of college students were killed while rafting on a flooded river in West Java. The newspapers would only report that they were killed. They would not give any information about why the students were on the river, what gear they used, and how they were killed. When I asked a mentor why this was not reported, he told me that people would blame the government. "How could they blame the government," I asked, "since the government was not involved in any way?" "It doesn't matter," he answered, "many people have a mystical idea that the government should not allow anything to go wrong. It is a sign of divine disapproval of the government." We found that this cosmology also applies to areas of church life.

NATURE OF MENTORING

Develop skills in being mentored

1. Accessing good mentoring requires skill. The effective church planter will develop this skill. There are not many people who have given thought to the kind of mentoring you will need in CC CP. It is helpful to read books on mentoring but they will give you only a few ideas because they are usually oriented to the concept of mentoring in an organization. You will need to find an established church to get this kind of mentoring. Perhaps some church planting team members can mentor you in the skills you need to start church planting. If not, you are going to have to develop the skills you need on your own.

Indigenous mentoring is a learned skill

At first, you will not be too concerned about mentoring because new information will come so thick and fast from so many quarters you will not be able to keep up. Some of it will just be a blur. It will be good if you have a spouse or a friend with whom you can discuss things. It helps just to recount what has happened and categorize your experiences. For example, the arrival process will include immigration, customs, your early trips through town, meeting team members, sounds and smells, and other experiences of the first few days.

It will be helpful to rehearse the conditions of your first residence, food, sleep, neighbors, and other particulars. You could describe the beginning of your language study. This would include impressions of your language teacher, place of study, materials used, and other details. Write down everything you do not understand about these experiences. Note questions you have about any of these activities, persons, or behavior. Record anything that was different from what you expected. You will be able to form your initial questions for a mentor from this diary. My wife and I had a language tutor who fell asleep most of the times we were assigned to read out loud. She would not correct our pronunciation when she was awake. While we never understood the falling asleep (except from boredom), we later learned why she would not correct us. It was a common trait of her culture.

Language learning enhances mentoring skills

2. Learning mentoring skills should not interfere in any way with your language study but it should be pursued in your spare time. Language facility without mentoring skills has little value for church planting because you need to use your language to implement the church planting models

Language is the basis of mentoring

that are contextual. You will not learn these in normal language study. However, you have to utilize your language to access mentors who can guide you in understanding the cultural models that are necessary. The more your language skills increase, the more you will learn from your mentors.

If you are an English speaker, you will doubtless be able to make acquaintances who speak some English. You can begin by asking them questions. But be cautious about getting in the habit of using a foreign language to probe cultural patterns. Many aspects of culture cannot be explained in a foreign language. The effective church planter uses the local language.

Cautiously check everything you hear

3. If people are willing to talk with you, record their answers. <u>Do not accept their answers as fact</u>. They may not understand your question or they may give an answer they think you want to hear. People are often confused by the many questions that expatriates ask. Some questions seem to be so obvious to them they wonder why we ask. They are liable to give any kind of answer if they become suspicious of us.

Verify the information you get

On the other hand, they might give you an answer just to make you feel good. If you ask directions to a street or location in Indonesia, many people who do not know will answer with made up directions because they want you to feel they are helping. Few people will tell you they don't know the way. In like manner, many people among the UPG hate to admit that they cannot answer your questions about cultural traits. They will tell you how they view the traits but that may not coincide with the way others see it. Also, there may not be an absolute way of describing some issues but rather, different perspectives on them.

4. People have varied styles of communicating and different ways of viewing events. We have worked for years with a wonderful man who is gifted as a pastor and evangelist. When he tells us a story we are not sure of the chronology of the event or even of the time frame involved. He can tell us of someone who did something 30 years ago as though it was presently happening. Often, we have to ask him specifically for a time frame or even clarification if he was personally involved.

The myths in our focus group have many variations. The same basic story can have details that are changed by the storyteller to emphasize some truth or to teach a particular point. This cultural trait can cause interesting interpretations of Bible stories. When we were showing films of the life of Christ, we had a narrator tell the stories in the local language as the film progressed. A mentor suggested that we just let the film run without the narration and the audience could make up their own story as they watched the events unfold!

Negative mentors are also helpful

5. Ask the same questions to people from various groups and compare the answers. You will begin to feel the differences between how people relate to

you. Some will be quite open and some will be fairly friendly while others will be guarded. You will begin to differentiate the potential mentors for they will be the ones who want to talk to you and answer your questions. Try to converse with these people as much as possible. Don't be put off by people who find you entertaining and just want to talk with you because they are bored. Some of these people can be annoying but you also have to learn how to understand annoying people. You will have some in the church you plant!

Do not argue with mentors

6. The effective church planter will not argue with the focus people about how they view their culture. It is important to process all viewpoints. We knew a young worker who argued with his language teacher about the use of words and even the pronunciation of words because he read language study books that disagreed with what the teacher said. He also heard pronunciations by people from other ethnic groups that were different from those of his teacher. After a few episodes, the teacher no longer corrected him, but rather let him believe what he wanted and say what he wanted. If we do not think that a mentor is accurate in his information, it is better to double or triple check with others. It is usually not wise to argue with nationals over their observations unless it concerns biblical truth.

Oh, I don't think it could possibly be like that, now could it?

Really, Really Wrong!!

Process your mentor's advice without prejudice

Seek religious mentoring

7. The effective church planter always keeps in mind that he or she needs mentoring in religious or spiritual issues as well as in secular areas. We may know Christian doctrine, but it is unlikely we will know much about the belief systems of the focus people. If you were to visit the grave of a famous person in Indonesia you will find a guardian of the gravesite.

This man knows the history of the deceased and, more importantly, he knows how to guide you in approaching the grave without encountering malevolent spirit forces. The graves of all people are believed to contain some power but those of the elite religious and political leaders have great power. People visit them to ask for blessing in many aspects of their lives. There is a complex culture of the dead and the church planter should understand it. We do not dismiss its importance just because we view it as false or silly.

Bobb Biehl writes that mentoring is helping someone "reach her or his God-given potential" (1996:19). When you study the religious beliefs of your focus group, you are learning the results of a worldview. There is a cosmology behind all their beliefs and it is different from a biblical world-view. Although few of our mentors will realize it, they are giving us the knowledge we need to explain the difference between biblical teachings and the beliefs of the focus group.

Prepare yourself to mentor a congregation

8. When you begin discipling a person or gathering be-lievers into a congregation, you will be mentoring your flock into mature faith. If you have applied yourself to gathering many mentors and learning from them the ways the focus people mentor one another, you will be ready. You will not be perfected in all the contextual skills of a mentor. There is still much to learn. But you will have sufficient knowledge to begin. At all times depend on the Holy Spirit to override your mistakes and empower your mentoring to connect with the real issues in people's lives. As you apply the gospel to their situations, lives will be changed.

> *There is:*
> *"A time to speak"*
> *– Eccles. 3:7*

The difference between mentoring and coaching

Another shift will take place as you begin to gather a congregation. You will begin to coach as well as to mentor. In this book, the process of coaching is defined as a more controlled process than mentoring. The effective cross-cultural church planter is well coached. First, you must be coached yourself into the CC CP model. Then you can coach others. This process is discussed in detail in Phase 5 - Engagement.

CRITICAL MODELS OF MENTORING

Although there are multiple cultural models involving a variety of mentoring skills, a few stand out as more critical than others. We have listed them in the following two categories:
1. Models that describe the way society is led
2. Models that relate to learning

There are many more models than these but it is impossible to cover them all in this small book. Even here, we are only summarizing the main ideas for your further study. From our experience of 50 years involved in and observing CC CP in three cultures, we have come to the conclusion that the three most important cultural models a worker needs to master are those describing the way society is led. These include: political leadership, spiritual leadership, and general social relationships. Each of these models has some special mentoring characteristics. Every culture has these models though they may vary from one culture to another.

Every culture has at least 3 leadership models

Models that describe the way society is led
1. Political leadership model

Every culture has a political leadership model. Sherwood Lingenfelter's (1985) categories on political leadership give a practical outline by which to study any culture. In Appendix 5, we have included a paper that uses these categories to evaluate the leadership model in a UPG. There are multiple leadership models in societies but the political model is usually the most powerful. For example, the Roman political model was copied by the Roman Catholic Church. In many cultures, the majority of its organizations use a political model.

We are not going to explain Lingenfelter's model in detail but an experience we had illustrates the value of it.

Selection model for leaders

Recruiting Process for an evangelist

A question was posed to a group of evangelists and pastors in a UPG concerning who sponsored them for their ministry. In general, they answered that they were not sponsored
but were called by God. Unwittingly, I picked one of the most
marginal of them to interview. When I asked him who sent
him to Bible School, he responded by saying he went on his own. His pastor and his church did not send him. When I asked him if he had filled
out an application, he said that he had. "Was there a question about references on it?" I asked. He responded that there was. "Would the school
have accepted you without those references?" He admitted they would not.
"Therefore," I said, "You were **recruited** by the school." He agreed.

Leaders are recruited and selected

When I asked him who paid his way to school, he said that no one
did. He had no sponsor. Then we discussed how schools operate and why
someone had to give the money to pay for his food, utilities, classroom
materials, and other things. He confessed that someone did pay for them
though he did not know who it was. He agreed that whoever paid was his
sponsor who helped **select** him for the ministry.

Next, we discussed criteria for ministry and he agreed that he would
have had difficulty getting a job if he had not finished Bible school. That
accomplishment proved he was qualified. Thus, the Bible school provided
him with **criteria** to be an evangelist.

Following this, we discussed how he got a job with a church and he
explained that the Bible school leaders recommended him for a job with
a pastor they knew. In light of this, I pointed out that their **esteem** of him
gave him credibility for the job. Also, it showed that he had belonged and
had functioned in an **organization** that was related to the church. In this
way, the evangelists and pastors saw the five elements of the recruitment
process.

Leadership selection

As it worked out, it was most impressive to the group when we showed
how even a marginal person was mentored through the process of leadership selection without him realizing what was happening. One does not
suddenly pop into a leadership position. Every culture has a process of

selecting leaders. That means that every organization in the UPG mentors their leadership through a proven system. When I asked the evangelists and pastors why anyone in the village or city would accept them as a leader, they all understood. Though they were leaders in their churches or para-church organizations, they would not be recognized as leaders in the UPG. They would have to earn that recognition by fulfilling the leadership model of the UPG. In some way, they would have to be mentored into that leadership model.

2. Spiritual leadership model

Church planters are spiritual leaders

The spiritual leadership model is the second of the three most powerful models that every UPG worker should master. Although it varies from one religion or belief system to another, it is <u>influenced</u> by the same categories that define political leadership. There are a variety of Muslim, Hindu, Christian, and inner self-discipline leaders, but they are all recruited, selected, have criteria, esteem, and belong to an organization. In other words, all these leaders are mentored into their office and they are <u>recognizable</u>. Most go through an apprentice type process in which someone who is already a spiritual leader mentors them. Frequently, this type of leadership is passed down in families.

Shaman as spiritual leader

An example of a spiritual leader is given in Appendix 7 where the position of the shaman is described. One finds this type of spiritual leader everywhere in Asia and Africa. The shaman gains power by being successful in the estimation of those he or she helps. When the people do not feel that the shaman is helping them, they go elsewhere. Thus, the shaman must be a purveyor of power. This involves the interplay of supernatural forces as they relate to the health and well being of the people. A Muslim teacher, who believes that the ploys of the shaman are fake, said that the <u>perception</u> of his power puts pressure on people to follow.

This perception reaffirms the way people see the ordering of their world that places the natural under the domination of the supernatural. When the shaman demonstrates control of power, it gives him legitimacy. He can find lost articles, make people fall in love, locate jobs, help people clear their house of malevolent spirits, conduct the spirits of the dead to their resting places, and many other such services. In Appendix 7, the story of the shaman burying the baby of a Christian woman illustrates his strong position in the community. The evangelist left the village to arrange the baby's funeral and this gave the shaman opportunity to take control and override his desires. The shaman pressured the mother to accept his authority over that of the evangelist. His standing in the community enabled him to do this.

Evangelist as spiritual leader

The evangelist or pastor in the UPG will have to reconcile his ministry with that of one of the spiritual leaders familiar to the people. This does not mean that you have to be like them in every way. You can be a spiritual leader with a biblical worldview, values, and actions. But, in order to be accepted, you will have to be recognizable to them as a spiritual leader. They have to accept you as their mentor in spiritual matters. You will have to show in some specific ways that you are connected to power that has control

The pastor as mentor

over the world that UPG people know and fear. This happens when the gospel changes lives physically, mentally, spiritually, or even economically.

A biblical leader

The biblical view of leadership is one of servant leadership. This will likely not relate to the worldview of the UPG. In order for your congregation to understand servant leadership, you will have to reorient their worldview. Mentoring converts in this area is one of the most difficult tasks. If they have something in their worldview that can be related to the biblical leadership model, it will give you leverage. If you cannot find any such value or tradition, you will have to lay the groundwork with biblical teaching. When they understand and accept the manner in which God leads people into deeper relationships, their worldview will change.

While you are living in the physical world, you must also show that you are connected to the spiritual world. When the evangelist goes into the UPG and prays for people to be healed or to find a job or to have a child, the people will likely assume that he is operating in the realm of the shaman. His first priority is to show that his connection to the spirit world is not like that of the shaman, though his ministry is similar in ways. Rather, he is operating under the authority of God and that the power being manifested is from the Holy Spirit of God. There must be a differentiation of the worldview. Sometimes this comes through what some call a "power encounter." But mostly it occurs when people experience Jesus and their lives are changed.

3. Patron/client model

The Patron-Client model is wide & deep

The third critical model every UPG worker should master is that of the patron-client. The patron-client system is powerful throughout Asia and Africa and also operates in many other areas of the world. Appendix 6 gives a short review of some of the major characteristics of this model. Most people are mentored into this cultural model from childhood. Experts differ somewhat in their expositions of this system of social relationships. However, the basic behavior of people within patronage is very similar.

Universal cultural application

For the newcomer, the most important aspect of the patron-client model is its universalism within the cultures where it operates. If you go into a UPG that uses patron-client patterns to order its social relationships, everyone relates in that fashion. You will be expected to fit in but no one will volunteer to mentor you about the process. When my wife and I moved from a Chinese cultural orientation where the patron-client pattern excluded the outsider to a UPG where they included the newcomer, we were confused. People wanted to borrow money and possessions. They asked us to give them things. They seemed to want to treat us as a patron though we did not understand what was going on. Later, when we did understand, we realized that the model was not operating in a reciprocal manner as it should. The outsider was allowed to be a patron but the client did not have to fulfill the obligations of a client. It was many years before we realized how the system should function.

As this book illuminates the various phases of church planting, you will see ways in which the patron-client model determines how an evangelist has to adjust to the community. The evangelists we worked with in a UPG were poorly supported by their church and they did not have the funds to be a patron. In addition, they had never been mentored into the patron-client system as adults. Nevertheless, the people tried to treat them as patrons and the evangelists were hard pressed to provide for them. They were able to help converts to find jobs and to get medical aid, but their status as patrons was low. This was a drawback as far as getting a hearing for the gospel because a potential leader who cannot be a patron has difficulty becoming a leader. The evangelists and pastors must be patrons to some extent in order to belong in a community.

The Patron-Client model affects the church

Because evangelists from the focus people are conditioned to operate in their social systems, they will continue to do so in the church. Many evangelists in our UPG continue to appeal to their patrons to give them money so that they could, in turn, be more effective patrons to their flocks. This system has negative aspects in our UPG because it encourages dependency in the evangelists and undercuts their accountability to the church. Some churches do not allow their evangelists to work in a secular job but they will not pay them sufficiently. These churches are trying to mentor the evangelists into a faith system but the evangelists look for patrons who will subsidize them. Often they have greater loyalty to their patron than to the church that has ordained them.

An evangelist from our focus group took me with him to visit one of these patrons and I was amazed at the change in his personality when he talked with this man. In my previous exchanges with this evangelist he had the air of self-assurance and set forth his ideas with confidence. However, when he was with this patron from another ethnic group he became subservient (even servile) and hesitated to express his opinions. Although the patron knew very little about ministry in the focus group, he was bold in giving orders to the evangelist concerning approaches to ministry. During the conversation, he repeatedly referred to "my evangelists" even though he had nothing to do with recruiting, training, and supervising their ministries. However, he was giving them money and this gave him power.

The effective cross-cultural church planter will identify and master these social models. Without this knowledge, you will not be able to understand the way people relate to one another. This is critical in the training of young evangelists, many of whom will not normally be mentored to function in this system until they are married. If they operate outside the social systems they will not be able to plant a contextual church.

Models that relate to learning

Although there are numerous cultural models to learn, it is imperative for the cross-cultural church planter to begin as early as possible to investigate them. Besides the three described above, there are two more that should be given early attention.

1. Communication models

Fortunately, much has been written about these models so we know that they go far beyond simple language facility. Paul Hiebert (1976) writes about symbolism and communication in his excellent book. Symbols can be anything to which people have assigned value. Dogs and pigs are important to some focus people while they are anathema to others. The worldview of the UPG will affect the way that many symbols are used in the culture. For example, rice has a mystical nature to many peoples because it is connected with supernatural beginnings. Rice can be used in many ways to bring blessing. In some focus groups, water left in a rice bin overnight is used to heal the sick.

John Condon and Fathi Yousef (1985) have an excellent book on communication. The writing is engaging and not technical. They emphasize an "awareness of our own culturally influenced patterns of communication" and the fact that "each intercultural encounter is unique and complex" (p.ix). Even if you have studied extensively in communication theory, the portions of this book that deal with value orientation and cultural beliefs will likely be useful. The authors focus on how communication functions in categories such as self, family, and society and in human nature, nature, and the supernatural.

Roat's story

Roat was a focus person who was injured by falling construction material. His back was seriously hurt and he was in great pain. The city doctor said there was not much they could do without an operation because his back was broken. An operation was planned but in the meantime, Roat returned to his village where his family and the local shaman convinced him that his back could be healed. He allowed the shaman to walk on his back in order to "adjust" it and this caused him excruciating pain. However, the shaman told him he would get well. Not only did he not get well but his back was damaged beyond repair. The city doctors said that he was permanently paralyzed and they could no longer help him.

Roat's story illustrates all of Condon and Yousef's categories listed above. Communication among the focus people operates to include self, family, and society. Many problems such as Roat's involve human nature, nature, and the supernatural. These become obvious when we look at the whole. These are the initial areas in which worldview is created. Persons with no formal education have a well-formed worldview because they learn it as they engage with people, nature and the supernatural.

Roat becomes a leader

Roat learns a new worldview

Roat's boss was a Christian from another ethnic group. He continued to support Roat and his wife and children but he wanted to do more. He asked evangelists from Roat's focus group to visit him. As time passed, Roat came to faith in Jesus but his body continued to deteriorate from lack of exercise. He became despondent and lost the will to live. At God's appointment, a German physiotherapist visited the area and Roat's spiritual mentors took her to the village to consult about Roat's condition. She convinced him that he could become active again even though he probably would not walk. She explained physiotherapy exercises that would strengthen his entire body and pictures were drawn that showed him what to do. Her foreign directions were communicated and validated by the mentors. Roat's wife helped him exercise and, in time, he began to recover strength and mobility until he could move about in a wheelchair. Twenty-five years later Roat is the head of a thriving congregation of converts from his ethnic group.

Through God's mercy, Roat's worldview changed from one of fatalism to hope. The combination of biblical teaching and Christian love moved him from a non-biblical worldview to a biblical worldview. In his case, the communication models were suited to his needs and learning process. Some of the implications of these kinds of models are discussed in *Communication Theory: The Asian Perspective* (Dissanayake, 1988). This book covers aspects of communication from the viewpoints of Indian, Chinese, Japanese, and Islamic scholars. The Islamic article is written by a scholar at Nehru University in India.

People learn in different ways

2. Teaching/learning models

This is another set of concepts critical to cross-cultural church planting. This is not usually an area that is investigated by the average worker but they are of extreme importance when we go cross-cultural. The field of neuroscience is discovering new information about the way the brain functions and how the chemistry of our bodies regulates our physiological state. Food and drink, rest, and stimulation affect learning. Even though we know these things, they may be areas that the cross-cultural worker cannot control.

However, cognitive learning styles is an area that the cross-cultural worker can utilize. It is being investigated by scholars in ways cross-cultural workers can study and implement. For example, research of three Indonesian ethnic groups sought to understand how the individuals in these groups selected and organized information dealing with problems in order to obtain solutions (Suyata, 1986). The study confirmed that "differences in field-dependent-independent (FDI) performances, in analytic (ANAL) style, and in non-analytic (NONAN) style were better explained from students' personal attributes, familial background, familial experiences, learning experiences in school, and environmental conditions" (*quoted from the Abstract*).

Adapting various models

These models are concerned with learning styles in schools but they can also apply to home life as well. The story of Roat illustrates worldview change through societal interaction. In schools we can evaluate worldview change through organized lessons. It is more difficult in the field because teaching/learning models may vary between the old and the young and between the urban and the rural person. The effective cross-cultural church planter will seek to know these models and recognize how they function in society.

It is critical that the cross-cultural church planter understand that his focus group will process information in ways not familiar to him. The salient question is whether these ways of learning will prevent the focus people from comprehending the messages communicated by the evangelist and also making decisions concerning these messages. The Coleman Report (1966) showed "that the student's family, peers, and general social milieu exert much more of an effect on learning than does the school" (Cohn, 1987:377). Cohn and Rossmiller's article is about research into the influence of the school but they recognize that the personal culture of the student is more important.

Conveying biblical truth

You must teach biblical truths using local models

If the cross-cultural church planter cannot tap into the social milieu of the focus group, it is highly unlikely that he will be successful in planting a contextual church. Some workers try to do this by imitating the religious practices of the focus group. This approach misses the crucial factor of changing worldview. The worker must seek to create a plausible biblical explanation of the natural and supernatural forces at work in the culture of the focus people in such a way that it will be an alternative worldview for them to consider.

About the year 1869, a Javanese Muslim convert named Sadrach moved to a city in central Java and began to gather converts through evangelism. Following the example of other Javanese evangelists, he established a new cultural configuration that included elements of Javanese mysticism and Islam. However, these were all reinterpreted in biblical terms. Because his teaching varied from European Christian practices, Sadrach faced opposition from some missionaries as well as from Javanese Muslims. Sadrach's exploration of ways to guide Javanese from an Islamic/spiritist worldview into a biblical worldview helped establish Javanese Christianity as an alternative worldview. Today, there are more converts from Islam among Javanese than in any other ethnic group in the world.

EVALUATING MENTORS

In this chapter we have surveyed various kinds of mentors and some of the areas in which the cross-cultural church planter eventually will have to be a superior mentor. If that is your goal you will need to keep the following factors in mind.

Working through the cultural patterns

Holy Spirit

1. A superior mentor is led by the Holy Spirit and empowered in all he or she does. The task is overwhelming and not possible for the church planter without supernatural intervention. We are aiming at nothing less than worldview change. This is like spiritual rebirth. It does not happen unless the Holy Spirit is at work in the individual. Our task is to seek to know the mind of God in the creation and organizing of our mentoring lessons so that they are understood and processed by those we mentor. The outcome is in God's time.

Mutual Respect

2. A good mentor will like and respect those who are being mentored. As it is with evangelism, it is hard to mentor a person you do not like. And in a similar manner, it is hard to receive mentoring from a person you do not like. For many of us, learning to truly love those of the focus group is not a simple matter. When we come to the focus people, our hearts are following God and we are hypothetically loving them. However, after we begin to get to know them and experience their bad traits, we can come to disrespect them and even dislike them. Loving and respecting the focus people is often not a natural thing but rather it is a special work of God in our hearts.

Agape love means we respect everyone

A defining moment in my life came when I became angry with a man who was working at our house. His boys were sick with TB and worms and I helped him get medicine for them and follow-up care by a physician. The medicine for TB had to be taken for six months. Every few weeks I asked him how they were and he gave a good report. After a few months, he told me the children were no longer taking the medicine. When I asked why he told me that they seemed well and the family decided not to give them the medicine any longer.

I berated him severely for his arrogance in thinking he knew more than the doctor who had helped the boys. When I entered my house, I asked myself why I was so angry and the Lord impressed me with the words, "Because you don't really love these people." That experience was the beginning of a radical change in my attitude toward the people.

Interest in the subject

3. When a person is interested in your questions it is the sign of a good mentor. Follow up that person and learn all you can. A good mentor will not only explain cultural concepts clearly but he or she will be willing to go over the same subject time and again. It is a mistake to think you will understand a focus group concept or worldview the first time you hear it even though it is clearly rendered. These matters are deep and have many levels of understanding. You may grasp one important aspect of a cultural myth while missing most of the lessons in the myth. Explain the gospel over and over to those you mentor. Expand on the biblical worldview so that they will understand more and more deeply.

Aware when you do not understand

4. It is a rare mentor who will comprehend when you are missing something important and will define the issue so that you can discuss it. But these are the kinds of mentors for whom you need to be praying. And these are also the kind of mentors you should seek to be for others when God places them in your way. When I told my mentor that I understood something about the insecurity and low self-esteem of my focus group because I had learned from their myth that they had a dog for an ancestor, he led me to think deeper. He told me that gods were often incarnated as animals. That dog might, in fact, be a god.

Correct you politely

5. The mentor should be polite and wise so that you are corrected in such a way that you will learn. They will be patient when you are slow. My first

language teacher was sympathetic when I learned so slowly. One day, she gave me an analogy of a train.

She said that there are express trains and local trains. The express trains go fast to their destination while the local trains stop along the way. However, they both arrive at the same destination. It is just a matter of timing. Remember to be polite and kind and patient when your disciples seem to learn so slowly to trust the Lord.

CAUTION !! Be cautious about using mentors from one's own culture in evaluating the focus culture. We need to be constantly cross checking all information we receive.

EVALUATION of END RESULTS - CHECK LIST - PHASE FOUR

[ ] am willing to learn from anyone

[ ] have actively sought out persons who can teach me about all aspects of the culture (name 4 of these)

[ ] have mentors in particular areas of importance to me at this time, such as local church life (name 3 of these & which areas they represent)

[ ] have mentors from at least 3 status groups; above me, below me, and from my same level

[ ] am not getting all my information from expats

[ ] am checking all information with more than one source

[ ] have begun to identify those who are most wanted as mentors by the indigenous people (give the profile of 2 of these)

[ ] can objectively define what kind of mentor pleases me (name 6 characteristics of this mentor)

[ ] have begun to recognize different mentoring styles (mention 2 of these)

[ ] can specify some areas where my mentoring style differs from that of the indigenous people (write them out)

[ ] have begun to observe the models listed in the section on CRITICAL MODELS OF MENTORING

[ ] can describe 1 learning model of the target group

[ ] am able to describe the Team strategy

[ ] am praying regularly for personal mentors in areas critical to church planting success

Tips: 1. PRAYER will open doors of opportunity.

2. You can learn about your focus group from other ethnic people, but beware of stereotyping/ generalizations.

3. Don't get drawn away from your calling to more easily evangelized people groups.

4. Learn all you can about the inner workings of an indigenous organization/church.

5. A good mentor allows people to make mistakes. When a person is not allowed to make mistakes, you are managing, not mentoring.

NEXT PHASE!

CHAPTER SEVEN

PHASE FIVE - ENGAGEMENT

"Whenever you enter a town and they receive you, eat what is set before you. Heal the sick in it and say to them, 'The kingdom of God has come near to you.'" Luke 10:8-9

By now, you are probably asking yourself this question, "Why does this book keep talking about lessons I need to learn? Why aren't I being given assignments to evangelize, and disciple, and lead worship, and all those church related tasks? Why am I not giving out instead of taking in?"

As we see it, more than half of CC CP is taking in all we can learn about our focus group so that we can create and structure contextual church planting tasks. People adjust and master language and other lessons at different rates. You may move through the Phases as fast as you can. But please do not fool yourself into thinking you can do effective and lasting CC CP without preparing yourself adequately.

Structure must be created

In structured situations such as medical work, education, and established church ministry, you can fit in much more quickly. By definition, CC CP in a UPG is <u>unstructured</u>. Your approach cannot be fashioned overnight or simply by strategizing with a group of expatriates. You need to spend time in Orientation and Mentoring in order to learn the skills you need to <u>engage</u> the focus group. Here in Phase 5, we shift more into that mode. But the effective cross-cultural church planter will never out-grow the learning areas we discussed in the first four phases. The greater your preparation, the better you will be able to serve others.

Engagement tasks

Engagement means pioneering social structures

You may start to do some of the engagement tasks in earlier phases. However, at this point, it is good to look at them on an-other level. Basic to all our tasks is our CC CP national team. At this point, it will probably be nationals from outside the focus group. Even if you have many nationals on your team who are more in tune with the focus group than you are, they will need to do the same things you do. It is crucial to continue building a national team that is strong in faith and in the skills they need to do the job. Your engagement with the focus group will be traumatic. Effective CC CP is a team effort.

DEFINING ENGAGEMENT

While you may think of engagement as any exchange you might have with the focus people, we prefer to define it as *initiating and structuring a ministry* to plant a church. Preparing yourself is like studying math-ematics while engaging the focus group is like studying calculus. CC CP involves the competencies your team will need to integrate the mul-tiple tasks of a contextualized church as you move into the Development Phase. These tasks include the following: evangelism, teaching/preach-ing, preparing music and other worship aids, preparing literature and other mass media for different age groups, developing infrastructure for education, medical care, job training and other needs that arise when people express faith in Jesus Christ. Engagement also involves many un-expected challenges such as a burial ground for converts. Very often, converts will not be allowed burial in the cemeteries run by other reli-gious groups.

In this Phase 5, we will discuss the beginnings of engagement and in the following phases we will describe how engagement is matured through Phase 6 -Negotiation until it reaches full bloom in Phase 7 -Development.

FIRST STEPS IN ENGAGEMENT (See <u>Second Steps</u> in Chapter Eleven-Phase Seven – Part Two)

Faith building in the Team.

1. This is the Achilles heel of many teams. Some do not understand the magnitude of CC CP in a UPG and they do not prepare themselves spiritually. Before you reach Phase 5 in your development, you will begin to feel the attacks of the enemy. As you share Christ with the focus group, these attacks will increase. Satan will not stay away from you. The more you learn how to share Jesus with others, the more the devil will try to stop you. You have to claim the UPG for Christ and plant the flag of the gospel. God will make a way for you wherever you go. Nothing should be allowed to convince you to withdraw on your own. You should stay until a church is planted or you are forced to leave. If you do not have this level of commitment, the devil will drive you out.

Know your enemy, know your Helper

2. Public and private prayer should increase rather than decrease. Public prayer will not substitute for private prayer. Each team member will have to learn to walk with God on his or her own. The Team will teach and encourage but the inner person of each team member must be in harmony with the Lord. Conflicts between team leaders and team members have caused some teams to disband. Expatriate and national teams have fallen apart when some members drifted into sin. No one is so spiritually great that they cannot be tempted.

Prayer is an absolute

3. Do not allow members to work alone, as the pressure is too great for individuals. Every team member should worship weekly with the team. Absence from these times of corporate worship is an indicator of potential problems. Attendance at weekly team worship was one of only two rules we had on our UPG team. The other was they agreed not to borrow money from outside people. We did not want them obligated to anyone outside

the team. In the section on Phase 6, we will explain why and how outside people might raid your ministry. We call these hostile takeovers.

Guard against team members spending time alone with members of the opposite sex as the temptations are enormous. For example, one of our focus team members was interested in a girl. When he went to visit her family, her parents left them alone in the house. Her parents wanted them to get intimately involved so he would have to marry her. Expatriates as well are enticed in these and other ways when they are depressed, confused, or frustrated. Be your "brother's keeper."

Survey the field of your focus group.

1. There are many good books and courses that suggest various ways to survey your focus group. Some may use ethnographic research, community mapping, neighborhood surveys and the like. Members of your team should be assigned these important jobs. Those members will have the tasks of finding the best approach, getting the training materials, structuring the training for the team members, supervising the implementation of the survey, and tabulating the results.

> *Always be studying your focus group*

2. This survey of the focus group should inform the team about the status of religious beliefs, places of worship, spiritual strongholds, how the language is used, family loyalty, community cohesion, political orientations, educational opportunities, medical facilities, economic strength, and other aspects of the culture. The church that is planted must live and flourish in these contexts. It is folly to try to structure and develop a church without first assessing these critical features of society.

Identify the most open inquirers.

We suggest finding the soft spot in your focus group. Others may want to strike at the heart of the most adamant opponents of the

Which would you approach first?

gospel. Each person has to decide where his or her call may be. However, in general, we have seen that the gospel attracts people from the margins of society where there is more openness and it then moves through them into the heart of the culture. People in any given area of a UPG normally have fairly extensive kinship ties. If we are successful in evangelizing and nurturing new believers, they will carry the gospel to other less open members of their family web.

Make friends and create a trust bond with prospective believers.

The trust bond is discussed in Phase 3 under "Hindrances in the Focus Group." If outsiders are not careful, they can have conflicts with focus group people. An outstanding worker we knew from New Zealand had conflicts because his language facility was so good his cultural learning could not keep up with his speaking ability. People did not tend to easily forgive his cultural mistakes because they thought he should know better. An expatriate who is stumbling along in the language is forgiven much because people have low expectations for a beginner.

We should be careful about criticizing anything until we understand the context. Humor also can be a pitfall because it is not used the same way in every culture. Crying and laughter in some UPG conveys meaning different from ours. For example, among some focus people no one is supposed to cry at the funerals because it makes the spirit of the departed more lonely and sad. Avoiding mistakes in cultural adjustment is important in forming a trust bond with new friends.

Deepen your understanding of the focus group's worldview and basic values.

Paul Hiebert (1976) describes a focus peoples' worldview as "the basic assumptions they use to organize their conceptual worlds…" (p.363). Worldview is the concepts and values that inform every aspect of one's culture. If a person believes that God is remote, he or she is not likely to respond to the idea of God as Father. Another example of worldview values can be seen in the Batak tribe of Sumatra. They do not allow anyone to marry a cousin on their father's side. However, maternal cousins may marry. The rule is clear for the outsider while the reasoning behind that rule is not.

In your research, try to delineate the value system of your focus group. You may not understand it at first, but knowing as much as you can about it will help you formulate the gospel in a way that will be coherent for them. Many cultures have books that will give you guidance in research-ing values. For example, Dr. Asrul Zamani (2002) describes Malay ideals. Sometimes the value system promoted by writers is idealistic and does not function in real life. This is true of cultures around the world. However, these values are important for us to know in proclaiming the gospel. More will be said about this in the following sections on evangelism and church theology.

Formulate & implement a contextual evangelistic model.

This is easier said than done. Such an evangelistic model usually does not exist in most UPG and it is one of the most difficult tasks to accom-plish. Some workers import contextual models from other groups with similar religious affiliations. For example, one might think that a model from India would apply to Balinese Hinduism. It is not impossible that such a model would work but it is not wise to follow that plan until one is convinced that the worldviews of both focus groups are compatible. To give another example, most Indonesians are Muslims but the major-ity of them practice an Islam quite different from that in Arab cultures. They need an original approach.

The effective CC CP worker creates an evangelistic model

Begin to formulate contextual Christian nurturing.

In many UPG, this is the most difficult model to develop and is the area in which church planting tends to fail. Sharing the gospel always seems to attract people. We believe that the Holy Spirit has ap-pointments for us in the focus group. When we proclaim the saving work of Jesus Christ, they respond. Sometimes, their con-version is swift but most likely it will take time. However, if we are faithful to evangelize, people will receive Jesus. After they are truly converted, they need to be discipled. This is pastoral work, the area of Christian nurture. It is here that we will lose many believers if we do not know enough about their worldview to speak to their daily issues. In the UPG where we worked, most believers contin-ued to keep their magic amulets even though they said they had thrown them away at baptism. Some persisted in going to the shaman when they were sick because they did not yet have complete faith in Jesus as their healer. Many fell away because those who pastored them did not know enough about their culture to speak to the needs of their hearts.

Christian nurture deals with faith problems

Start developing infrastructure for a focus group congregation.

The effective church planting team will not delay this until they have gathered a congregation. They will start preparations as soon as there is a team member ready to do so. Church infrastructure has many features and we will expand on this throughout the remainder of this manual. In brief, critical infrastructure includes adult, youth, and children's ministries. Literature and teaching aids are needed. Equipment and furniture might also be important. The Bible must be translated into the focus language so that it can be studied. Worship music and hymnody is vital. When a team is adapting focus group music to use in worship, expertise is needed. See the example we gave in Chapter Four about the selection of the proper musical instruments.

"The minister at Wonosari (Kediri) once replied to a question of Harthoorn, as to why the Christian Javanese should not be allowed to play the *gamelan*, whereas the European can play his piano without criticism, in the following manner: 'Because the European is indeed just playing his piano, while the Javanese who plays the *gamelan* evokes associations with the dancer, who provokes sexual excitement among the spectators with her more or less erotic song and dance'" (Van Akkeren, 1970:83). This is the kind of information you need to process before you involve new believers.

EARLY PROBLEMS IN ENGAGEMENT

Your major problems will occur within your team.

1. Remember the quote in Phase 2 from Andrew Murray about the missionary problem. With few exceptions, you will have more serious problems from within your team than you will have with those outside your team. Years ago, an American cartoonist named Walt Kelly drew a political comic called *Pogo*. In the strip, he had one of his animal characters say, "We have met the enemy and he is us." This is often the case in UPG teams. The stress is so high that internal disputes often derail a team.

> *"The missionary problem is a personal one"*
> Murray

2. It is very hard to get unity in an expatriate team unless the members are skillful in resolving problems. The very nature of expatriates who go to a UPG predicts that many on a team will aggressively promote their points of view. Sometimes a strong team leader will be able to pull everyone into

consensus. In other cases, the team members will partition the tasks and carry out their assignments. However, there are many cases where this kind of unity is not accomplished and the team flounders. Even team leaders give up and leave their teams. Some major mission leaders have experienced this in their early careers.

A dysfunctioning expatriate team cannot properly integrate national or focus group members. (See: Five Dysfunctions of a Team under TEAM BUILDING in Phase 3).

First of all, their spiritual condition is not conducive to inspiring trust. Members will tend to vent their disagreements more than they will share their agreements. In addition, expatriates who are so rigid in their points of view that they have difficulty negotiating with fellow expatriates will also have difficulty negotiating with nationals or focus people. This is particularly true if they control the ministry money. Language is another problem. Developing strategy and tactics in a second language creates additional communication problems. You neglect your team building skills at your own peril.

Established Christian churches may be suspicious.
If there is a church in your UPG, you will likely have more trouble bonding with them than with focus people of another religion. This is frequently the case with churches founded by historic European or American missions. They have learned to exist in what they perceive as a hostile environment and they do not want outsiders coming in and possibly stirring up resentment among the focus people. In many cases, these churches have enculturated the believers among the focus people into a context that only approximates their original culture. Their physical looks are like other focus people but they do not live like them or participate in their religious gatherings. Those early Christians in our focus group who were led to Christ by the Dutch missionaries were called stingy because they did not follow tradition by providing ritual meals for the community during their religious ceremonies.

When we were passing out tens of thousands of tracts during the early 70s, there were more serious complaints from church people than from focus group leaders. The church people were afraid of a reaction to the tracting. They had some basis for that fear though trouble never materialized from tracting. Differences of opinion in outreach can cause serious friction. The focus group church that existed previous to the formation of our focus team accused us of violating a basic community value. They said we promoted our agenda without first asking permission from the presiding focus church leaders. The idea that we should ask them was left over from comity agreements under the colonial government that allocated geographical areas to certain churches. It is probable that even if we had known to ask them, they would not have given us permission to evangelize. Research from their own scholars showed that they had become a non-evangelizing church. But perhaps there was a way of negotiating this issue, had we known we needed to.

Unity is hard to maintain; love difficult to foster.

1. Although it is very frustrating to maintain, much effort should be given to promoting unity with co-workers and with all believers in your vicinity. John 13:35 records Jesus' observation that people will know his disciples by their love for one another. If we avoid other Christians, we will never be able to know them. If we do not know them, we cannot adequately pray for them and we will never love them. This is not a good witness to the focus people who come to know the Lord. They cannot grasp the nature of the worldwide fellowship of believers if we do not even have fellowship with Christians in our own neighborhoods.

There may be some problems with church people

Incorporate problem solving models

2. Lines of communication must be established and kept open as much as possible. We can explain to new Christians why we want them to develop their own contextual church, rather than copy the churches of other groups. They will understand that non-believing focus people will feel more comfortable in a culturally familiar gathering. However, communally oriented people have difficulty understanding arbitrary separation from the larger community. If we model an isolationist, independent attitude in respect to existing Christian churches, it will not lay the grounds

for the love among believers that Jesus desires. In fact, there is danger it will become a model of domination.

Physical & emotional problems waste the energy of your team.

1. There are few expatriate and national workers who do not experience new physical problems when they enter a UPG. The physical problems may result from adjusting to new bacteria in food and water. Stress is a big problem in cross-cultural workers and it can weaken the body so that it is susceptible to various diseases. This can be exacerbated by overwork and lack of proper rest. One of our colleagues had to go back to his native land because he tried to work as hard as the national evangelist who was his mentor. Over a period of years his health broke down. In the book, *How to Beat Burn Out*, Dr. Frank Minirth (1986) describes how to manage emotional health. One of the key indicators is the amount of changes one experiences in a short time. The authors developed a scale of various stressful changes that one might encounter. Each of these changes is given a numerical value, which represents relative emotional pressure. "A total of two hundred or more stress points can indicate the presence of or likelihood of burnout" (p.116).

BIG TIME BURNOUT

2. We also know a considerable number of people who have had phantom illnesses that mirrored the real thing. They had symptoms of such serious conditions as heart attacks, tumors, numbness in the limbs, weight loss, invalidism, and other similar complaints. But when physicians examined

them, no reason for the illnesses could be found. Some expatriates were medically evacuated to their homeland where doctors could not find a physical reason for their condition.

3. It is a serious mistake to underrate the attacks of the enemy against our physical and emotional health. William Taylor (1997) tells us that poor health is one of the five top reasons workers leave the field. It is wise for team members to monitor each other's health because they are the ones who will have to take care of the sick and pick up the slack in their work assignments.

Keeping workers well is a challenge

Consequences of imprecise negotiations and misunderstandings.

1. During the time you are in orientation, relationships with focus people will be free and easy. You will be studying language, asking a lot of questions, and generally getting to know people. Usually, you will not be perceived as putting pressure on them in any way. Most people will be curious about you and many will want to interact with you. Now that you are

The Many Faces of Burnout

at the point of engagement there will be times when you will negotiate with people about miscellaneous important things. For example, you may rent a house, buy a motorcycle or car, talk with church leaders about evangelism, or bargain with your visa sponsor about the amount of time he wants you to work. Phase 6 is about serious negotiating but any negotiating runs the risk of misunderstanding.

2. Misunderstandings and conflicts will begin to surface when you are seriously engaging people. Before this, you have probably had a free ride. But when you are involved in a program in which people have assignments, make reports and give accountability, you are almost sure to encounter difficulties. Focus people will operate on a different wavelength from you. When you are locked into a specific pattern of life with people of other cultures, differences arise and cause stress. Your concepts of time, space, energy, work style, and responsibility may vary widely from those of

the people with whom you work. These and many other values can cause relational problems.

Security is not possible for an evangelist.

1. Many cross-cultural church planters are extremely concerned about security. They are afraid to reveal their faith because they fear the reaction of the focus people. Some will pretend that they are following the religion of the focus people. Others will admit they are Christians if asked but will never offer that information. These workers believe that as long as they are incognito, they will be able to live and work among the focus people. This is fine if one is only interested in learning language and culture. But if one's purpose is to plant a church, it is impossible to do so without evangelism.

2. In many focus groups, openly evangelistic workers do not encounter persecution. In these groups, it is rare for foreigners to experience severe pressure before focus people begin to be baptized. As long as focus people are not being baptized, it is likely the expatriate will not be challenged. Even when persecution begins, it is generally aimed at new believers, inquirers, and nationals who are team members rather than at the expatriate team members. You can get national Christian leaders to counsel you concerning the degree to which you should behave as a spiritual leader. Your spiritual leader model may be modified as you enter the focus group.

Supporting new believers.

Engaging people means dealing with problems

Engagement also means that you will begin to interact with new believers. Perhaps you will be used by the Lord to evangelize some of these or guide them in their new faith. It is critical to pray for and with these believers and to participate in teaching them by word and deed. They will be looking at you as an example of the Christian life. Your team members will be their models in Christian love and service. In our UPG, a focus person told us that it takes about ten years for a person to really grasp the meaning of salvation in Christ and the victorious life they

"Let the peace of Christ rule in your hearts, since as members of one body you were called to peace.
Col.1:15

could live in him. Many focus people were kind and humble believers but it took time for them to inculcate the biblical worldview.

CUTTING EDGE MINISTRY

During the period when you are beginning a serious engagement with your focus group, it is important to remain aware of certain cutting edge aspects of your ministry. Many workers tend to forget these essentials in the busyness of life. CC CP demands an almost total focus in your life and it is important to remind yourself of these features. We divide this section into Primary Concerns and Implementing Cross-cultural Skills.

A. Primary Concerns

1. Spiritual warfare will intensify as time goes on.

It is imperative that you keep your family and your church planting team spiritually sharp. The biggest mistake you can make is to let spiritual relationships slide. Many church planters and church planting teams tend to exclude wives from discussions on theology and strategy. They only want to strategize with men and this excludes women from the grand adventure of church planting. Some teams include single women in all discussions but other teams tend to marginalize them. Great spiritual power is evidenced in teams that include all members in prayer and planning.

Avoid chauvinism in your team

2. Maintain close communication & unity with visa sponsor.

Do not forget that you are a guest in the country and can only stay through the good graces of those who sponsor your visa to live there. Churches and Christian schools who sponsor you may know you are a

Christian worker but may not know your ultimate goal is to penetrate a UPG. You should fulfill all your obligations to them. Remember that Christian ethics directs us to do the job we agreed to do. Some workers have gotten so involved in their UPG activities that they neglected to fulfill their agreement with their sponsor and thus have lost credibility with them as a Christian witness.

Guard your integrity

If you are a tentmaker, your sponsor will perhaps not know that you are called to the UPG. You have to be careful not to cause any suspicion by the government to fall on your sponsor. We always risk dishonoring the Lord if we pretend to our sponsor that we are not serious Christians. We have agreed to serve our sponsor and we should not betray that trust.

3. CC CP requires both evangelistic & pastoral skills.

As we have already mentioned, in the early days of our UPG work all the activists were using an evangelistic model. They did not have a vision for a UPG church and they had not prepared themselves to pastor converts using a focus group model. From early stages, you must train your team in both evangelistic and pastoral models that are appropriate for the focus group. If not, you will find yourself losing many of your converts who cannot relate to a non-focus group pastoral style. This experience is described as believers coming in the front door of the church and leaving through the back door.

4. Develop coaching models.

In Phase 4 we mentioned the coach. We perceive of the function of a coach in the following way. The CC CP coach is similar to a sports coach. This person does not actually do all the ministry himself. In fact, the ideal is that the focus group converts will be the ones doing most or all of it.

You need a culturally appropriate coaching model

The expatriate coach may not be able to perform certain ministry skills as well as the focus people but he or she can guide them in what needs to be done. When we taught focus people how to do evangelism, we found that most were more gifted than we were. Empowering spiritual gifts is perhaps the greatest contribution of an expatriate.

A coach does not have the insider knowledge of the culture like a mentor but an experienced and well trained coach can tell the focus people where to find that information. The expatriate has to prepare himself for a number of years before he can be an effective coach. Of course, we have to know what we are talking about. A mentor can give you information but he cannot necessarily tell you how to implement it. A successful coach has to be able to guide a focus person in ministry skills so that they can implement them. In this way, an expatriate can become a coach for focus people in developing various ministries of the church. Expatriate church planters tend to think that they are the ones who should structure such ministries as evangelism, spiritual nurture, biblical leadership, and pastoral ministry. The real story is this. A contextual church will have to be conceptualized by the focus people. The expatriate's job is to coach them as well as possible in doing the church planting tasks.

COACH : This is what you need to do.

MENTOR : This is how people will respond if you do that.

Coach versus mentor

5. Becoming a Coach.

Reg Hamilton (1993:62-70) defines coaching as one type of mentoring. While we define it differently, we can still appreciate Hamilton's stages of coaching. They are: 1. Observation, 2. Analysis, 3. Modeling, and 4. Practice and review. In the area of observation, "the coach sees, in detail, the level of performance and area for improvement" (p. 63). Obviously, one cannot become a coach in CC CP unless one has both participated in and studied the discipline. We will not be able to identify anything in detail until we actually experience it.

Analysis has to do with detecting the cause of poor performance. The coach is able to debrief the person learning the skills. Our focus group team met every Friday to debrief all their experiences during the week. Gradually, they came to understand more and more about what was going on around them. In the modeling phase of coaching, "the coach demonstrates or explains correct performance" (Ibid.). Once when the sister of a home church member was having a baby, we asked the evangelists what they should do in ministering to her. They had not thought about it. When we asked what the focus people do when a baby is born, they did not know. We advised them to go to an older woman in the village and ask her what the tradition was. They did this and were able to minister to the new mother. They were coached into seeking a mentor who could tell them what to do.

The practice and review stage of coaching is when the new behavior is tried out under supervision. A training program for home church leaders in our focus group teaches ministry gifts through role-play and rehearsal. Although it is not possible to observe all the home church leaders in action, the program includes extensive evaluation within a short time.

6. "Church planting is best done by the indigenous person."

From the time we arrived on the mission field, we heard that mantra over and over. As time went by, we learned that it was true <u>provided</u> the indigenous person is well trained and spiritually fit to do the job. An un-trained focus person has no idea of how to begin church planting. One of the teams we coached consisted of Bible school graduates. They had learned evangelism and were skilled in it. However, they knew little about the pastoral ministry. They could lead people to faith but they did not know how to gather and structure a congregational ministry. They needed coaching in all that entailed. When they gained those skills, they were able to pastor their flocks into mature Christian service.

The indigenous worker will also need training

7. Conflict resolution.

Conflict resolution is not a subject one usually takes in Bible school or seminary but it is one that should be studied by every cross-cultural church planter. Conflicts and potential conflicts will constantly arise. It is like what Jesus says about wars and rumors of wars. It is amazing how many petty issues can threaten to set a team into a tailspin. And beyond that, there are potential conflicts with various ethnic people and with those of the focus group. We found that many cultural concepts were vastly different between western and eastern cultures. Space between people, concepts of time, ways of borrowing, and multiple other differences in cultures give rise to misunderstandings and potential conflicts. The cross-cultural church planter must be prepared to resolve these as quickly as possible even when it means sacrificing one's own "rights."

8. Church planting is most stable when sponsored by a recognized church or denomination.

Many church planters want to jump into the fray and evangelize and gather a congregation without thinking about the consequences. Some focus people will accept Jesus as their savior with no idea that the religious leaders of their community will react against them. They have never experienced a time when anyone in their community left their corporate religion. When the persecution comes, new believers are frequently taken off guard and thrown into confusion. At such a time, the support of a recognized church or denomination can make the difference between the survival or extinction of a village congregation.

Partnership in ministry

In many countries, the government only recognizes certain Christian churches or organizations. Many para-church ministries operate without such approval. If these groups plant home churches that are not recognized, it is likely they will experience confrontations with the dominant religious structure. The governments of many countries are not primarily concerned with Christian activity. However, they have to be concerned with the reactions of politically powerful religious leaders who do not want the Christian church to thrive. It is critical for believers to have as stable and secure a church plant as possible.

B. Implementing Cross-cultural Skills

1. Accelerate language learning.

One of the most careless mistakes cross-cultural church planters make is to stop language learning. This process should accelerate during the engagement phase. Some people feel they have learned enough language to understand what people are saying and they do not realize that they may not grasp what people mean by what they say. This is true for both expatriate and national workers who are learning another language. Every language has nuances and ambiguities in meaning that are not apparent to the outsider until one has had years of experience. The focus people we served used their language in a roundabout manner that was sometimes obscure even for them. On one occasion, a man talked to an evangelist for an hour about various subjects. When he left, I asked the evangelist about the purpose of his visit. His purpose was not clear to the evangelist. Various mentors agreed that this was characteristic of the focus people.

2. Continue recruiting mentors.

The effective cross-cultural church planter continues to seek out mentors in various areas of the culture. Contextual church planting is so complex that one will never stop learning its distinctive features. Each difference in theological or sociological expression creates questions we can bring to our mentors. Rarely can one mentor answer many of these questions. We need to find mentors who will give us information about all phases of church and cultural life. Then we can assimilate, integrate, and blend this information into a composite picture.

> *Engagement means going deeper in cultural knowledge*

3. Cultivate appreciation of focus people's music & art.

By the time you reach this phase of engagement, you should be reading about music and art and developing an appreciation of it. This may not be a pleasant task for you. One of our focus people teams (actually mixed ethnic makeup) began to study the local music with a professional teacher. After a few weeks of practice with the musical instruments, one of the focus group team members said that the constant striking of the gongs gave him a headache. This team was made up of young people who had not grown up appreciating this music. It was hard work for them to learn to play the instruments but their ability to do so opened unimaginable vistas for them both on a personal level and in their acceptance by the non-believers.

4. Evangelists/pastors need to become experts in cultural customs/ traditions.

In Phase 4, the spiritual leadership model was introduced as one of the critical areas in which you should be mentored. Spiritual leaders are expected to be experts in religious belief systems and ceremonies. People in Africa, Asia, and S.E. Asia look to their religious practitioners to explain to them the unseen world. Ordinary people do not make up religious beliefs or pretend to be knowledgeable in the area of religion. This is the arena of the practitioner and his or her apprentices. When your church planting team begins to think about the scope of a contextual church, the average church member will not be helpful. They have never thought about the way organizational structures conform to the culture and they will have no idea how the church should conform.

The evangelists and pastors are the people who will be responsible for designing the beginnings of a contextual church. It is unlikely that any of them will have been trained to do this before they come to the work. Learning culture is a critical part of their job description. They need to learn how to think through issues such as how the focus people feel about medical care, education, labor and livelihood and how those issues would relate to the church. Coaching them to do this is one of the top priorities of the expatriate and focus group church planting team. This is one of the hardest jobs the team will undertake. Several members need to spend considerable time observing religious orientations and seeking acquaintances with religious practitioners. The repetition of religious ceremonies determines worldview. In writing about the Javanese, Niels Mulder observes that new events and changes "must be ritually acknowledged before they can be accepted" (1983:48).

5. Social organization.
When you begin to truly engage the focus people with the intent of gathering a congregation, you will have to intensify your attention on the ways they organize themselves socially. There may be a few differences between men and women and between adults and youth. But all of their patterns will emerge in a focus group church. Leadership is probably the most important of these models (see: Phase 4 & Phase 7-Part 1). Secondly, family systems will impact any church. Frequently, faith spreads through the kinship web. People will tend to organize themselves in the churches in the same way they do at home.

Another example is status and role. Respect will be shown in the church depending on how the members understand status and role. This is true around the world despite the clear biblical teaching against ranking members in terms of importance. Knowing how the status and role system functions will enable the church leaders to speak to it from a biblical worldview.

6. Identify leaders and try to make their acquaintance.

Leadership will operate in the church in the same way it does in the community unless you are able to affect worldview change in this sphere. When you are able to make friends with leaders, you will access some important mentors. These mentors will help you become informed about the strength and weaknesses of their models. This will enable you to process these models in terms of biblical standards. All cross-cultural church planters should be familiar with leadership models so that they can explain both their similarities to and differences from biblical worldview. This will give them competency in constructing a biblical leadership model for the church.

7. Systematic observations of material culture.

During this engagement phase, seek as much information as possible. This will include descriptions of material products that are in everyday use in your focus group. The location and type of houses in use reveal social concepts. For example, they show the need for shelter against weather or protection from other people. The presence of certain animals such as dogs and pigs indicates important worldview orientation. Most people view life through their labor and the types of jobs they do will indicate their ability to grasp new concepts. One of the young people first recruited for a focus group team was cutting grass for goats when the evangelist asked him if he wanted to go to Bible school. He really had no gifts for study but he said he preferred that to cutting grass. Despite his inauspicious start, and his lack of conceptual skills, he was a faithful evangelist and pastor until his death.

We need to note the presence or absence of schools and medical facilities. Information like that may indicate an opening for the gospel. Locating and mapping political strongholds often gives us indicators about people's religious orientation. In the decade of the 60s, many counties in Indonesia voted for the communist party even though the citizens were all nominally Muslim. Look for opportunities.

BARRIERS TO FAITH & SPIRITUAL GROWTH

Lack of understanding spiritual questions.

1. As we engage the focus people beyond the normal social amenities, our language and cultural experience should deepen dramatically in many categories. The most important of these is that of spiritual concerns. Our natural tendency is to address our own spiritual questions because that is what brought us to faith. Also, our faith deepens as Christ answers our spiritual questions. However, the spiritual questions of other cultures can be different from our own. We must learn the spiritual questions people ask in order to answer them with the gospel. This involves listening to the way focus people structure their spiritual experiences. A middle-aged friend of ours described an experience she had while staying at a friend's house. When she was reading in bed in the evening, the books in the bookcase at the head of the bed slid along the bookcase. She thought it was odd and was her imagination. Then the books moved back. We questioned what might make books move but she explained it as spirit activity. Part of her spiritual questions centered around spirit activity in the world and how that might affect her.

2. Fear of all kinds of spirits is part of the worldview of people in many of the UPG. This fear is manipulated by religious leaders to keep people dependent on the spiritual power of the leaders. Social behavior is also formed as a result of this fear. In some UPG, dusk is considered a dangerous period because of increased spirit activity during the boundary between day and night. Most people try to be inside a house or building at this time. You will discover many such beliefs that determine the way people live.

Answer their spiritual questions

In some cultures, people believe that political leaders also have spiritual power and some leaders play on this fear as a control mechanism over their citizens. It is important to begin to observe and catalog such influences. When you share the gospel with people, it must speak to these worldview areas and the spiritual questions they raise. If people do not feel that the gospel answers their questions and the important problems they face in their daily lives, they will not be drawn to it.

Lack of a model of evangelism.

A barrier that correlates with a lack of understanding of spiritual questions is the lack of an evangelism model that answers those questions. One of our mentors told us that our focus people do not believe that their personal sin is so great that God has to sacrifice himself for it. They can do good works and overcome the effects of their sin. In addition, their tradition teaches them the king does not die for the people but rather the people have to die for the king. This pattern of structuring spiritual understanding means one has to restructure the gospel message to emphasize the meaning of our human condition before that of a holy God. Evangelism must speak to the nature of God and how he responds to human sinfulness.

Each focus group will have its own spiritual questions that we must answer with our evangelism model. It is useless to keep using our own model, or any model, if it is not answering the aspects of life that are most important to them. Friendly visits and long conversations with people is one of the ways a worker can begin to define these issues. There may be books and other materials that explain religious orientation and practices. One of the goals our son-in-law had when he studied under a religious practitioner in his focus group was to learn how that religion answered spiritual questions.

Survey those who have believed.

Surveying new believers from the focus group is an excellent way to gain information as to why people come to faith in Jesus. Testimonies are good but people do not always include pertinent information about what attracted them to Jesus. Carefully crafted survey questions will bring out various aspects of the ways people are influenced. Dreams and visions are often mentioned in publications but there most certainly are experiences and mental strugglings behind those dramatic encounters. It is important to gain as much knowledge as possible about the process through which the focus people move to faith. These survey results will guide you in creating an evangelism model that is relevant to the spiritual questions people want answered. Survey believers who are still close to their conversion experience. Their answers are usually different after years have passed.

> *Worldly Christians in your area will make a negative impact*

Counter productive testimony of traditional Christians.

One of the distressing barriers you may face is the negative testimony of the lives of Christians who live in and around your focus group. In many cases, these traditional Christians are only nominal in their commitment to Christ. Their daily lives do not radiate Jesus' love for the focus group and there may be a background of conflict between them. In some cases, there may be a colonial history by governments perceived to be Christian. These "Christian" governments may have persecuted and/or deprived people of opportunities for a better life. In other situations, it may be businesses from so-called Christian countries that are exploiting the focus people for their own financial advantage. All of these situations put the cross-cultural church planter in a negative light.

Lack of effective nurturing models.

1. The lack of effective nurturing models will affect the results of the evangelism model.

Even with an effective evangelism model, you will lose members unless you develop effective nurturing. It is not sufficient to simply evangelize people. When they believe, we must nurture them in a way that speaks to their hearts. This was mentioned in **Begin to formulate contextual Christian nurturing** under FIRST STEPS IN ENGAGEMENT. (Phase 5- Engagement) Nurturing, like evangelism, has to be oriented to the emotional and spiritual nature of the people. In our focus group many converts were lost because the non-focus group pastors criticized or corrected them in a way that was not appropriate. The national pastors thought they were being very understanding but their focus group members could not endure the words they used.

2. Focus group leaders know how to get angry without breaking the spirit of the people.

They can cajole, criticize, reprimand, and insult in such a way that the people will recognize that this is the prerogative of the leader and not be devastated by it. We might say or do something that is incon-sequential to us and people freak out. We had a friend who told us that an expatriate worker had pointed with his foot at a picture on the floor. "My spirit was shocked," he said. "If I did not understand that a foreigner has not been properly taught, I could not be friends with him." It is staggering to Westerners to think that pointing with one's foot can break relationships but these are the kind of cultural issues we have to master.

EVALUATION of END RESULTS - CHECK LIST - PHASE FIVE

[ ] seeking to deepen personal & family spiritual life

[ ] participating in faith building with the Team

[ ] being careful to move together as a Team

[ ] have established an identity as a spiritually oriented person

[ ] have begun to formulate an evangelistic approach & a nurturing model

[ ] regular in personal evangelism & witnessing

[ ] am identifying and seeking a trust relationship with truth seekers

[ ] continuing to hone skills as both a mentoree and as a mentor

[ ] am going deeper into cultural customs and models

[ ] giving quality and quantity attention to the sponsoring church body (if one exists)

[ ] deepening study and implementation of the focus group's music and art

[ ] am continuing to do regular evaluation of both Team & team members

[ ] name 4 characteristics of the successful indigenous spiritual leader

[ ] write out 3 spiritual questions of your unreached people

[ ] survey those who have come to faith in your focus group to see what answered their spiritual questions

Tips: 1. Your contextual leadership principles & practice is one of the crucial factors in success of CC CP.

2. A personal kingdom complex & pride can bring you down– 1 Corinthians 10:12.

3. Don't be misled into thinking no one has ever tried to penetrate your unreached people (focus group). Most people groups are unreached mainly because attempts have <u>failed</u> rather than never been tried.

CHAPTER EIGHT

PHASE SIX - NEGOTIATING

"Do two walk together unless they have an appointment?" Amos 3:3

CONGRATULATIONS: If you have made it thus far in your effort to engage an unreached people group without being diverted to an easier job (<u>most</u> other jobs are easier), you are now at the critical stage.

INTRODUCTION

Definition of negotiating

Webster's Dictionary defines negotiate as "to confer with another so as to arrive at the settlement of some matter" and "to arrange for or bring about through conference, discussion, and compromise." These definitions describe the process through which a cross-cultural church planter will be able to implement procedures that bring success. Normally, we do not explain spiritual endeavors in terms of negotiation. Traditionally, spiritual ministry is related to the Holy Spirit and how he works through the various actors to accomplish the goal of founding a church.

It is not our intention to undercut or minimize that understanding. Our purpose is to highlight the way the Holy Spirit accomplishes this through the interaction of cross-cultural church planters with indigenous people. The effective cross-cultural church planter continually engages in exchanges with everyone who is a stakeholder in the church planting process. By stakeholder, we mean the evangelists, pastors, and leaders of the congregation, the converts, the workers creating the infrastructure for the congregation, and the community that is the focus of evangelism and church planting. The cross-cultural church planter does this through negotiation. For the purposes of this CC CP description, negotiation encompasses dialogue, discussion, and consultation. Essentially it includes everything involved in reconciling two separate and possibly different agendas.

Importance of negotiation

The cross-cultural church planter and the stakeholders will bring the church planting project to a successful conclusion through negotiation. A young American worker was sitting in a meeting that had lasted almost two hours and seemed nowhere near ending. The focus people were discussing a matter back and forth. He asked whether they were anywhere close to finishing and arriving at a decision. The answer was no to the first part of his question and uncertain as to the second because they might not arrive at any decision. The American was frustrated and asked if they had not discussed the issue enough to make a decision. The answer was yes but they were still not ready to do so. The process of negotiation had to be carried out according to their indigenous pattern.

Be alert to learn to negotiate

NATURE OF NEGOTIATION

Negotiation models

1. Anthropologists have discovered that all cultures have social contracts of various kinds. Some are ancient and experience little change such as the relationship between the shaman and his clients. Others, like marriage contracts, are renegotiated by society from time to time depending on changing needs. Church is also a social contract that needs to be negotiated. The Muslim mother of one of our evangelist colleagues did not want to become a Christian because she would be nailed up in a coffin when she died. She believed she would not be able to get out on judgment

day. The only way to settle this issue was to negotiate a social contract that would answer her fears. The church had to guarantee that she would not be buried in a coffin.

2. There are many types of negotiation in a society and someone in the church has to know how to negotiate them. Pastoral counseling encompasses some of these issues but there are many more that have to do with civil affairs and judicial matters. One of our evangelist colleagues was locked up for distributing tracts too close to a mosque during Friday prayers. The police said they wanted to protect him but they kept him in jail for four days. We felt they were trying to frighten him. Finally, we contacted a lieutenant colonel from another police station to talk with them. When they saw that someone of importance was negotiating for the evangelist, they let him go.

Negotiate from a position of power

Although the cross-cultural church planter cannot do every kind of congregational negotiation and probably little of the political or civil bargaining, he or she must be able to guide trainees in understanding the importance of these concerns. If the cross-cultural worker cannot do this, his contribution is severely reduced. We need to know how these negotiations can be done and who can do them. This is imperative if we are going to teach workers in a UPG how to minister to a community that may not be friendly. This is mature mentoring in contextual church planting.

3. Learning how to mediate issues in a cross-cultural situation takes years of experience. One has to know the language well and understand the relationships between various parts of society. A soldier was stationed in every village in our focus group to observe what was happening among the people. Even though that soldier may have only had the rank of corporal, he held considerable power in the community. Only the most powerful village leaders could

You must learn how the focus people negotiate

afford to offend that soldier. In Western society, a corporal who lives in a village community would hardly be noticed and certainly would not have any power to affect the activity of the residents. However, in our focus group this low ranking soldier could stop any activity he did not like.

Negotiation necessary for church planting

1. All phases of church planting must be negotiated.

All church programs and activity have to be negotiated in the beginning. Concepts have to be approved and planning is required before workers are recruited and trained. You can check Appendix 4 "Envisioning the CP Project" to get an idea of a typical process in planning any church program.

2. Negotiating sensitive situations.

This relates to one's skill in organizing and implementing a ministry. The following are examples. 1) In our UPG we had to reconcile differences with an existing church that opposed our work. 2) When contact was made with village leaders, some allowed Christians to live in their communities while others did not. 3) Converts could be baptized openly in some villages while others would reject them. 4) Natural leaders cannot always be installed as congregational leaders before they change certain non-biblical lifestyles. These are examples of sensitive areas that need negotiation. The cross-cultural church planter needs to develop skill and wisdom in these matters.

3. Some leader of status usually is required to negotiate on behalf of the church.

It is not impossible for others to do it but usually status and role have significant impact. When our focus group wanted to have a large meeting in a public facility, they needed to have permits from the police and from the local community leaders. That job was given to a leader who would be credible to those granting the permits. It may seem obvious to some to pick such a person but inexperienced workers have made many mistakes in this area.

4. Credibility as a negotiator is necessary for church planting success.

The cross-cultural church planter is not an owner, director, or supervisor. Instead, he or she is a mentor and a facilitator. When the cross-cultural church planter is perceived as owning the project, everyone does not feel free to relate to him or her. Every team member must feel that he or she has part ownership in the project. When that happens, the cross-cultural church planter will have freedom to be a negotiator and not a manager. A mentor negotiates with people while a manager gives them orders.

Mentoring for team ownership

It is easy to see that this is impossible if the cross-cultural church planter controls the finances of the church planting team. This would mean that he or she is the owner. The same is true if all the orders come from one particular worker whether he or she is an expatriate, national, or a focus person. If our goal from the outset is to have a hand-off point when this church planting effort will be completely operated by focus people, every team member needs to feel that they have ownership.

TWO PHASES OF NEGOTIATION

Negotiation can be divided into two phases. One is preliminary and the other is advanced. Preliminary negotiation involves working through the building blocks of church planting. It has to do with laying foundations. This does not mean that it is less important. Laying the foundations is crucial to the ultimate success of church planting. However, these negotiations are not as difficult to achieve as those of the advanced phase which require more experience and greater knowledge of the culture.

Preliminary Negotiation

1. Discovering opportunity

This would take place primarily in the first two years a cross-cultural church worker is in the UPG. It requires some facility with language but is dependent more on a learning mindset. Learning how to relate to people is the most important aspect of this period. Good relations with focus people leads to discovering opportunity to experience various types of negotiation in the society. For example, we can learn how the negotiations of life cycle ceremonies are carried out between the people and their practitioners. In the UPG, most important ceremonies have to be negotiated.

2. Studying recruiting practices

During this period, we can examine the ways in which people recruit leaders and workers to participate in community affairs. If we are spending time with our neighbors, we will hear such concerns being discussed. When we have friendly ties with them, we can ask about various processes that are taking place in the community. People are usually open about discussing matters such as the election of leaders, the way village organizations operate, and which services are run by the area or regional governments.

3. Developing partnerships

Learning how to negotiate can be done by trial and error

Another area for investigation is partnership structures. We have a friend who began negotiating a partnership with focus people within five months of his arrival. Some focus friends thought he was distributing money unwisely but they applauded his openness in learning how partnerships should operate among focus people and between expatriate church planters and the focus group. He was learning by trial and error. If we do not discover how to negotiate partnerships, we will continually fail in our projects. At one time, we negotiated a chicken-raising project where we supplied the capital and the focus person did the work. We understood that he was supposed to return all our investment by giving us chickens. He understood that giving us a few chickens over a few months period was sufficient even though it covered only a small portion of the investment. We failed to negotiate that partnership successfully.

4. Determining boundaries

Every people group has boundaries that are important to understand. Negotiations are not easy to implement if one has not mastered boundaries. In our UPG, we had to negotiate with both city dwellers and village people. Their boundaries were different and even their use of the language varied. It is extremely difficult for an expatriate church planter to appreciate the boundary subtleties that run through a society. This is why it is wise for the expatriate to limit independent negotiations as much as possible. There are times when we must react to unfamiliar forces but generally our negotiations should be with and through the nationals on our church planting team.

All of our national or focus people team members will not have the same skill in determining boundaries but they will usually be better than we are. However, there are always a few areas in which our experience might help them improve their skills. For example, when our team began, no members had ever negotiated renting a house, performing a life cycle ceremony, obtaining a police permit for a meeting, or inviting a village chief to a Christian program. The experienced expatriate church planter can help team members think through the ramifications of these kinds of negotiations and evaluate their outcome. In this way, the national or focus person team member increases his or her negotiating skill.

5. The relationship of form and function

One aspect of negotiation that is important to know from the outset is the relationship of form and function. For example, Americans usually want to negotiate the form of a project/ministry before they practice it. All facets of it are negotiated in detail so that everyone knows the theoretical framework before any work is actually done. Miscellaneous adjustments are done after the process begins.

Negotiating a starting point

In many UPGs, function is more important than form. In fact, many people may not be concerned with the form or structure of a project/ ministry as long as they are convinced about the function of it. In these groups, ministry may begin anywhere and continue until it proves efficacious. When this happens, the management team constructs a form to encompass all the useful aspects of the ministry. If you are trying to structure a ministry with people who believe that form follows function, you may have some difficulty adjusting to the process.

Advanced or Critical Negotiation

1. The time frame.

Generally speaking, the cross-cultural church planter will not be capable of advanced negotiations before he or she has had two or more years of experience in the focus group. This applies to national workers of other ethnicities as well as to the expatriate. Unless a person is very gifted in cross-cultural adjustment, it takes that long or longer to get the needed experience.

2. The status and role of the team member is critical in advanced negotiations.

Learning to negotiate takes time

This was mentioned in the sections on Team Building in Phase 3 and in Social Organization in Phase 5. This will be explained in more detail in Status and Role later in this chapter.

A person can rarely negotiate upwards and this can result in a hostile takeover threat to the ministry. Experienced workers from the city churches visited our young team members and pressured them for an invitation to see their work. Our workers felt unable to refuse them. Then, when these senior leaders had learned where the ministry was, they visited on their own and enticed the believers to follow them. One example of this was as follows. The senior Christian visited a group of new believers who were being taught about baptism. He told them it did not matter who baptized them and took them to his city church where they were baptized and registered as members. Our team member was then not allowed to visit them and teach them anymore. To prevent this from reoccurring, our sponsoring church forbade the young evangelists from taking anyone to their ministry locations.

3. Working relationships with churches, teams, and other organizations.

Those in leadership capacity generally do these kinds of negotiations. The margin for error is reduced here because the church planter is usually negotiating with people who are from similar social classes and educational backgrounds. If there is some misunderstanding involved, it is easier to identify and rectify. However, this is included in advanced negotiations because a young worker will not likely have the credibility to do it.

4. Envisioning the church planting project with teams and churches.

This is another area that is not as difficult to negotiate as some but it requires extensive knowledge and experience in the way people work together to implement a project. It will be explained in detail in following sections.

5. Financial involvement.

While finances may not be the most difficult area to negotiate, the risk of failure is enormous. One may do everything right in deciding how finances should be used and accountability structures should be organized but still experience a disintegration of the entire process. The influence of money is so powerful that one has to keep in prayer for all involved.

Some areas of negotiation are tricky

We had a pastor friend who traveled abroad and was enamored by the way society functioned outside his country. When he returned, he had trouble converting his foreign funds into local currency. This experience seemed to exacerbate his feelings of frustration and started him on a downward spiral that ended in a debased lifestyle. This was a strange experience from one perspective but many strange things happen where money is involved.

6. Implementing contextual principles.

Negotiating contextual ministry is one of the most difficult of all negotiations because it requires a profound knowledge of the theology, history, and socio-political concepts of the focus group. It took ten years to negotiate a successful church planting model in our UPG. Parts of the process like evangelism functioned adequately but others such as Christian nurture failed. We had to navigate our way through hindrances from a preexisting Christian church, government persecution, opposition from local religious leaders, and continual turnover among the workers. At the end of the decade, we had not trained any second-generation leaders and had to start afresh with a young cadre.

CATEGORIES IN NEGOTIATION

There are two general categories in negotiation. One is groups and individuals. The other category of negotiation concerns topics. Topics are the items that are negotiated. Thus, one needs to remember that there are two important aspects to keep in focus. We have to understand <u>who is negotiating with us</u> and <u>what we are negotiating</u>. In our personal experience, too many negotiations to mention have gone astray into topics other than our purpose. Once we were negotiating a church planting training program to be implemented in a Bible school. We could not understand why it was proceeding so slowly. Finally, we realized that the director of the Bible school was negotiating a master's program in missions. This was entirely different from our original proposal and all negotiations collapsed at that point.

Groups and Individuals

1. Counterparts (Church Planting Team).

Counterparts are national co-workers on the church planting team or equivalents in the focus group. They should be on an equal footing with you and able to negotiate as an equal. These are workers who are central to the success of your mission. It is vital that you understand the way they negotiate because they will not likely be able to understand your preferred style. The cross-cultural church planter always has to adjust to the national.

2. Friends.

This category refers to friends in the focus group (or nationals from other ethnic groups). You will negotiate with friends on many occasions concerning doing something together such as a project, a trip, or a vacation. The more complicated the issue is, the more careful you have to be in negotiating it.

EXPECT THE UNEXPECTED!

Always be up for surprises

People in our UPG are very prone to alternatives or variety so they are unconcerned when plans do not work out. However, the expatriate might not be so tranquil. Many a joint venture can disintegrate into chaos due to imprecise stipulations.

3. Patrons

Considerable explanation about patrons is given in Phase 4 under Critical Models of Mentoring. Part of the theoretical basis of this model is found in Appendix 6. This is one of the major models that every cross-cultural church planter in Africa, Asia, and S.E. Asia will have to master. You will be negotiating constantly with people you consider to be your patrons and others who would like for you to be their patron.

4. Clients

Those who look to you as a patron are relating to you as your clients. You must learn how to negotiate with clients because there are many pitfalls involved and it is not sufficient to expect them to understand your terminology if it does not correlate with their system. In our UPG, many clients understand the evangelists' concern as a commit-

Negotiating goes vertically as well as horizontally

ment to help them. When the evangelists told people that they would pray for them to get money or a job, some people interpreted that as a promise to help them. In a few days they would return to get that help. When it wasn't forthcoming, they said that the evangelists were not trustworthy to do what they said they would do.

5. Evangelists and Candidates to be Evangelists

Another group with whom you will be in constant negotiation are the evangelists and the candidates to become evangelists. You might help educate some of these and you will be involved with others in training or in ministry. Even though there may be a procedure by which the candidates are vetted by a national church or Christian agency, they may still come to you for special help. Your negotiations with candidates and with evangelists must be carefully confirmed with their focus group leaders. An expatriate worker should never agree with an evangelist on anything before checking with his or her team or church leader. Even the simplest matters can escalate into unforeseen difficulties.

6. Support Ministries

The cross-cultural church planter normally takes an active role in support ministries that make up the infrastructure of a contextualized church. In usual circumstances, workers who have expertise in these support ministries have been oriented to a traditional church and may not have any experience with a UPG. Therefore, they tend to implement their ministry in a traditional way. If you want to adjust such a ministry to the UPG, it will mean extensive negotiations with the workers. First, you must familiarize them with the needs of the UPG and then assist them in walking through the process of contextualizing the ministry. Even a fairly simple ministry such as producing Sunday School materials can consume months in working through the process.

7. Training Programs

Another area in which the expatriate will probably help is the training process. This may include informal as well as formal programs. The expatriate might teach at a Bible school or seminary. Evangelism training and Bible teaching are two other common areas of service. Each one of these assignments should be negotiated in fairly clear detail. Some UPG groups are not prone to negotiating in detail. They prefer to be open ended as it lessens the obligation to carry through on agreements. This can be a source of irritation to any person outside the UPG. We have seen many nationals from other ethnic groups leave the UPG work because the people did not follow through on their agreements. If you have negotiated clearly, you cannot be faulted for withdrawing. If your negotiations are vague, people are likely to blame you.

8. Cooperating Church Leaders

Much of the UPG work is done under the auspices of a sponsoring church or parachurch. Some of these may be underground movements.

You may negotiate with other churches or parachurches

The strongest political entity is an established, registered church that can be accountable to the government for the existence of the church plant. Negotiations with these church leaders must be precise so as not to mislead anyone concerning your ultimate goal of planting a contextual church. In our UPG, there were only a few churches of other ethnic origin that were prepared to sponsor outreach. Although they said that they would take responsibility, we taught the evangelists to settle all issues in the villages and not bring any conflict to the city church. This avoided direct negotiations between the sponsoring church and the focus group community. The evangelists handled all negotiations. This will also be the case if your church planting efforts are not sponsored by any established church.

9. Local Authorities

The evangelists and pastors will do most of the negotiations with local authorities. Rarely will an expatriate be involved in these matters. However, there can be exceptions. Several of us were summoned to the government agent after we had finished one of our tours to distribute tracts among the villages of the focus group. A church member had reported us for tract distribution. Our national colleague said that he would do all the talking. As we sat in the office of the government agent, our national colleague took complete responsibility for the action and negotiated a satisfactory conclusion to the matter.

Topics of Negotiation

1. Agreement on Non-negotiables

The effective cross-cultural church planter will not ally himself with anyone without clarifying one's non-negotiables in theology, ethics, and values. This does not mean that one may not work with a member of the UPG who has some different theological, ethical, and value standards. Their non-negotiables are affected by their worldview and some of them surely have to change. But it is critical that everyone understands each of the areas in which you have non-negotiables. If they understand and accept them, it may be possible to work with them.

Unify different worldviews

2. Theological or Biblical Differences

Some examples of theological positions are the mode of baptism and criteria for church membership. Since the three major church governments are common around the world, one may have to accommodate with Episcopal, Presbyterian, or Congregational systems. In addition to the mode of baptism, two of the thorniest issues are eternal security and the baptism of the Holy Spirit. In any case, honesty and openness require us to be clear on our positions. It is not ethical to pretend there are none just to get along.

3. Evangelistic Approach

A model of evangelism will be an area that undergoes almost continual modification as we search for a contextual way to share the gospel. Some western models begin with the concept of sin and others start by proclaiming God's love. The philosophical and religious background of your UPG will affect the way you present the gospel. This is a model that must be negotiated by everyone involved and it usually takes a long time to discover the most effective approach. The cargo cults of New Guinea illustrate the varied ways people can interpret spiritual activity.

4. Reconciliation/ Peacemaking

If you have ever been involved in a conflict that was seemingly unsolvable, you understand the difficulty of reconciliation. Each culture has its own understanding of bringing two wounded parties together. In many UPG, shame and guilt are two major causes of estrangement. One of the evangelists on our focus group team loaned money to a believer who agreed to pay it back at harvest time. However, for some reason he did not pay it back. Whenever the evangelist would visit his house, he would escape out the back so that he did not have to face him. There was no way to heal the breach. After a year we decided to forgive the debt because it could not be repaid. After that, the believer was willing to rejoin the fellowship. But some people will not reconcile if their feelings of shame or guilt do not change.

DANGER! Satan seeks to disrupt personal relationships and thus destroy leadership.

5. Finances/fund raising & Use of Funds

This is one of the most difficult of all negotiations to manage because the consequences of error seem out of proportion to other negotiations. One of the teachers in our training school wanted the teachers to have a raise. The expatriate in charge disagreed with him and he quickly became hostile and threatened to quit. When the expatriate sought counsel with his colleagues, he was advised to give all the teachers a raise because they deserved it. He gave them the raise but the discontented teacher quit anyway. He got what he wanted but wasn't satisfied. Sometimes, emotions about money can sabotage the best of negotiations.

6. Standards of Living for all Team Members

The experience of many expatriate agencies and missions has shown that negotiating living standards for team members is like threading a minefield. When one of the largest mission agencies in our country voted in their convention to set lower limits for house size, some of the senior missionaries refused to honor them. Living standards are a very difficult element to negotiate. When cross-cultural church planters live on a level that is far above their focus team colleagues, it establishes artificial criterion for leaders. Focus team colleagues can become frustrated in striving for the same standard and can create dissension in a team.

7. Control & Management of Ministry

When an expatriate team comes to a UPG, they usually have agreed on how they will control and manage the ministry. However, they frequently forget that this should be negotiated all over again when nationals or focus group workers join their team. Every team should have a plan to shift leadership from the cross-cultural church planter to the focus person. This is also true for the national leader who is working cross-culturally. If the team does not have a plan, it is unlikely that leadership will be transferred at the appropriate time. Unfortunately, there are many examples of UPG ministry that failed because focus group leaders were not empowered by the church planting team.

Renegotiating team parameters will happen with every change

8. Contextualization

The next chapter deals exclusively with contextualization but it helps to continually remind ourselves that contextualization is a process that is negotiated between the stakeholders in church planting. Nothing can be more counter-productive than arbitrarily imposing a "contextual" model from another culture. Many church planters do this because they do not understand contextualization or the necessity of negotiating new concepts and structures in the culture. A contextual model blends with some worldviews and causes changes in other worldviews. An imposed model disrupts this process and can derail any attempt to find a truly contextual model.

9. Purpose & Goals

The diagnosis of church planting in Appendix 4 emphasizes that purpose and goals are defined when a team envisions the entire church planting project. While there is a similarity in all church planting, the nature of the UPG may determine how one sets purposes and goals. Our UPG team decided to evangelize and start home churches without adequately considering things such as the number of workers we would need to pastor those groups. Purposes and goals are about more than merely establishing contextual churches. There are many short range purposes and goals that have to be negotiated in order to be successful in the long term purposes and goals.

Negotiating can be upsetting

STATUS AND ROLE

Status/Role Model

1. Status has to do with one's position and role is the behavior associated with that position. Many young people go to other cultures to minister to people without observing simple things like clothing. Three young men who had been trained in a reputable organization asked us to help them find a sponsor so they could evangelize in our country. After we got an appointment with a lieutenant colonel in the army, we discovered that they had only short pants and sandals to wear for the interview. We had to cancel our appointment until they could buy suitable clothing. In our country shorts were not worn in public or for social visits.

Blend with your status group

Many young workers are not taught to fit in with their desired role. Most cultures have a criteria for the clothing and personal appearance of a professional. Personal appearance gaffs may include such things as improperly cut hair, clothes in disarray, and tattoos showing. It is important that your appearance agree with the status that you are seeking. In our focus group, one must put on a 'proper' shirt before greeting a visitor.

2. Status and role are seldom confusing for the focus people because they know what the standards are. The outsider is the one who must adjust to their customs. When the church planting team is a combination of people from different cultures, status and role will be more difficult to determine. Such elements as age, education, and experience will affect how status and role are perceived. When the team leader is younger than team members, it may cause some difficulty for focus people. When we were recording radio programs, the editing team disagreed about theology with the man who wrote the script. He said he

Be conscious of your appearance

could not change it so we told him we would just skip that program. He was older than any of us and he was offended. The only thing that saved our ministry team from a possible collapse was that I was an ordained minister. Later, he said that he felt he had to give in to a clergyman. In this case status was critical.

3. The class (or in rare cases, caste) system falls into the status/role category. It is often very difficult to mix UPG people of different classes. In our UPG, mixing urban and rural people is not easy. We found that many city people will not attend worship with rural people who have become house help in the city. The same is true with rural people for different reasons. They feel very insecure mixing with professional or wealthy people. Although they are not acting from a scriptural standard, their worldview has not changed enough to make the adjustment. There are many similar class problems with which we have to contend.

Networking of Statuses and Roles
1. Status and role clarification should begin with the expatriate team. Although every team member may feel that they are equal, it is clear to the focus people that members are not of the same status. For example, there are classifications such as "team leader." Even for the expatriate members, this puts a person in a special category. There may also be older persons

on the team and that may automatically give them more status with some people. In our UPG, young people generally have very low status. If one does not have inherited status, an important job, high education, or lots of money, high status is unlikely. Young expatriates have an advantage over focus group youth because they are an unknown quantity.

Keep clarifying status and role

2. When the team receives national or focus group members, status clarification has to be reassessed. It is critical that they are accepted as having equal status as team members. However, the UPG group may not be willing to assign them that status. In the early years, believers in our house churches did not perceive that their church planting team had much status. This was because the sponsoring church only recognized them as evangelists. The house church members would try to go over their heads when there was a disagreement. The church planting team continually blocked that effort so that the members would realize that the evangelists were empowered as their leaders. As time passed, the sponsoring church eventually ordained the evangelists as ministers and secured their status.

3. This episode illustrates the significant role of the sponsoring church in assigning and affirming status and role. Although the ministerial candidate can achieve status in the church community by completing all its requirements, this does not usually carry over into a UPG society where the church has not been culturally valued. In a situation where the church is being planted, there is usually no way for an evangelist to achieve or be assigned status by the community. Therefore, the new believers generally appreciate his or her status because of the affirming action of the sponsoring church.

4. The way other churches, agencies, and partnerships relate to the status and role of the evangelists is likewise dependent on the good graces of the sponsoring church. When the church is not prepared to affirm the importance of their workers and empower them in the community, it is impossible for them to accrue meaningful status with anyone. With few exceptions, independent church planting teams do not have this kind of influence in either the Christian community or among the focus people. If church planting teams continue to operate as para-church

organizations, they will probably have difficulty in affirming status and role in the UPG.

Profiles of Status and Role

1. In the beginning, the church planting team should develop a status profile for a successful church planting evangelist and pastor in the focus group. This should include the personality characteristics and conditions of an ideal leader in the eyes of the society. As we mentioned in Phase 3, (sections on Team Building and Learning Culture) status and role generally have defined categories among

Every status has advantages and disadvantages

most UPG. The people in our UPG valued age over youth, males over females, married over unmarried, and parents over those who had no children. In their early years, our church planting team of young singles were on the wrong side of the profile and had little or no status in the UPG communities. They were therefore not expected to fill any role.

This meant that someone with status had to sponsor and/or promote their status and role. Christian merchants who had business relations with UPG people accomplished this. They introduced the evangelists as qualified to minister to their spiritual needs. Several UPG people accepted the Lord and began to introduce the evangelists to their family and friends. In this way, the young evangelists began to gain status and role.

2. The next big challenge that the evangelists faced was developing a profile as community leaders in the focus group. In the case of our church planting team, this was difficult to accomplish because there was no profile in our UPG community for a Christian minister. They had two kinds of spiritual leaders. One led the formal religion and the other was that of a shaman who was the practitioner for their informal belief system. Although several communities have tolerated the presence of Christians, they have only understood the status and role of a pastor as

Developing leadership status is a major hurdle

being similar to that of a teacher in their formal religion or as a shaman in their informal religion. They have not yet given full recognition to the pastors as community leaders.

3. It is imperative for the church planting team to maintain focus on establishing these profiles in both the church planting team and in the community. Of course, the process begins in the church planting team. If it is not done there it will not be done in the community. However, having the profiles clearly delineated in the team does not mean that it will automatically be done in the community. Carelessness in this area will cause your team members to lack a precise goal toward which to work. They will tend to be satisfied with their status in the team or in the sponsoring church and will not struggle with achieving the status they need in the UPG community.

NEGOTIATING WITH A NATIONAL TEAM

When your expatriate team has come to the place of Engagement, it should have developed relationships that allow it to begin to negotiate the formation of a national church planting team. This may happen within a year or two but normally it takes longer for expatriates to learn enough about the culture and also to gain credibility with nationals. Skills in negotiation are also necessary for this sensitive task.

The Church Planting Team
1. Begin with National Leaders

This negotiation should begin with national leaders, not with trainees that you are supporting. Some expatriate teams recruit believers and then train them in their chosen church planting model. It is rare that such trainees will have enough status to challenge the expatriate who provides their livelihood. Because of this, trainees will give little correction to any program the expatriate devises. On the other hand, leaders in an established church, or focus group leaders who become believers often have enough self-confidence to give input about evangelistic and pastoral models.

While every variety of church planting model may have its strengths and weaknesses, it is frequently best if one can facilitate a church planting team with a sponsoring church. A church that is already registered and authorized by the government is better prepared to support the ministry. However, many expatriate teams have chosen to work outside all established structures because that was the best way they could implement their chosen model. Each team has to decide which road to follow and this is a critical decision. I have already mentioned David Kyle's advice but it should become a mantra for you, "The seeds of any organization's success or failure are found at its very beginning." **Make As Few Mistakes As Possible At This Point!**

2. Three Types of Teams

When you are prepared to form a team composed of expatriates, nationals from other ethnic groups, and members of your focus group, you can choose from three main types. The three are: create a new team, join an existing team, and a combination of those two.

THREE TYPES OF TEAMS

1. NEW - EXPATS AND NATIONALS
2. EXISTING – EXPATS AND NATIONALS
3. MERGER – NEW AND EXISTING

a. A new team will mean that your expatriate team will then restructure itself into a team that includes focus group believers and/or nationals from other ethnic groups. This means that your team is no longer an expatriate team. While it is not always possible to form a team that includes focus group members, it will still be closer to a contextual team than it was. With rare exceptions, the movement toward contextualization is very slow and measured. See Phase 3 in the section RECRUITING A NATIONAL TEAM.

b. Another choice is to join a team that is already in place. Unfortunately, many expatriates isolate themselves in their own team and fail to explore the potential in various national teams. The most successful church planting will involve nationals because they are able to make the cross-cultural adjustment more quickly and efficiently. The effective cross-cultural church planter will relate to and interact with as many national CC CP teams as possible in order to gain knowledge and experience.

> *Expatriate teams tend to be rigid*

c. The third choice for a new team is a combination of a new team and an existing team. Unifying the restructured expatriate team with a team already in place does this. This is not easy to do because it will expose the weaknesses in your expatriate models. The larger your expatriate team, the more difficult it becomes. Expatriates will generally have more problems than nationals coalescing into a new body because they are generally more rigid in what they desire and face considerable culture shock when blending into a new environment.

In our UPG, we followed this third course of action several times. We had only a few expatriates on our initial team and they were willing to recruit nationals and focus people to join the team. In one case, we negotiated with a cross-cultural church team that was failing. The blend benefited both parties as we brought trained evangelists to the table to cooperate and work with a registered church body. Nevertheless, it took years to develop a smooth working relationship where we were not undermining each other.

3. The Most Comfortable Team

You will correctly assume that forming a national team is not a comfortable job. The most comfortable team you can form is one that you recruit and lead. However, you have to be careful about that for several reasons. First, it will reflect your weaknesses. You will bring to it your expatriate models that have to be renegotiated with each member of your team. Secondly, an expatriate led UPG team automatically raises the specter of being a foreign religious mission. When expatriates are in the foreground, challenges to their role are sure to rise. Frequently, this happens within the team as well as without.

4. Indigenous Leadership

One of the main goals of your team is to raise up indigenous leadership. This should be an early milestone in your planning. In the case of some infrastructure projects such as literature and mass media production, an expatriate can supervise in the beginning phases. However, as long as the expatriate has a high profile in the ministry people will consider it a foreign endeavor. When the expatriate's role is shielded behind indigenous leadership, it can be highly significant without being noticed by the average person.

The Philosophy of the Church Planting Team

1. "Envisioning the Church Planting Project"

When you have formed your national team for the UPG work, it is important to revisit the church planting project. See the Phase 3 section-ENVISIONING YOUR STRATEGY AND METHODS FOR CP. You cannot expect new members to understand and own a vision for church planting unless you go through the entire process with them. They have to work through the Critical Issues, Milestones, Turn Over Points, End Results, and other aspects of the project. Failure to go through this process with your restructured team will result in a confused and uneven approach to the ministry.

"Envisioning" ensures that every worker/participant has a clear idea of what is expected of him/her. Your strategy must be clear to the end and understood by all your co-workers (as far as it is possible). They need to know what they are trying to accomplish. Church planting may not be easy for them to conceptualize, particularly if there are few or no concrete

Envisioning your goal is an ongoing exercise

examples for them to observe. Seek to make this as concrete as you can. Remember that many people do not think or learn conceptually. They may not be able to remember much detail, but at least you must make the steps of the process clear. Our national team had to interact with each other many times about these aspects of church planting before they began to own the ministry. "A number of subprojects are almost always preferable to one large project" (Kyle, 1990:2).

2. Agree on a philosophy of ministry

You can read a sample Philosophy of Ministry in Appendix 8. This seems like a simple procedure that would include all the non-negotiables in your team's theology. But it is not an easy task to bring an entire team into agreement on a philosophy of ministry. We have already given a number of examples in previous sections of this book about disagreements among team members on such mundane things as housing and willingness to carry out critical tasks one is not trained to do. Our UPG team had a philosophy of praying for God's provision in every need of the congregations we served. But we had one member who continually violated this position by escorting focus people to the homes of wealthy city dwellers to ask for money. This caused confusion about our philosophy of ministry and we eventually found him a job elsewhere.

3. Unite your team in strategy as well as vision and philosophy

If your team is not unified in strategy as well as in vision and philosophy the results will be chaotic. An example of this on our UPG team was the requests from distant places for evangelists to come to them. Our team was united in vision and philosophy but we had difficulty with agreeing on a common strategy. Some of the team wanted to minister to everyone who requested help. In some cases, doing that meant opening new house churches in locations that took hours to reach. It was impossible to unite these believers in a central place and the evangelists were wearing themselves out with the travel. The believers were not being ministered to in an adequate way with the infrequent visits. We had to restrict our team's strategy to an area where we could maintain regular contact with the house churches.

4. Clarify boundaries

In many cases church planting team members in the UPG are young and unmarried. It is important to work through cultural issues with the entire team so that they will establish boundaries. One of our home church congregations was destroyed when an evangelist kissed the daughter of a member. This would not have created much reaction in the city but the village people were highly offended. It is best to make as few rules as possible but the team has to agree on boundaries and be willing to enforce discipline. Many teams have disintegrated over violation of boundaries.

5. Team worship

It is important for a team to worship together because Satan's pressure is extraordinarily strong against those who are trying to plunder his goods. "No one can enter a strong man's house and plunder his goods, unless he first binds the strong man" (Mark 3:27). In order for the team to maintain biblical principles, and strengthen its members against temptation and false theology, it must continually reaffirm worship, prayer, Bible study, and fellowship.

6. Mutual accountability

The team's commitment to penetrating the UPG requires mutual accountability. A team leader cannot carry a team spiritually. Members cannot expect their colleagues to carry them. Every member must accept accountability for the purpose and goals of the team. This includes spiritual disciplines, an equitable workload, and

Pray for one another

the sacrifice of personal preferences and desires. The leader may be the catalyst for everything that happens but each worker must respond to the challenge personally. Friedrich Wilhelm Nietzsche wrote:

> "If you would go up high, then use your own legs!
> Do not get yourselves carried aloft; do not seat
> yourselves on other people's backs and heads!"
> (*Thus Spake Zarathustra. Chap.73*)

OUR WEAPONS: "All prayer and supplication" (Eph. 6:18) Paul summarizes our major weapon of warfare. This indicates transparency in communication, no hidden agenda, not serving self-interests, brutal self-examination, absolute self-sacrifice.

NEGOTIATING WITH A CHURCH

Nearly every church planting team eventually has to negotiate with a church. In our area there were a number of para-church efforts that later registered themselves as churches and implemented some kind of typical church order. However, the most secure church planting is done in association with some church denomination or body that is registered with the government or is recognized by other churches as having authority to start new congregations. Recognition is important because any negative reaction from other churches always creates insecurity in a congregation of new believers. This section explains some of the important aspects for an expatriate or national in negotiating with a church in order to start a church planting effort under their auspices or, if you have already started, in order to negotiate an ongoing relationship.

Established churches may or may not be helpful	See Appendix 9- BECOMING INVOLVED IN A LOCAL CHURCH for an explanation of some important peculiarities to look for in a church.

Develop relationships

1. Be active- Create a presence

Don't forget that you are a stranger and an outsider to the area. This means that people will know little or nothing about you or people from your ethnic background. It will take time for people to get to know you and you must take the initiative. Your presence will eventually be less novel to them and they will want to know more in depth about you.

2. Identity as a spiritual leader

When you first visit the church, you may use the identity you have on your visa as a tentmaker or student. However, if your intention is to become a partner in church planting, eventually you have to establish yourself as a spiritual leader. Church leaders are unlikely to open up to someone who is incognito and has nothing to lose when problems arise.

Note the demeanor of a spiritual leader

3. Express some interest in the focus group

When you feel comfortable with the church situation, you can begin to express your interest in your people group and try to promote interest among church leaders and members. You do not have to tell anyone what your ultimate plans are. It is best to be open to questions and suggestions and just discuss church planting in general terms. If the church leaders do not respond to your suggestions about an outreach to the focus group, you will not lose anything. In one case, we spent four years negotiating a partnership with a local church to reach a focus group. The result was the most successful church planting team that we experienced.

4. Let your vision emerge

It is better to let your plans emerge gradually rather than abruptly. At first, just express interest in what is being done to reach your focus group. Next, you can talk with church leaders about the possibility of their church being involved in some sort of outreach to the focus group. When the time is ripe, you can explain your vision and commitment to reach the focus group with the gospel. When people get to know you, they will not be surprised to hear this. Don't feel you have to do everything during your first year in the focus group area.

5. FEAR is often the major problem

Church people frequently have some negative history with unreached people. It may be that they belong to a hostile religion or that they have been oppressors in the public arena. The most common problem that church people have about outreach is fear. When we investigated outreach to our focus group, practically every church leader warned us that we would not be able to do anything useful and it would be better if we did not try. They were afraid of the focus group leaders who were aggressive in opposing Christianity and they did not want an outsider to stir them up.

6. Make friends with church leaders

Before you start any ministry, win the support of as many church leaders as possible. You will doubtless have difficulty with some church leaders and you may need someone to come to your defense. In the Pentecostal churches the pastor is the key person as he or she usually controls the church government. The church board as well as the pastor is responsible in most Protestant churches.

Clarify structure

1. Describe ministry proposal

It is best not to assume that the church leaders understand what your team is trying to do. It may take a lot of presentation and discussion before they do and some may not grasp the concept before actually seeing it implemented. Since church planting is the responsibility of the sponsoring church or organization, your goal is to outline your model as well as possible and win their approval.

Be a networker & a resource person

2. Mentor the model

Mentoring the church planting model is a better style than managing it. Managing gives the impression of control. When people think that you are managing a ministry, it can stir up anti-colonial feelings or other counter productive responses depending on your ethnicity. It is very difficult to guide or coach a ministry when one does not have authority but often it is better done that way. Some cultures do not have a tradition of delegating authority to underlings. You have to learn to work around this and other difficult cultural patterns.

3. Integrate your team

As much as possible the church planting team should be integrated into the sponsoring church structure and the workers should become part of the hierarchy. Doing this enhances the functions of the team by making it an integral part of the administrative structure of the sponsoring church or organization. Some teams function as a special unit of a church department. For example, they may be part of the Committee on Evangelism. In any case, the members of the team should become part of the church clergy team. This will empower them in their ministry and provide a future for them in the church when their focus group congregations are recognized as official congregations.

4. Prayer support

It is imperative to create prayer support early on in the church planting scenario. Paul tells us in 2 Thessalonians 3:1, "Pray for us, that the word of the Lord may speed ahead and be honored, as happened among you." One of the primary tasks of your church planting is to mobilize churches to pray for you. In the beginning phases of your outreach this may not be possible because of security reasons but as soon as possible, it should be implemented.

Pray for one another

5. Financial guidelines

Many churches do not want to finance work among the UPG even though they are willing to take credit for it. Our focus group team worked for years without sufficient income from their sponsoring church to support themselves. When this happens, workers are forced to get secular work or beg from their family and friends. Some unethical persons can take advantage of the evangelists' financial need to insinuate themselves into decisions concerning the house churches. Such meddling has ruined many good works. If possible, work out financial guidelines with the church for support of their church planting team. It can be a difficult negotiation but it should be done.

DANGER ! The person initiating a project will probably have to take full responsibility for the project. He/she is given credit for success and blame for failure. Many unreached peoples' cultures do not understand delegation of responsibility. That is considered in the province of the leader.

EVALUATION of END RESULTS - CHECK LIST - PHASE SIX

[ ] have understood that most everything has to be negotiated in one way or another

[ ] can outline several models of negotiation used in focus group

[ ] can describe the most common negotiation model in the church, the para–church organizations, and the training institutions (Bible schools, etc.)

[ ] have negotiated a role (established credibility) as a type of spiritual leader in the church

[ ] have allowed vision for an unreached people group to emerge naturally in my church relationships

[ ] have given time and effort to gain the sympathy & support of as many congregational leaders as possible (particularly the pastor and church board members)

[ ] have gone through the process of "Envisioning the CP Project" and can clearly describe strategy used and end results anticipated

[ ] have decided what type of team to form and how to do it

[ ] if your team is formed, have done the "Envisioning" process with them

[ ] have negotiated a philosophy of ministry with my team

[ ] can describe status/role relationships in the areas of my church planting team, my church, my secular work, and between expatriates and nationals

[ ] have agreed with Team on organization, discipline, finances, and priorities

[ ] have set up an accountability structure for the cp team which is integrated with sponsoring church (this implies agreement and support from the church)

[ ] have developed a profile of what a successful church planting evangelist and pastor would look like in the focus group

[ ] can describe the profile of a focus group community leader

[ ] have tried to train the church planting team to be able to fulfill the requirements of these profiles

[ ] have experience in negotiating with leaders in the church, the church planting team, evangelists outside the team, and some persons from the focus group

[ ] have worked at creating prayer support in the church for the focus group

[ ] am continuing constant in prayer and spiritual warfare

[ ] am aware of specific "hand-off points" & "deliverable ministry"

PRAYER GOAL: Within a year of your arrival in your focus group, God may have led you to at least one viable church planting counterpart. But this does not necessarily mean you can start immediately. You may first have to lead that person to the Lord and disciple him or her. This may add to your church planting time frame.

Tips: 1. **If God brought you to this people, he is moving ahead of you. Look around prayerfully to see whom he has selected to work with you. Be realistic! It probably won't happen overnight. Frequently, it takes 8–10 years to plant a church (if all goes well).**

2. **Every additional expatriate or national co-worker will potentially complicate the negotiation process for a focus group team. Expatriate and national team structure and responsibilities must be clear.**

3. **Constant evaluation is needed to pinpoint potential hindrances within the church planting process; especially those coming from within any of the teams.**

4. **Circumstances will vary from rural to city churches, lower economic class to higher, young and old, etc.**

5. **No one can arrive at a goal without identifying it first. The clearer your church planting vision and specific goals, the clearer you can make the philosophy of ministry and strategy needed to reach it. This, in turn, will make the process more real to your team.**

CHAPTER NINE

CONTEXTUALIZATION

*"Surely it should disturb us that after 2000 years of ministry,
missions have such divergent ideas on our methods and goals."*
Warren Chastain, "Contextualization: Some Cautions and Criticisms,"
An unpublished paper

INTRODUCTION

Unfortunately, only two kinds of description have dominated this field. One is erudite theory represented by the exposition of scholars such as Hesselgrave & Rommen (1989) and the other is illustrated by a simplistic presentation such as the C1-C6 Spectrum (Travis, 1998). The former is difficult for many cross-cultural church planters to understand and the latter gives a misleading perception of the issues involved. In "Contextualization That Is Comprehensive," Scott Moreau (2006) outlines a structure that not only highlights the complexity of contextualization but also gives us characteristics that help make it practical.

Gathered into one statement these categories are: 1) *"Concerned with the whole of the Christian faith, 2) both propositional and existential, 3) grounded in Scripture, 4) interdisciplinary in its approach to culture, 5) dynamic, 6) aware of the impact of human sinfulness on the process, 7) a two way process in which all sides contribute."* (Moreau, 2006:325-327) [*numbering added*].

The Javanese church experience is a clear example of Moreau's theory and gives us a practical view of ministry with other UPG because it took place among people who were oriented to the world religion of Islam. The early history of this church reveals specific steps that any cross-cultural church planter must consider in engaging a UPG. There were no missionaries involved in this work for the first 20 years but there was European influence. Later, some of the missionaries clashed with Javanese leaders over theological and cultural understandings of Christianity. It is difficult to neatly fit the elements of the Javanese church experience into Moreau's framework because some features flow among his categories and the time frame covers decades. Nevertheless, his framework is applicable and guides us in exploring and understanding true contextualization. The later Javanese church contextual history can also be applied to this model but space does not permit for that task.

This Javanese example covers the seven factors Moreau suggests and at the end of each explanation, we include an application for present day church planters.

1) *"Concerned with the whole of the Christian faith"*

Coolen

Many of the early Javanese Christian leaders were oriented to a comprehensive Christian faith and to a contextualization of that faith to the Javanese culture. These people included both men and women who were Javanese, Eurasians, and Dutch. Opposition came from their Javanese Muslim neighbors, from Dutch colonial government officials, and from some Dutch missionaries. Their history is so complex that it is impossible to recount it in these pages (See Dixon, 2002). One aspect stands out above all others and that is their great leaders who forged the foundation on which a contextualized church could emerge. In their struggles, these leaders were concerned with the whole of the Christian faith.

Coolen began the early Javanese Christian philosophy

The earliest of these was Coenraad Coolen, the son of a Russian father and a Javanese mother. All his life he imbibed the traditions and emotions of his Javanese mother. About 1817, he came to faith as an adult, but he never left his Javanese roots. When Coolen retired from government service, his wife refused to move with him to an isolated area of East Java. Later, he remarried illegally (according to Christian standards) and raised a family in that new location. His Christian beliefs were syncretistic. He believed that one of his sons was a reincarnation of an early settler and guardian spirit of that region and he followed his son's suggestion to open a new clearing in the jungle near the village of Ngoro in East Java. Coolen developed a prosperous village and invited Christians and Muslims alike to live there. He established a new set of community morals for Javanese and led in Christian teaching. The citizens there were known for their honesty. The village became a prosperous area and this increased Coolen's prestige among the Javanese.

After Coolen had a vision of the prophet Noah telling him to preach to the people, he never flagged in spreading the gospel as he conceptualized it (van Akkeren, 1970:67). He believed that the Javanese "could not comprehend the Gospel in its New Testament or European Form..." (Ibid., 77), so he began to teach them in Javanese stories, myths, and other forms. According to van Akkeren, Coolen began the process of clarifying the difference between Christianity and the other religions that had come to Java. Christianity was presented as a "new foundation for the life of the *desa* [village]" (Ibid., 151). From the beginning, the gospel stood in stark contrast to the worldview of other religions. He taught about the Trinity, using many concepts from daily life such as the flame of a candle. The one area in which he differed from orthodox belief was in baptism. He did not baptize and, as a result, many of his most promising apprentices left him to join another church.

Some aspects of Coolen's church theology can be seen in his mixture of European customs intermingled with those of the Javanese. He seated the congregation according to the cosmology of the Javanese, with men on the right and women on the left. None of the Javanese believers wore European clothes or cut their hair like their Christian counterparts in the city of Surabaya. Coolen, himself, wore Javanese clothing except when he led the Sunday services. However, at that time his dress was typically Dutch and he sat at a table. The people sat on benches or stood. Later, when a missionary had charge of the congregation, he removed the benches. Even so, in 1900 the members replaced the benches (van Akkeren, 1970:64). This vignette of life in Ngoro illustrates how believers were grappling with Christian faith and practice for more than half a century.

Coolen demonstrated the worldwide fellowship of believers with Christians in other parts of Java. Some Javanese near Surabaya had become Christians and they followed the Dutch style. Even though Coolen did not agree with that approach, he did not isolate himself spiritually from other Christians. He had contact with many of the Indonesian evangelists working in different parts of Java (Partonadi, 1988:46). There are records of visits to Coolen by both Indonesian evangelists and European missionaries who later became leaders in the Javanese church. He was known and liked by the earliest Dutch missionaries even though they disagreed with some of his theology. The villagers of Ngoro also exchanged visits with their relatives in many parts of East Java and spread the news of the development of their church.

Sadrach

Our second example of a Javanese leader who was concerned with the whole of the Christian faith is Kiai Sadrach, who ministered in Central Java in the second half of the 19th century and into the 20th century. He developed a church similar to Coolen's but more closely related to and influenced by Islamic practices and Dutch church leaders. Converted from a Muslim background, Sadrach had studied at a *madrasah* [Muslim school] and was considered a teacher of Islam. Before he began his Christian work, he had visited Coolen and many other Christian leaders among the Javanese, the Eurasians and the Dutch expatriates, observing the ways they evangelized and nurtured believers.

Sadrach adjusted the original models

The Dutch mission agencies came into Java around the middle of the 19th century so Sadrach interacted with missionaries as well.

Sadrach extended the contextualization process started by Coolen, although at first his community was not as clearly distinguished from others as Coolen's was. In the beginning it "could be compared to the New Testament Christian community which initially was regarded as merely a new Jewish sect" (Ibid., 111). One of the Dutch Residents considered it a Christian sect influenced by Islam while the Muslims thought it was a new sect of Islam with a Christian color. Sadrach arranged a

Sadrach observed Javanese social patterns

complete creed in the form of the Islamic *syahadat* [Statement of Faith] (Ibid., 135). As we describe later, Sadrach incorporated many aspects of Islam as well as those of Javanese *adat* [customary law].

Sadrach began his work by helping two Eurasian ladies who were active in evangelism among the Javanese. His approach to the Javanese was very successful and he gathered many converts. Although Sadrach was committed to a Javanese church, he emphasized the major tenets of Christianity. He was able to read the Malay and Javanese Bibles and he taught from them concerning the Trinity, salvation by grace through faith and all the biblical tenets. He could not baptize or administer the communion because he had not been ordained in any church. Therefore, he invited Dutch pastors and missionaries to perform these ceremonies. Even when Sadrach was under attack by the Dutch missionaries who wanted to take over his congregations, he continued to be willing to work with some missionaries. He was ecumenical in every way, but he did not allow the Dutch missionaries to take over leadership of his congregations. This caused some to push him away.

APPLICATION

Effective CC CP will be concerned with promoting the theology of a worldwide communion of saints. Although your ministry may occur in an isolated place, biblical theology shows that believers are integrated into a fellowship that extends far beyond their cultural boundaries. They must not be allowed to isolate themselves physically from Christians of other traditions because this impoverishes them spiritually in their attempts to contextualize the gospel to their culture.

They must be allowed to interact with various worldviews. As the Javanese wrestled with biblical worldview as it related to those of Islam, their own *adat,* and the European influences, they were able to make informed decisions concerning the expression of their own faith in every day life. In today's world, some cross-cultural church planters isolate their converts so that they can create a "pure" contextual situation. But separation from the larger Christian community is not biblical contextualization.

2) *"Both propositional and existential"*

Propositional

If we look at the cultural reasons why the Javanese had both competency and validity for engaging in the contextualization of the gospel, one would have to consider their intense immersion in *ngelmu* which can be translated as esoteric knowledge. The search for *ngelmu* can be described as a major characteristic of the Javanese. Previous to hearing about the gospel, they had already developed their own ideas and truths about themselves and codified them into a social system called *kejawen*. This involved everything related to their *adat* [customary laws] and to their indigenous religion. In addition to this, they had incorporated Islamic beliefs into this system so that they operated with two belief systems or two worldviews simultaneously.

> *Theology must be formulated*

At first, Coolen began to postulate about Jesus and the gospel in a way that varied from European forms. For example, he incorporated the structure of the Islamic statement of faith (*syahadat*) to read, "There is one God and Jesus Christ is the Spirit of God" (Bentley-Taylor, 1967:69). Later, the missionaries challenged him concerning that statement saying that Jesus is the Son of God and not the Spirit of God. But Coolen felt that the concept of Spirit was more attractive to the Javanese. He also compared Jesus to mythological Javanese characters (Ibid., 70) because he believed it would attract the minds of the people. In 1841, Walter Medhurst was the first missionary to visit Coolen and he was pessimistic about these approaches. But Coolen was undeterred.

There were also differences between Coolen and the city Christians on "...sacraments, baptism, clothing, language (Malay/Dutch or Javanese), the arts (the *gamelan* orchestra and shadow plays), circumcision, etc.,... attitude toward Islam" (Sumartana, 1993:47). Coolen arranged the Creed in a form similar to the Muslim *syahadat,* and with the Lord's Prayer, it was set in *Tembang*, a Javanese musical form (Partonadi, 1988:134). These propositional aspects concerning Christianity among the Javanese would be debated for over 100 years.

Later, Sadrach followed Coolen's example by trying to expose ways the message was already in the culture (van Akkeren, 1970:75). "Before beginning his own community, Sadrach himself had made several tours to Javanese Christian communities in East Java. He had been very much impressed by Coolen's community, and seems to have derived some aspects of the liturgy used by Coolen's community" (Partonadi, 1988:134).

He emphasized the parts of the gospel that spoke to the Javanese spirit, "...the importance of good deeds, piety, obedience to God's law, following Christ as an example, and the ministry of healing and exorcism." (Ibid., 224). Sadrach created a Christian marriage ceremony to replace the Islamic one (Ibid., 145). In effect, this changed the believers' worldview concerning marriage. In ways like this, these early leaders embedded an entirely new set of ideas and truth in the culture.

Existential

It is not enough for leaders to define new ideas and truths to be incorporated into the lives of Christians but they also have to interpret the way they should be carried out in the everyday life of the church. Javanese life cycle ceremonies illustrate this. All of these ceremonies were oriented around the appeasement of spirits. Sadrach maintained most of the ceremonies but omitted the aspects of spirit worship and simplified many of them. Children were dedicated in the church and circumcision was continued because it was linked to being a Javanese as well as to being a Muslim.

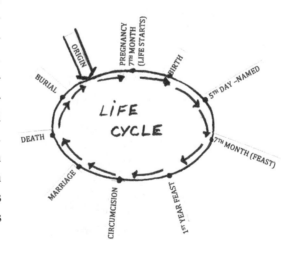

Life cycle includes important ceremonies

Sadrach continued the annual harvest festival but reoriented it to God's creation and the goodness of God in place of the traditional cleansing ceremony to prevent evil and disaster. Many other Javanese holy days were reinterpreted for the Christians. Public celebrations closely linked to Islam were

You will be expanding theological principles in your church plant

rejected (Ibid.,149-151). In this way, biblical worldview was embodied in the daily lives of Christians.

They set up rice barns in every community where the church existed so that they could care for the needs of the poor. Believers were encouraged to give money for this purpose. (Ibid.,117). Their church buildings were simple structures made from local village materials. Like the Muslims, they called them mosques and used a drum or hollow bamboo to call people to prayer. These churches were placed in the leader's (imam's) yard to show the theological centrality of the leader. The church in Sadrach's yard was "built in the old rural mosque style" with "a *cakra* (a disc with several protruding arrows) on the roof in place of a cross" (Ibid.,131). [The *cakra* is the weapon of Dewa Wisnu in the Hindu myth (*wayang*) that is the end of all life.]

Van Akkeren comments on Coolen's village, "One gains the impression that this Javanese *desa* must have been like an Old Testament community, with hardly any division between the civil and the religious aspects" (1970:62). People sought to live out the implications of their faith. This is illustrated by the life of the church in Sadrach's time. "In general, members of Sadrach's community did not participate in gambling, polygamy, or the use of opium." "...the life of the community was marked by simplicity, modesty, and honesty" (Partonadi, 1988:154).

APPLICATION

When people of the UPG come in contact with the gospel it will introduce new ideas and truths into their concept of the world. They should be encouraged not only to wrestle with these new ideas in their biblical context but also to confront them with their own traditions and tenets of faith. Some cross-cultural church planters seem afraid to let the cultural systems of the UPG challenge the gospel while others seem afraid to let the gospel challenge the culture. For example, some want to allow circumcision without letting focus people work their way through the issues involved, using the gospel as their touchstone. Other outsiders translate the Bible to minimize or obscure terms such as Son of God because they think those terms would be repugnant to the people. As the Holy Spirit leads, believers can make the right decisions in these matters. This tendency on the part of outsiders to encourage withdrawal from a struggle with the scriptures can be illustrated in many ways, such as teaching the poor that they don't have enough money to give a tithe, or insisting that the dead be buried in coffins.

Holiness is the scriptural model for the Christian life. It is the existential life of the believer. The early Javanese leaders knew this instinctively. Although Coolen was remarried illegally, he never justified it before the people. He required them to live by Christian standards or leave his community. In Sadrach's case, "Emphasis was placed on Christian ethics and the obedient fulfillment of the divine law which was taught by *nabi* [prophet] *Ngisa Rohullah*. Jesus was the exemplary figure whose entire life, as viewed by Sadrach, consistently proved the truth and triumph of his Christian *ngelmu* through obedience to the law even unto death" (Partonadi, 1988:220-221). Sadrach's life was dedicated to emulating Jesus in all that he did and said.

Some have questioned Sadrach's approach to both the Javanese belief system and the Islamic religion as an example of the position of the modern "Insider Movement." However, the major difference is seen in Sadrach's orientation to the future as compared to the modern Insider Movement's retreat into the past. Sadrach contextualized to the Bible in an attempt to move away from syncretism with the former religions. He was consistently moving into the future toward a model based on a biblical worldview and away from the worldview of both *kejawen* beliefs and Islamic doctrine. Unlike the Insider Movement paradigm of our day that promotes orientation to the socio-religious community, Sadrach's adaptation of either *kejawen* or Islamic models was addressing the future of the Church and biblical theology rather than retreating into the existing socio-religious condition of the new believers.

3) *"Grounded in Scripture"*

The Javanese evangelists and pastors owned a Bible and taught from a Bible. At no time in the development of Javanese Christianity did the leaders fail to consult with the canonical scriptures and the church tradition. The Bible was translated into Javanese as early as 1828 but was not used widely until a better translation of the New Testament was made in 1848 (Bentley-Taylor, 1967:53). The Javanese Bible has always been translated on a word for word correspondence model and has not been adjusted to Islamic terms or theology. The interpretation of the scriptures in Islamic contexts has been left up to the evangelists and pastors.

Bible based theology exposes syncretism

Despite the complicated process of trial and error in contextualizing the gospel to a culture which was previously influenced by both *kejawen* and Islamic religious systems, the Javanese Christians never blurred the unique status of Jesus as Son of God and Savior. For example, all the translations of the Javanese Bible have used the name *Yesus* (a transliteration of the Greek) instead of the Arabic term *Isa Almasih*. Like the Shellabear Malay Bible's use of indigenous Malay terms in place of Arabic, the Javanese Bible has always used indigenous Javanese terminology (See: Hunt,1996:164). The Javanese translations support the historic creeds of the Church concerning the person and work of Christ and other theological foundations of Christian faith. Surely, endless discussions and great amounts of prayer were behind these decisions.

Coolen and Sadrach were characteristic of most of the Javanese evangelists and pastors. All of them were influenced by Christians of long standing who came alongside them to discuss theology and the gospel message. Although Coolen never had a missionary at his village, reports by missionaries show that he interacted with them on many occasions and also with Dutch officials who were Christian. When his disciples, Paulus Tosari and Abisai moved to the village of Modjowarno they related closely with the missionary Jellesma.

Javanese shadow puppet

Coolen realized the importance of Bible stories and taught them using *wayang* (Javanese drama) and other art styles (Kraemer, 1958:74). He also wrote prayers that would counter the power of sacred places (Partonadi,

1988:67) and he translated hymns from the Dutch hymn book (van Akkeren, 1970:65).

Sadrach worked with mature Christians throughout all of his first twenty years in ministry. He was strongly influenced by F.L. Anthing, Christina Stevens, and many others in the formation of his Christian doctrine. The missionary, Jacob Wilhelm, had the most influence on his congregational teaching during the height of his ministry. This missionary also corrected misunderstandings of the Bible and guided the believers in searching the scriptures for themselves.

F.L. Anthing & housemaid

Sadrach used worship aids from Coolen, Wilhelm, and others and also arranged the Ten Commandments in *tembang* (Partonadi, 1988:137). Although he did not use a fixed liturgy, Sadrach composed a handbook for services with the Lord's Prayer, the Ten Commandments, and a summary of the law from Matthew 22:37-40. He added prayers to this collection (Ibid.,132). In addition to this, Jacob Wilhelm translated materials that would enhance the teaching of biblical knowledge among the congregations (Ibid., 80).

Partonadi reports that "...the distinctive and basic Christian doctrine of the resurrection of Christ became the main theme of the preaching of Javanese evangelists in the nineteenth century, including Sadrach." "Christian obedience became the second emphasis of preaching." (Ibid.,144). These men and women worked out a contextual theology for Javanese but it was done in a biblical framework. The interaction of both worldviews was constant throughout the formative years.

Differentiate biblical worldview from local worldview

The clear differentiation of the gospel from their other belief systems has allowed Javanese to make a choice between worldviews.

The gospel is not considered the completion or the apex of other systems. It stands alone as the revelation of God. It is a choice, not an echo. At certain periods of the church's development, it depicted Jesus as the "*Ratu Adil*" (the Just King) who was to appear for the Javanese (Yoder, 1987:85). At other times, Jesus was presented as the "*Imam Mahdi*" who completes the Muslim faith and delivers the people from spiritual bondage. Eventually, however, the dominant view of Jesus Christ became that of the Savior God who delivers from sin and demands total obedience from all people. This uncompromising message has produced good fruit in Java's soil.

APPLICATION

Bible translation should be faithful to the text and not adjusted to an Islamic or specific cultural context. The interpretation of the scriptures should be left up to the believers themselves but not without input from more mature Christians. The evangelists and pastors used Javanese art forms that they deemed appropriate but there was a continual evaluation of these teaching aids. Miscellaneous other Javanese and European teaching models were also used to teach the Bible and Christian doctrine. All these models were adjusted as biblical worldview became clearer.

Leaders should seek worship forms that will convey a biblical worldview to the people. Experimentation with worship aids was a process that lasted for many decades among the Javanese and both Javanese leaders and European missionaries were involved. Their goal was for all aspects of church life and worship to be grounded in scriptural truth. Tension with the Javanese culture complicated this endeavor.

4) *"Interdisciplinary in its approach to culture"*

The way in which comprehensive contextualization encompasses all the complexity of culture is perhaps the most difficult concept for cross-cultural church planters. Even workers who are trained in missions seem to struggle with this concept. Many workers have difficulty understanding how the church can and should be involved in all the structures of a culture. Some are isolated on the religious aspect of culture whereas the church's task is not simply to change the religious worldview and habits of a people. It must be involved in modifying all the cultural systems. We can observe some examples of this comprehensive contextualization in the Javanese church experience.

Psychology

Hendrik Kraemer writes that Coolen's "main idea was that the Javanese embracing Christianity should remain Javanese" (1958:74). To do this, they must truly belong to the Church and truly belong to the Javanese. Coolen believed that the struggle with the Surabaya group over baptism had psychological and cultural implications. If the Javanese were baptized, he felt that they would be identified even more with the Dutch colonial masters and would be further ostracized from Javanese society. His main goal was to keep the Javanese in their local society. Although he lost the short struggle over baptism, Coolen established the principle that Javanese must stay within their cultural environment.

An example of this is the strong psychological bent of the Javanese toward belief in the spirit world. When the early evangelists introduced Jesus into the Javanese worldview, he was portrayed as the most powerful of all supernatural beings. Coolen created Christian forms to mark the transitions in life because he knew that Javanese were "accustomed to accompany the joys and sorrows of life by fixed ceremonies" (Kraemer, 1958:78). Sadrach was honored partly because he had the "... ability to control the devil and evil spirits" (Partonadi, 1988:66). He could cultivate haunted rice fields without experiencing harm. The gospel spoke to the worldview of the people.

Help converts to wrestle with their culture

The principle of staying within the culture was not an easy transition for either the Christian Javanese or for the majority Muslim population. "Javanese Christians were considered as outcasts by their fellow-countrymen- to profess Islam and to be a Javanese were practically the same thing- and it was not until more than a century later that Christians were recognized as Javanese and Indonesians" (van Akkeren, 1970:76).

Sociology

Government influence cannot be ignored in the development of a church. In the Javanese church history, permission to be baptized came from government officials. They were afraid of the reaction of local Muslim leaders if persons were allowed baptism. They also had control over who was authorized to baptize. In the early days of the church, believers were baptized by the ministers of the Dutch Reformed Church and, after the mission agencies came, by missionaries. Only much later were Javanese pastors allowed to baptize. Government officials controlled church documents such as baptism and marriage certificates because these were considered legal records. Officials were involved in giving permits to bury one's dead, to develop land, to build, to move one's residence, and to perform many of the functions of a church such as evangelism. Many of the Javanese leaders had serious conflicts with the government.

The early leaders sought ways in which they could integrate the life of the church into the existing Javanese society. Although Sadrach differentiated the gospel from Islamic theology, he maintained close ties to the sociological aspects of Islam. "The organization of the community grew up and developed along the lines of Javanese culture... comparable to the *pesantren* [Muslim school] system. Personal and emotional relationships were emphasized..." (Partonadi, 1988:114).

Sadrach's network operated like a Javanese extended family with the leader of the family playing the dominant role. In church life, this is called an episcopal system. Sadrach appointed elders and delegated responsibility. "In short, all things dealing with the life of the community as a whole were discussed and the problems tackled. From these meetings the elders gained new insight into the Christian community's life and a broader vision of what Christian community meant" (Ibid.,113).

For a period of time, the Dutch missionaries influenced Sadrach to install a Presbyterian system where authority was divided among elders in the various village churches. However, when Sadrach joined the Apostolic Church in 1899, he reverted to his natural Javanese family model.

Economics

One of Coolen's goals was to make the Javanese church community financially self-sufficient. His rules for work were stringent and those who stayed in his village were successful economically. When famine hit East Java in 1852, Coolen's community had sufficient rice to sell and give away.

A spin off of Coolen's work was the development of the most famous of the early Christian communities at Mojowarno. This also was a farming society. Its influence was such that Javanese Christians were primarily farmers for the next 100 years. However, farming allowed them to have economic stability and to develop their own type of Christian Javanese group. This enabled them to gain leadership experience in operating their own society. The churches in Central Java also continued to keep their members in touch with Javanese culture so that they would never develop a ghetto mentality.

APPLICATION

Utilize the gospel to engage and change non-biblical culture

Contextualization that results in a strong church will incorporate and transform such cultural forms as politics, education, economy, labor, social organization, and family systems. The list is too comprehensive to include here. Contextualization is not simply about whether believers sit on the floor, or chant as they pray, or bow toward a certain place. While knowledge and understanding of all religious and cultural forms is important, contextualization encompasses more than that. It is important for all missiologists to develop a comprehensive model of contextualization and not get diverted by inadequate conceptions.

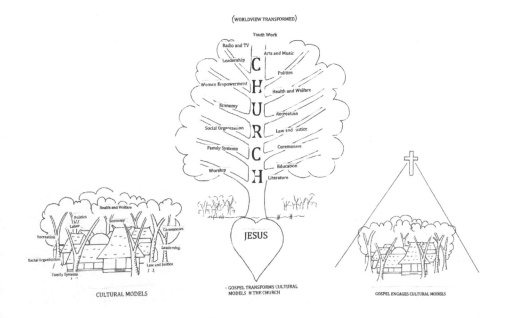

The Church engages and transforms cultural models

In the early days of CC CP, it is highly unlikely that the majority culture will welcome and value new believers. Rejection, ostracism, and persecution are common experiences for new believers. The Church, however, should never allow members to isolate themselves from their wider society whether it is their original community or another ethnic Christian group. The role of the Church is to be a blessing in changing every facet of society that is ungodly.

5) *"Dynamic"*

Many workers will likely not feel the dynamic aspect of comprehensive contextualization because progress and change comes slowly. Many cross-cultural church planters expect to establish a flourishing congregation in months or at least in a few years. The actual growth, however, may be far slower. Even though the Javanese churches developed slowly over more than half a century, they were still dynamic. Both progress and failure involved insiders and outsiders. Change went on continually.

The effective cross-cultural church planter looks for dynamic changes in the lives of individuals, for it is through those people that the church will come into being and grow. The Javanese work in Central Java began as house churches and did not have much organization. As Sadrach led more people to faith, he had to appoint elders to carry out leadership duties. As members increased, multiple cultural issues came into focus in the lives of the members. The church had to wrestle with these issues.

Spiritual growth in individuals will be dynamic

Growth was characterized by the interaction of Christian theology, church life, cultural issues, the Javanese religions, and traditional culture (*kejawen*). Leaders have struggled with the relationship of the gospel to the culture up until modern times. For example, the 1974 Synod meeting of the The East Java Christian Church (GJKI) in Malang was challenged to relate the Christian theology of farming to *kebatinan* beliefs [inter-life disciplines] (*Benih*, 1976:245).

This continuous contextualization creates a dynamism that keeps believers focused on the work of the Holy Spirit. An example is the interplay of Javanese *ngelmu* [esoteric wisdom] and biblical teaching. During the first half century of the church, the believers' understanding of the *ngelmu* was superior to their knowledge of scripture. The greatest contribution of the missionaries was their concentration on biblical worldview. Even though they can be criticized for many mistakes in cultural adjustment, they did not fail to constantly relate the Bible to the lives of the Javanese.

The dynamic interaction of biblical worldview with that of the Javanese created a gradual shift in their theology and cosmology. For example, aspects of the culture that were spirit related gradually began to fade in importance or to disappear altogether. Even today, it is not unusual for a convert to continue to keep his magic amulets even though he will not admit it to the church. When one understands the sovereignty of God, the amulets become invalid. The dynamic transition of the believer not only to saving faith but also to a holy life is the goal of the church planter.

APPLICATION

The cross-cultural church planter must not be deterred by personal failures, collapses in ministry, persecution, or other outside problems. They will happen on a regular basis but they do not mean that the ministry will be stopped or even crippled in the long term. In our UPG, many workers fell away for various reasons. Government opposition and persecution by other religious groups has slowed forward movement in our UPG for short periods of time. But the work is far stronger now than it was 40 years ago.

Biblical worldview should dominate contextualization efforts

The single most important aspect of the dynamic factor in comprehensive contextualization is biblical worldview. As the Bible is faithfully taught as the living word of God, people's lives will continually change. They will relate God's word to their cultural situation and discern the similarities and the differences and make their own decisions concerning it.

6) *"Aware of the impact of human sinfulness on the process"*

Some aspects of this characteristic of comprehensive contextualization have already been mentioned but it is good to reflect on it in a deliberate manner. All the problems we face in CC CP come from the human heart.

At times, those outside the church are at fault but frequently the fault lies with the believers. Hendrik Kraemer quotes one of the Dutch missionaries concerning the motives of the Javanese in becoming Christian.

> Encouragement by more or less influential persons, above all by Europeans, sometimes coupled with the prospect of increased material prosperity; inclination towards equal status with Europeans; tendency towards imitation in general, especially among relations; marriage, supposed or genuine concurrence between Christian teaching and *ngelmu* desired or long sought after, sometimes coupled with striving after morality or with the recognition that some points in the Christian teaching are clearer or better, the latter in connection with disapproval of the teaching or behaviour of their own *gurus* or priests; seldom free from superstitious notions about baptism, which often occasion making a vow (1958:82).

In the same breath, we can relate the despicable actions of some of the missionaries who sought to take over Sadrach's work through devious and dishonest means. History records that one such missionary was P. Bieger. "Bieger was very ambitious and had been attempting to take the leadership of the community away from Sadrach ever since his arrival in Bagelen. When his attempts failed, he became impatient and accused Sadrach of disloyalty to the government" (Partonadi, 1988:73). This false charge resulted in Sadrach's arrest. Bieger then became the head of Sadrach's churches. Fortunately, this situation did not last long.

Sadrach's flock was quite large. The Dutch missionaries had very few converts. Some of the missionaries were jealous of Jacob Wilhelm when he negotiated a working relationship with Sadrach. This continual pettiness on the part of some Dutch missionaries eventually caused a break with Sadrach and drove him into the Apostolic Church.

The Dutch colonials who were members of the State Church were also resentful that their pastor was helping Sadrach. They felt that he should not spend time in Javanese ministry. The Dutch colonial government also obstructed Sadrach in various ways. "The rapid expansion of the community independent from Dutch control aroused the suspicion of the local government" (Ibid.,73). These are but a few of the examples of human sinfulness that impeded church growth.

APPLICATION

The cross-cultural church planter must expect opposition. When we enter land that Satan has controlled for centuries, it is not easy to establish a new worldview in a short time. Everyone who has an agenda in controlling some aspect of society is going to react to the gospel as a threat. Those who rule do not want things to change. This applies to religious, political, and educational leaders.

Many problems will arise from within the church and even from within the church planting team. Church planting is hampered and even destroyed by people. The sinfulness of the human heart is our biggest problem.

7) *"A two way process in which all sides contribute"*

The Javanese church experience is valuable as an example of comprehensive contextualization because the gospel was introduced in a passive way. By this we mean that the initial contacts were not pro-active evangelism done by a foreign missionary but rather indirect approaches through literature and by way of personal relationships. The Javanese who received the gospel began to process its meaning through conversations, by reading the Bible, and in fellowship with others who were also investigating this new message.

When the missionaries came to Java, there were already growing congregations of believers who could trace their Christian heritage to Europeans whom they did not personally know. The missionaries brought their ideas of social life, church life, and political life. But the gospel message had already impacted the Javanese concerning those concepts. Coolen had struggled over the meaning of baptism with the group in Surabaya. At the time the Dutch missions entered central Java, Sadrach had already been interacting with numerous Indonesian, Eurasian, and Dutch nationals concerning how the gospel should be proclaimed and lived out in Javanese society. The missionaries wanted to take control but both Coolen and Sadrach resisted them.

Eventually, Coolen grew old and some of his apprentices joined the missionaries to form new congregations. Leadership of the church in East Java gave way to Dutch missionaries. However, the story in the south of Central Java was different. "Those who were acknowledged by the government and ordained by the church were not accepted by Sadrach's congregations as their leaders" (Müller-Krüger, 1966:179) [author's trans.]. Although Sadrach did not openly reject them, it was understood by the people that he did not give way to them.

The tension between the Dutch missions and the Javanese leaders was beneficial for the church because it impressed on them their role in dialogue about their faith. Local church lay leaders

Tension between east and west

New believers and church members should dialogue

were strengthened by this vitality. Elders in Sadrach's community attended regular meetings at which they shared mutual concerns about local authorities, other religious leaders, new buildings, health, education, labor, and general livelihood (Partonadi, 1988:113).

Missionaries, like Jacob Wilhelm, introduced Reformed church organization and biblical worldview. Wilhelm formulated a confession that included the church, the worldly government, and the Christian attitude toward the government to guide those who were persecuted (Ibid.,115). The give and take between all the actors invigorated the church and encouraged new growth in other areas of Java.

APPLICATION

Introduce the gospel in such a way that people are not threatened when they interact with it. Encourage inquiry even if it means that people challenge both you and the gospel. When people consider a new worldview, they must process it through the lens of the one they have. It is not possible for people to adopt a new worldview without working through its many facets. Translate the Bible as authentically as possible so that people can wrestle with its uniqueness and the Holy Spirit can affirm its truth.

Understanding how Christian theology and practice impacts a culture comes more quickly when many people collaborate in reflection and agreement. This is always a long process in a UPG taking years to resolve many aspects of the culture. Contextualization should be done by the leaders of the focus group. The expatriate church planter should only be a catalyst to enhance this process. Any model imposed by the expatriate will only hamper the natural development of contextualization. The expatriate can introduce various models and ideas as long as leaders are not required to abide by those suggestions.

EVALUATION of END RESULTS - CHECK LIST – CHAPTER NINE

[ ] am relating all aspects of contextualization to biblical worldview

[ ] am relating a contextual church to the worldwide fellowship of faith in Jesus

[ ] am concerned with the whole of the Christian faith

[ ] am using the Bible to answer the spiritual questions of the focus people

[ ] am careful about using structures of the local religion that contain elements that are not biblical (such as inequality for women in marriage and ritual prayer postures)

[ ] am applying biblical teachings to all aspects of culture and learning such as psychology, respect for life, business ethics, etc.

[ ] am praying for dynamic changes in the lives of converts

[ ] am seeking God's power to deal with the sinful persons and institutions in the society

[ ] from the beginning, am involving focus people in the process of contextualization

If only we understood mission history

217

CHAPTER TEN

PHASE SEVEN - DEVELOPMENT
PART ONE - LEADERSHIP

"Unless the LORD builds the house, those who build it labor in vain."
Psalm 127:1

In an Andy Capp comic, a young rugby player is chasing Andy, who has the ball. Andy's wife thinks he is young and daft to engage a devious player like Andy. However, the young man gets the ball and runs over Andy, whose wife then philosophizes, "Success seems to come from doing things you wouldn't dream of attempting if you had a bit more sense."

As you move into the development phase, you may be challenged again and again with the fact that you really do not have a handle on everything that is going on. Don't let that bother you because the Holy Spirit is doing this work and if you have been faithful to prepare yourself, He will carry you along.

CONTEXTUALIZATION REVIEW

The effective cross-cultural church planter must have a grip on true contextualization as described in the last chapter. It is all about grounding your biblical model in the non-biblical culture. A primary problem with some workers is that they restrict contextualization to mean simply religious and cultural forms. Contextualization must include a theology of the Fatherhood of God, the person and work of Christ, the activity of the Holy Spirit in Christian faith and practice, the nature of the Church, and Christian ethics. We begin with that and consider every aspect of our focus culture to determine how those biblical truths can be manifested in evangelism, Christian nurture, and the life of the church in the community.

Contextualization that results in a strong church will engage and transform all cultural forms. The following partial list will alert you to its scope: politics, education, economy, labor, social organization, family systems, politics, law and justice, leadership, religion, traditional customs, language, basic values, social behavior, coping mechanisms, social control, land, and livelihood. If you have been active in engagement and negotiations, you will be able to process these factors as you assist in the contextualization of the church plant.

The Church should transform society

Role of the Church Planting Team
1. Begin with the best model you can conceptualize

You may follow a pattern someone else has formed, provided you process every part of it for your culture. In our UPG, one western parachurch group tried to do contextualization on the basis of some model they had read about that was reportedly successful in another country. They were primarily concerned about religious forms and did not understand the factors of comprehensive contextualization. Within a short time their converts were contacting leaders of our church planting team to ask them why their evangelists seemed to be talking about a different culture.

Church planting occurs in a process

While it is easier for your church planting team to copy or modify a successful local model, you always have to be open to adjustments. This is the essence of development. You are in a process and nothing is static. Development means you must be open to continual change as your contextual model grows. Do not attempt to use a model that has not been effective in the past unless you have corrected the cause of its failure.

2. Have your Team adapt to contextualized leadership

If you have not already done so, this is the time to reconfigure your national and focus group team to involve local leadership. Since my wife and I were the only expatriates on one of our church planting teams, we became coaches and the evangelists were given complete leadership of their church plants. Even though they were not culturally qualified because of their youth and unmarried status, our team promoted them as leaders. It took several years for the new believers to get used to this. They kept coming to the sponsoring church leaders but they were sent back to the evangelists. Eventually, they accepted this contextual leadership in their congregations and subsequent leadership change was not difficult for them.

The servant leader

This stance takes a great deal of effort and commitment to a servant model. It is very difficult to convince your team and the emerging congregations to be led by people who are essentially novices. However, contextual leadership will be stronger sooner if you operate on biblical principles and coach them to maturity. This does not mean you will not have failures. That also is part of development but you will learn from them.

3. Coach and mentor rather than manage

Many expatriate led church planting teams practice a strong leadership model. Some even go to the extreme of controlling when their members can marry. Any kind of dominance model that promotes control by expatriates or non-focus group people is a weak model for long-term success. There are teams claiming to be "contextual" who isolate new believers from believers in other ministries. They are afraid that other believers will negatively influence their doctrine and practices. Their isolationism is a denial of the theology of the fellowship of all believers, and in many contexts, a cultural deviation. We must be careful to coach and mentor rather than control.

4. Involve the new believers

| *Local people must evolve as leaders* |

A truly contextual approach cannot be devised solely by outsiders. It requires input by all believers as well as by the church planting team. Each person can be active in bringing his or her contribution to the table. No one needs to be reticent about engaging in the contextualization discussion and no one should be excluded. Contextualization is a very complex equation requiring extensive knowledge of the culture and of the biblical record. Everyone can contribute.

Role of the Congregation

1. Focus people must engage

New converts will become involved in contextualization provided they are given the opportunity. This happens when they are not overwhelmed by traditional church or imported models. Many new believers in our ministry questioned why we continued to celebrate some focus group festivals when believers in other churches did not. We always guided them to the Word of God to investigate whether the festival had practices or connotations that were non-biblical. We never assumed that everything had already been said about any issue.

2. Believers must be grounded in the Word of God

As we saw in the chapter on comprehensive contextualization, probably the most important contribution of the experienced Christians on the church planting team is teaching the word of God. The entire contextualization process must be continually held to God's word. We want the emerging congregations to say what God says about the Church. They will not be able to do this if they do not know their Bibles. When they know the word of God, they can interpret its meaning both for the individual and for society. The Westminster Shorter Catechism says this as follows:

"What is the chief end of man?"
"Man's chief end is to glorify God, and to enjoy Him forever."
"What rule has God given to direct us how we may glorify and enjoy Him?"
"The Word of God...is the only rule to direct us how we may glorify and enjoy Him."

3. The contextualization process is generational

It is sheer naivety to imagine that true contextualization will take place in a single generation. This long-term process must be passed on for each succeeding generation to wrestle with their issues. There have been Christian congregations in Java for 120 years and contextualization issues still arise as

The Bible must guide the dialogue

Christians interact with culture. Some church planting teams condition their converts to follow a model they have imported from another culture and deceive themselves into thinking that they have established a contextual church. The true contextual church will emerge from the dialogue between the Word of God and the culture.

Leadership Training

If you have been reading through this manual you have already seen multiple references to leadership in CC CP. We have mentioned some books on leadership and there are many others that we have not cited. Our major theme is that leadership requirements and practices vary from culture to culture. You have to immerse yourself in the culture to learn what the leadership model is in your focus group. Leadership principles and practice are linked to worldview. Worldview is another topic that we have touched on from the beginning of this manual. By the time you get to Phase Seven in your cross-culture church plant, you should already be cognizant of your focus group's leadership models.

One of the most difficult areas in CC CP is the development of leaders for the churches that are formed. There are many reasons for this. For example, new believers may not come from families that have a culture of leadership. In most UPG, leadership is assigned rather than achieved. This means that it is passed down from genera-

Pray specifically to obtain local leaders

tion to generation within the same group of families. Families that are outside of this group do not seek to achieve leadership. In fact, they tend to shrink from it. Because of this, there are very few converts who feel that they can move into leadership positions. We are sure that the early apostles felt the same way. But the Holy Spirit changed them and he can change converts today. This is accomplished by grounding the candidates in biblical theology and worldview. As long as you leave them in their focus group mentality, they cannot change. When the Holy Spirit impresses them with a biblical theology and the worldview that emerges from it, they can change.

Worldview and Theology

Their focus culture leadership principles are based in their worldview and the theology that springs from it. You have to train them in biblical worldview and biblical theology. Biblical worldview is embedded in the Bible stories. When Jacob dreams of the ladder to heaven, he understands that God is always with him wherever he goes. When Samson receives his strength back, he understands that God forgives and answers prayer. When Jesus teaches about the shepherd who leaves his many sheep to look for the lost one, he is teaching about a God who is like a Father who loves all his children and will seek them wherever they may be. These stories have application for both children and adults. However, they must be taught in a way that applies to each group.

There are worldview considerations in all the Bible stories. And these stories are about truth and how God reveals it to mankind. The Bible presents many examples that focus on truth which can be understood and absorbed by new as well as experienced believers. It lays the foundation for understanding more of God's truth as one grows in relationship with him. As the biblical teachings are compared with other cultural and religious beliefs, people see the significant differences that exist between them. A change begins to take place in their worldview.

The Bible should be the basis of worldview

The gospels as well as the writings of Paul and the other authors of the New Testament letters show a particular concern with the differences between the gospel and the non-biblical philosophies and cosmologies of their day. Since most of these non-biblical constructs have continued in one form or another, you will likely wrestle with some of them in your focus culture. The type of teaching that Paul develops in his letters emphasizes the worldviews that counter non-biblical teachings. These worldviews become apparent from the biblical theology that Paul explains. This is the theology that gives believers an entirely new concept of who they are in their new koinonia.

I'm learning!

Teaching Worldview through Bible Studies

In a particular leadership-training program developed in Indonesia, the candidates are instructed in various aspects of ethics and biblical character traits using Bible stories where worldview is embedded. We attempted to correlate as many of these stories as possible with theological categories. I can't relate all of the categories and Bible verses because there are more than 72 theological topics with nearly 100 passages of the Bible that illustrate them. We offer the following as a brief example.

For the theme of God we chose the following 6 sub-themes: Father/Child Relationship, Faithfulness, Nearness, Goodness, Love, & Forgiveness (mercy). These were the lessons about the nature of God that we gave to show the difference between the teaching of the Bible and that of Islam. Each of the 6 sub-themes was illustrated with Bible stories. For example, under the first sub-theme (Father/Child Relationship), we used the following:

The God of all creation is not impersonal but longs to relate to us as a Father.
A. God is a personal father to those who believe in him.
   Luke 15:11-32 – The Prodigal Son
B. God is a redeemer father to those who believe in him. Judges 6:11-18 - Gideon
C. God, the Father, gives good gifts to those who believe in him.
   2 Samuel 5:17-25 - David defeats the Philistines

Under the sub-theme of Faithfulness, we made this statement: *God the Father is faithful forever. He will never abandon us; he will always be with us.* We illustrated it with the following:
A. God, the Father, is faithful to keep promises. Exodus 4:1-17- God promises Moses;
   Genesis 15:1-6 - God promises Abraham

B. God, the Father, is faithful to never lie.

    Joshua 1:1-9 - promise to Moses given to Joshua

    2 Samuel 5:17-25 – David obeys God

C. God, the Father, is faithful to give us his salvation, which establishes us in faithfulness

    2 Chronicles 7:11-22 – God's promise to Solomon

We also had six themes under the heading of the Son. One of these was Immanuel. Here are some of our examples.

The Bible explains that God, himself, came in the flesh to dwell among humankind.

A. God, the Father, became incarnate in Jesus.

    Matthew 1:18-25 - Immanuel- God with us

B. God, Himself, is clearly manifest in Jesus. Matthew 8:23-27 – Jesus calms a storm

C. The Father and the Son are one. John 10:27-30 - "I and the Father are one"

When God became incarnate in human flesh, he revealed the name by which humans would know him.

A. God gave a name. Acts 4:5-12 - Jesus is the name

B. The name, Jesus, has a meaning.

    Matthew 1:18-25 – Jesus ...will save his people from their sins

C. The effect of the name of Jesus. Acts 16:16-24 - evil spirits obey

When the Word of God was incarnated as a human being, he was also called Son.

A. God calls Jesus "Son." - Matthew 17:5 – "This is my beloved Son"

B. God calls the Son "beloved." - Matthew 3:13-17 –"This is my beloved Son"

C. God calls the Son "God." - Hebrews 1:8 – "But of the Son he says, Your throne, O god, is forever and ever,..."

The six themes for the Holy Spirit include the following two:

Dwells In The Believer

The divine unity of God is not violated or compromised by the fact that he enters the life of a believer.

A. The Spirit dwells within the believer. Matthew 16:13-20 – Peter's confession

B. The indwelling of the Spirit is the only way to a relationship to God. (*We did not have a story for the course but there are appropriate verses.*)

C. We have the assurance of God's presence. Acts 2:1-13 - Holy Spirit filled the believers

Empowerer (Gifts, Fruit)
The power of God is available to the believer through the ministry of the Holy Spirit.
A. The Holy Spirit is power. Acts 3:1-10 - lame beggar healed

  Acts 13:6-12 – Elymas, the magician blinded

B. The Holy Spirit operates in power. Luke 13:10-17 – deliverance from satanic power

  Acts 8:4-8 - signs lead to faith

C. Believers are given power. Acts 9:36-43- Peter raises Dorcas

  Acts 19:11-20 - God gives Paul power

We constructed the same sort of worldview teachings for all the themes we chose so that the candidates for leadership would struggle with the incompatibility of biblical and Islamic doctrine and their cultural worldview. We did not want any of the candidates for leadership to remain in the confusion of Islamic doctrine. Although most of them were converts from Islam, we wanted to encourage them in their movement out of Islam rather than allow them to remain in it. One of our teaching models for doing this was to also introduce worldview questions that related to the Bible stories we used. This was an effort to get them to compare the biblical worldviews in those Bible stories with the worldview of their local Islamic community. As they recognized the differences between what the Bible teaches and what they had been taught in their former religion, they were able to grow spiritually. Although a convert's spiritual movement out of Islam may take many months or even years for some people, knowledge of biblical worldview will increase this movement drastically. We wanted these candidates for leadership to be able to facilitate that movement.

Train those who are willing

Leadership training is a long process and should begin as soon as you have converts. It is important that you do not make the decisions as to who is worthy. The selection process will develop if led by the Holy Spirit. A national colleague of ours pastored a church that started around the conversion of a crippled man. This man had the heart and gifts to be a leader but our colleague would not consider giving him that blessing. Largely because of this, the church has struggled for many years because no other candidate for leadership came forward.

EVALUATION of END RESULTS - CHECK LIST - PHASE SEVEN – PART ONE

[ ] am striving to focus on comprehensive contextualization

[ ] involving the entire congregation in comparing the Bible with their culture

[ ] comparing all the various structures of culture with the word of God

[ ] have reorganized the church planting team for local leadership involvement

[ ] am coaching and mentoring rather than managing

[ ] special focus is given to recruiting potential leaders

[ ] have developed a leadership-training module

[ ] am training leadership to deepen knowledge of biblical theology and worldview

[ ] am stressing a biblical standard of leadership

CHAPTER ELEVEN

PHASE SEVEN - DEVELOPMENT- PART TWO

"Launch out into the deep and let down your nets for a catch." Luke 5:4

SECOND STEPS IN ENGAGEMENT

The Team

These second steps are advancing from "First Steps in Engagement" in Chapter 7, Phase 5. They are separated because negotiating skills are needed to fully appreciate these steps. Only the rare person is ready at the beginning of the engagement phase for these necessary steps.

1. Continue deepening faith building in your Team

By now, you may have moved from an expatriate team to a mix with a national team. You might even have progressed to a focus group team. Each of these entities needs to continue to practice faith building disciplines such as worship, Bible study, and personal counseling.

2. Sharpen your evangelistic models

More will be said about this in the church planting evangelism section below. The key to developing a relevant evangelistic model is answering the spiritual questions being asked by the focus people. There is not much point in answering questions no one is asking unless you teach them what to ask. Sometimes we have to do that. In our UPG very few people have a sense of sin before a holy God. When we teach them about the Holy Spirit and how he convicts

Keep abreast of all aspects of the church plant

us of sin, then they realize that questions about sin are important to ask and to answer.

3. Intensify language learning of team members

Language learning can be a problem for national and focus group members. Of the four focus group members we had on our team, only one could handle the language well enough to minister to old and young alike. As young people they had been schooled in the national language and had not learned their mother tongue beyond the youth level. They had to study to improve their language abilities. Team members from other ethnic groups experienced a psychological barrier in learning the focus language. They felt that the status of the focus group was below that of their ethnic group and they were conflicted about identifying with the focus group by giving up their use of the national language. Our team had a principle that those who did not learn the language sufficiently well were really not called by God to serve with our team.

4. Develop your coaching models

In Phase 5, we discussed coaching models. They are similar to mentoring but we do not consider them as deep as mentoring. The coach can often tell the worker that they need to learn about a subject such as family systems but not necessarily give them the information they need about it. As the team deepens their experience with the focus group, they will recognize areas of knowledge that they should master and they can find a mentor in the focus group to teach them. In doing this, team members can learn how to coach younger team members in identifying cultural events and relationships that need explanation.

5. Widen study of cultural models

There are many cultural models that you will continually access in your relationships with the focus group. We described three of the major ones in Phase 4 (Chapter 6) and you can study them in Appendices 5, 6, & 7. They are the political leadership model, the spiritual leadership model, and the patron/client model. All of these models are extremely broad and powerful in their influence on most UPG and the success of a church plant depends on understanding and employing these models in light of a biblical worldview.

Review cultural models on a regular basis

Friendship (relationship) is another critical model to master. Team members must learn how friendship is defined by their focus group. This sometimes requires years of experience when one is a pioneer in engaging a UPG. In the book *Peace Child*, Don Richardson describes how one UPG extolled the betrayal of a friend. What seemed to be friendship was really a ploy to engineer an elaborate plot of betrayal. We cannot assume we know the reason why people act as they do. We can observe what their actions are but we must research what causes them.

The Church is a friend to the alienated

Kinship systems are vitally important to church growth. We know that congregations grow primarily through the kinship web but many teams fail to study the organization and dynamic of that web. We have consulted with teams that could not answer such simple questions as who makes the decisions in the focus family. One of our team's early mistakes was baptizing unmarried youth without their parents' consent. Almost all of them eventually fell away from fellowship because they were not allowed to make that decision on their own. Without parental support, they could not finish their education, get a job or make a marriage alliance.

A mutual help model is also common to many cultures. This usually involves a community where every family is obligated to help in community projects such as road maintenance. Our UPG has a strong tradition of mutual help in the community and emerging Christian congregations that participated in these projects deflected some of the criticism that they were leaving the tribe. Church planting develops best when we can convey the fact and feeling that followers of Christ are not leaving their focus group.

6. Integrate with your community

We have had team members who were not allowed to live in some communities where they were witnessing. When the village head knew they were Christian, he would not give them a resident card. Local citizens were ordered not to rent to them. Others were even forbidden to visit people who were interested in the gospel. Despite all these forms of opposition, we should follow scriptural injunctions to do our best to live as Christians in every situation. Our team learned that politeness was one of the highest values of our UPG and whenever we were polite, the opposition was deflected or in some cases defused. The church planters never demanded their constitutional rights as citizens but rather at the time of confrontation acquiesced to leaders who opposed them. However, they would always return at a later date to continue their ministry and sometimes they were not expelled a second time.

Some verses that serve a UPG team are these:
a. live in peace — Romans 12:18
b. serve others — Luke 22:27
c. share — Acts 20:35
d. bear persecution — John 15:20
e. accept despoiling of goods — James 1:2
f. live holy lives — Ephesians 5:1-11

The Congregations

1. Concentrate on a less resistant segment of the population

In Phase 5 under FIRST STEPS IN ENGAGEMENT, the third item was "Identify the most open inquirers." There are times when this is not easy for a beginner to do. In our UPG, voting records of various districts gave us clues as to which areas were open to change. However, sometimes these populations were not open to change that involved the gospel. Concentrating on a less resistant population will give you the best chance of successfully planting a church. Having a church plant is your best opportunity to learn more about how the gospel is understood and implemented in the UPG culture. This will be invaluable to formulating strategy to reach other more difficult portions of the UPG.

Review & strengthen the basic church models

2. Church theology & Evangelism

The team needs to have a theology of the Church and an evangelistic model that flows from it. One of the biggest mistakes made in pioneer church planting is concentration on evangelism as an end in itself. Workers have the attitude that

their calling is to seek souls and lead people to Christ. They conceptualize believers as being the Church without envisioning the function of that
body of believers in fellowship. At times, sacraments become secondary
and believers are not trained in Christian nurture. The life of the church
becomes simply winning souls and gathering for worship. That type of
church will not be able to function as a change agent in its community.

3. Social & theological terminology

The words you use to describe your church and the life of your
church will affect how the congregation understands itself and how the
community views it. Some examples are as follows: (a) The word "church"
has a lot of baggage in some UPG. Fellowship (*koinonia*) is a more neu-
tral term for outsiders and it expresses a biblical meaning for believers.
(b) "Christian" is another loaded term in many UPG. "Follower of Jesus"
has a lesser impact while conveying a biblical commitment. However, a
congregation's alliance with the fellowship of believers in the Christian
world cannot be hidden. One's identity as Christian will soon be known.
(c) Evangelism in some languages contains the term Injil (gospel) and
this is traumatic for various groups. Other terms such as "winning souls"
and "target people" are militant and create some fear in non-Christian
communities. The word "sharing" has the same context for believers as
the word "evangelism" and conveys a feeling of friendship to unbelievers.
(d) Conversion is terrifying to many focus people because it means leaving the corporate body. There is much less emotion in the terms "believing in Jesus" or "following Jesus." These are useful for a
transition period.

Christian nurture is a key to faithfulness

4. Continue formulation & implementation of a contextual
nurturing ministry

The church planting team must be proactive in helping
the congregation develop contextual nurturing models. In
our UPG, many new believers were surprised when they were persecuted. It came as a shock to them that their community wanted to expel
them. Without nurture that speaks to the challenges of their situation,
many converts will fall away. The team and the new congregation must
negotiate the kind of nurture that both informs and sustains the believers. It may include activities in cell groups, retreats, Sunday School type
education, worship, discipleship, personal spiritual disciplines and social

service projects. It is important for the team and the congregation to work together to figure out how to provide for their needs.

5. Develop leadership training

When leadership emerges along contextual lines, the congregation accepts them more easily. Leaders can then be trained in biblical principles. If the team imposes leadership that is not characteristic for the focus group, it becomes much more difficult to install those people even though they may have more spiritual maturity.

In the beginning, the fledgling congregation will most likely be led by a team member. However, prayer needs to be made for both lay and clergy candidates. Strive for local leadership because they are usually more productive in evangelism than outside leaders. It may take a little longer to train them and install them but they can be evangelizing while they are in training. In some instances, you may have to wait for a young person to grow older before he or she is accepted as a leader.

6. Work within a small geographical area

As we mentioned in the section on "The Philosophy of the Church Planting Team" in Phase 6, extensive travel in ministry depletes team energy. When our team members made the mistake of accepting invitations from distance places, the extensive travel time resulted in ministry to fewer church plants. It is better to work several communities in depth rather than work many in a cursory way. This will conserve the energy and focus of your team. Limit travel to any church plant to one hour by public transportation.

Define the area you can serve effectively

7. Cast a missionary vision

Emphasize the gift of evangelism among new believers. They are the ones on fire with the joy of God's grace. Don't be overly concerned about their lack of Bible knowledge or theology. Give them encouragement to obey Matthew 28:19-20. If they cannot give sound teaching, others can aid them in that. So keep in close contact and fellowship with them.

8. Implement infrastructure for social welfare

Start to implement infrastructure for social needs from the very beginning of your evangelism and your congregational nurture. Many of the believers who follow you will need guidance and possible financial help in matters like health, education, and job concerns. Our team found that many of the believers lost their jobs and some had their children expelled from school. When they were sick, the village leader would not sign a document that allowed them to get government aid. Infrastructure has to be created as early as possible for these needs.

9. Establish & clarify financial structure

When our team members were required to keep a simple expense account, they were not able to do it. They had to be taught how to set up a financial record. In doing this, they learned how to organize a financial structure for the church plant. If financial records are set in place and transparent from the very beginning, the believers will never question that they should be continued. The integrity of church finances is vital to the teaching of honesty in every aspect of the believers' lives.

DEVELOPING BIBLICAL CHURCH PLANTING

Biblical definition of church planting

1. Matthew 28:19-20

If we use the Great Commission as a guidepost, then church planting begins with "go therefore and make disciples of all nations." Unfortunately, some "church planting teams" interpret this as merely evangelism that leads to baptism. They expect someone else to do pastoral care and they move on to evangelize others. Put simply, they are evangelism teams and not true church planting teams. They can be very useful if they are connected with real church planting teams. Other teams go further and do discipleship. This is characteristic of many para-church agencies. Since Jesus instructs us to "teach them to observe all that I have commanded," some teams create discipleship ministries or cell groups for ongoing biblical teaching. They do activities such as we list in Phase 5 "Engagement."

However, true church planting involves more than that. In this Phase 7 we are describing in more detail what true church planting teams do.

A real CHURCH goes beyond a para-church model

The purpose of church planting goes deep into what Jesus refers to as "all that I have commanded you." It includes the teachings of Jesus. We need to consider what it means to be "the salt of the earth" and "the light of the world" (Matt. 5:13, 14). A church plant is a "city set on a hill" that cannot be hidden. Jesus says, "I will build my church, and the gates of hell shall not prevail against it" (Matt. 16:18). Through his Church, Jesus proclaims good news to the poor, liberty to the captives, recovering of sight to the blind, and liberty to the oppressed (Luke 4:18). Paul tells us that "through the church the manifold wisdom of God might now be made known to the rulers and authorities in the heavenly places. This was according to the eternal purpose that he has realized in Christ Jesus our Lord, in whom we have boldness and access with confidence through our faith in him" (Ephesians 3:10-12).

Matthew 5:14,15

Let your light shine

2. Maturing a congregation

The Bible always speaks of the Church in terms of the *koinonia* or fellowship of believers rather than in abstract terms such as a church plant. We describe the development phase of church planting as maturing believers within a fellowship to evangelize and nurture others to become an "aroma of Christ to God among those who are being saved and among those who are perishing..." (2 Corinthians 2:15). All the scriptures quoted above indicate that the Church is a transforming agent in the culture. To accomplish that, it must interact with all the institutions and activities of the community in which it exists. The local church engages the world around it and establishes itself as belonging to its community.

The church must not allow itself to be forced into a ghetto but instead must interact with all facets of society so that its members take their rightful place as full members of the focus group.

3. A new family and a new fellowship for believers

The church becomes a new family for believers. Those who are driven from their families must be able to find a new family in the church fellowship. The church intercedes for them to make up the difference for what they have lost, in the hope that they will eventually be reconciled with their biological families. As far as possible, Christian fellowship seeks to reconstruct the focus culture and society within a biblical worldview without isolating believers from continual interaction with the local community.

4. The testimony of holy lives

A true congregation does not exist without the testimony of holy lives. Some church planters define a church plant as the gathering of a few believers and others describe it as believers who have been baptized. Both of these views lack an essential biblical quality, which is the trait of holiness. A true congregation of believers is one that is not only baptized but exhibits holy living in their community. "As he who called you is holy, you also be holy in all your conduct,..." (1 Peter 1:15). This kind of congregation cannot be ignored by unbelievers because it sets forth a biblical style of living that is different from the worldview of the culture. Believers who present themselves for baptism should be able to give the testimony of a changed life. A church plant without that testimony is not a true biblical congregation.

EVANGELISM FOR CHURCH PLANTING

Evangelism models

Cross-cultural evangelism has many facets, but the most important is conveying the person and work of Jesus Christ. Since people may have no knowledge of this event in their history, we have to find a way to make this clear. There are many types of evangelism but all have to begin at the place where people are spiritually and philosophically.

A congregation is gathered through evangelism

Next, we must identify the spiritual questions that people are asking. One of the ways our team did this was through a newspaper survey that asked cultural questions which related to various spiritual beliefs. Such questions and answers need to be analyzed so that we can fashion evangelism to answer them. If our explanation of the gospel does not answer the spiritual questions of a focus group, it will have no meaning for them.

1. The goal is not only evangelism but also a congregation (Matthew 16:18)

Not having evangelism as one's primary goal may seem to be a strange position but it is not. To use the phraseology of envisioning a project, evangelism is a milestone in the development of the church, not the ultimate goal. Of course, evangelism must be done in order to lead hearts to the Master. It is one of the activities of a true church. The problem is that some do not go beyond evangelism. There are Bible schools which teach that an evangelism model is the goal. When outreach began in our UPG in the late 1960s, evangelism was the main goal of most workers. Discipleship was a secondary goal and congregational nurture was almost unknown. If we are to do true church planting, a <u>spiritually mature congregation must be the main goal</u>.

2. Evangelism model vs. a church planting model

The evangelism model can be illustrated by the following graphic showing the footsteps of the evangelist going only as far as the inquirer.

Model of Evangelism

A church planting model can be illustrated by the footsteps going with the inquirer to reach other members of his family who are open. Then the footsteps follow the kinship web and the friendship web to reach as many persons in that community as possible.

Model of Evangelism   *becomes a*   *Church Planting Model*

3. Characteristics of evangelism

While there are many characteristics of an evangelism model, one element that should never be neglected is God's word. Evangelism is simply sharing the gospel. Jesus is the gospel and our source is the Bible. We should always share our personal testimony but not to the exclusion of sharing what God says about the human heart, sin, and Jesus' sacrifice for us.

In many UPG, friendship evangelism is a context in which practically anyone can share the gospel with an unbeliever. Often, it may take weeks or months to establish a basis of friendship with someone. As we wait patiently, God will provide the opening. In many cases, this opening occurs when we discuss some of the spiritual questions that people have in our UPG. This can be done in an informal way so that the discussion is not directed at the focus person. In our UPG, most people enjoy hearing various points of view about their spiritual questions as long as they are not applied to them personally. For example, discussions about unseen spiritual beings is very popular.

Paul Hiebert's "Analytical Framework for the Analysis of Religious Systems" helps the evangelist define the worldview of the person being evangelized. Hiebert sets up various categories of worldview out of which people operate. If the evangelist can determine what kind of worldview a person has, it is much easier to formulate the gospel message to answer questions in that worldview.

AN ANALYTICAL FRAMEWORK FOR THE
ANALYSIS OF RELIGIOUS SYSTEMS

**AN ANALYTICAL FRAMEWORK FOR THE
ANALYSIS OF RELIGIOUS SYSTEMS**

ORGANIC ANALOGY
Based on concepts of living beings relating to other living beings. Stresses life, personality, relationships, functions, health, disease, choice, etc. Relationships are essentially moral in character.

MECHANICAL ANALOGY
Based on concepts of impersonal objects controlled by forces. Stresses impersonal, mechanistic and deterministic nature of events. Forces are essentially amoral in character.

UNSEEN OR SUPERNATURAL
Beyond immediate sense experience. Knowledge of this based on inference or on supernatural experience.

HIGH RELIGION BASED ON COSMIC BEINGS	**HIGH RELIGION BASED ON COSMIC FORCES**
cosmic gods	kismet
angels	fate
demons	Brahman and karma
spirits of other worlds	impersonal cosmic forces

OTHER WORLDLY
See entities and events occurring in some other worlds and in other times

FOLK OR LOW RELIGION	**MAGIC AND ASTROLOGY**
local gods and goddesses	mana
ancestors and ghosts	astrological forces
spirits	charms, amulets and
demons and evil spirits	magical rites
dead saints	evil eye, evil tongue

THIS WORLDLY
Sees entities and events as occurring in this world and universe

SEEN OR EMPIRICAL
Directly observable by the senses. Knowledge based on experimentation and observation.

FOLK SCIENCE	**FOLK NATURAL SCIENCE**
interaction of living beings such as humans, possibly animals and plants	interaction of natural objects based on natural forces

Hiebert, (1982:40)

4. Elements of the conversion process

"The Spiritual-Decision Process" (commonly called the Engel Scale) gives us an example of how one might illustrate the process of conversion. Although it is a western model, it seems to apply to the experiences of some Asian UPG. When evangelists have a sense of where people are in their movement toward the gospel, it helps them to fashion ways to move them farther.

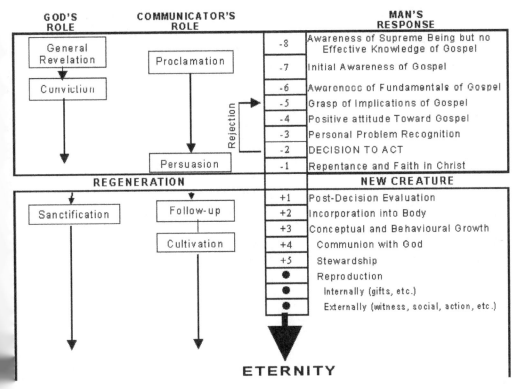

(Engel, 1975)

Continuum of Misunderstanding To Understanding

We devised the following model to illustrate how the Rational-Emotive Therapy of Albert Ellis can apply to the fear people feel when they hear the gospel. Some evangelists believe that the greatest obstacle to the conversion of followers of other religions to Christianity is fear. When fear is removed or moderated, people are able to consider change. The conversion of most people who are born and raised in non-Christian cultures relates to a movement from misunderstanding to understanding. Fear underlies misunderstanding. But misunderstanding can also create or enhance fears.

> *"We are so largely the playthings of Fate in our fears."*
> Hugh Walpole [1884-1941, English Novelist]

241

<u>Misunderstanding</u>   <u>Understanding</u>

Hate ---- Dislike ---- Distrust ---- Indifference ---- Trust ---- Like ---- Love
<--->

A. Hate
   1. rage
   2. violence

B. Dislike
   1. anger
   2. belligerence

C. Distrust
   1. suspicion
   2. threatened

D. Indifference
   1. ambiguous
   2. confused

E. Trust - Conversion takes place here
   1. attracted
   2. receptive

F. Like
   1. embrace
   2. peaceful

G. Love
   1. promote
   2. defend

Theoretical Basis
A. Rational-Emotive Therapy - (Hess, 1985, p.198-201)
1. ABC theory of personality (1962)
Ellis argues that the activating experience/event (A)
is not what causes an emotional or behavioral reaction (C)
but rather the person's belief (B) about what happened at (A).

EVENTS   HOW YOU FEEL
(A)   (C)

(B)
WHAT YOU TELL YOURSELF

People often think that an Event (A) will cause a Feeling (C)

In reality, what people tell themselves (B) about Event (A)
is what causes Feeling (C)

DARK STREET   SCARE
(A)   (C)

(B)
"I MIGHT GET MUGGED"

(Hess, 1985, p. 198)

2. The basic premise is that emotional problems are due to the person's irrational belief system. [e.g., what might happen if one becomes a Christian. The negative (persecution) outweighs the positive (peace, joy, & eternal life)]

3. If the person's beliefs are irrational, the evangelist's role is to displace them. A new behavior is achieved by changing the faulty reasoning which gives rise to irrational beliefs.

4. Perception, emotion, movement, and thinking are interrelated and operate in an integrative way. However, intense emotion, such as fear, generally interferes with the integration of these processes.

5. Ellis indicates that changes in reasoning, ideas, and values are necessary to produce substantive and permanent change and control. The challenge of maladaptive beliefs is the central task of therapy. [taken from: Leslie S. Greenberg & Jeremy D. Safran (1987). *Affect, Cognition, and the Process of Change*, p.41. New York: The Guilford Press.]

The Impact of the Theory in Evangelism

A. Understanding your focus group

    1. The effect of your evangelistic presentation (A) has less effect on feelings and behaviors (C) than what the person thinks (B) about Jesus Christ or Christianity.

    2. Your presentation (A) does not cause an emotional reaction (C) as much as does the person's belief (B) about what you are trying to do to him.

B. The importance of friendship/ relationship

    1. Friendship can function to show the person he is illogical about Christ or Christianity.

    2. One must relate to the person in terms which are non-threatening. This requires understanding religious background and systems of religious thought.

    3. Repetition and familiarity with the gospel under pleasant circumstances can begin internal rehearsal of positive beliefs.

> *A strong church needs strong families*

    5. Family/community focus

        Church planting needs families, and families need communities. Thus, we are concerned with the entire area in which families live. In our UPG, the family is more important than the individual and the community is more important than the family. It is very hard for a family to survive in a hostile environment. It is even harder for individuals. Sometimes, the family is driven out of the community but the goal of church planting is to create a dynamic congregation in the community. Many, if not most, UPG have this same kind of communal organization. It is imperative to contextualize to the wider society and not just to individuals. Try not to extract people from their community and work to prevent expulsion by the community. This will encourage converts to interact with their communities rather than withdrawing into isolation.

Seek the family

In order to penetrate society and plant the gospel, we must win families, not just individuals or separate units of society such as youth. Through families, we seek to share the gospel with entire communities. This is key to our ultimate goal of changing the worldview of society to a biblical worldview.

6. Evangelism should include community leaders

In the decade of the sixties and seventies, the evangelists in our UPG were afraid of approaching community leaders with the gospel because there had been a history of animosity toward Christians. Small groups of new believers sprang up in the villages but community leaders were suspicious of them and tried to destroy them. Gradually, the evangelists learned to contact leaders and share the gospel with them instead of trying to avoid contact with them. By answering the leaders' questions about their purpose in the community, the evangelists enjoyed more success. There were very few easy areas to evangelize but there was less opposition in some areas.

7. Approach all age groups

Evangelists will tend to approach those who are similar in age, gender, and social status. If all your evangelists are young *Spread your* and unmarried, you will probably have more fruit among the *net wide* unmarried youth in a community. People tend to gather with those similar to them. However, church planting evangelists must be careful to reach all age groups, both male and female, and all status groups. For example, it is often improper for males to approach females. In status conscious societies, lower status persons seldom impact those of higher status. Sometimes, you may not have evangelists who can reach certain groups. If so, it is a weakness of your church planting team and you should try to rectify it as soon as possible.

8. Cultural change is an ultimate goal

It is critical that we always remember that our goal is a change toward biblical values in the society/culture. While some people may think this is unrealistic due to the nature of slow change in society, we must pray and work for change no matter how long it takes. If we do not maintain our goal, we will miss God's opportunities. Javanese evangelism and church planting began at a time when there were "signs that in the interior of the country faith in Islam had been shaken" (van Akkeren, 1970:44). Major cultural changes can happen at any time.

Some changes are fun

There are three guidelines that help us decide about culture patterns. The first is we accommodate any cultural feature that does not conflict with biblical worldview. Styles of eating and dressing may not present any problems. Secondly, we reject anything in the culture that contradicts biblical worldview. For years, William Carey advocated the overthrow of infanticide and *Sati* [widow burning] in India. Thirdly, we try to change or modify those traits that are not biblical in their standard. In addition to many religious practices, these would include peculiarities like shortcomings in public health and a lack of concern for the poor.

NURTURING IN CHURCH PLANTING

Nurturing models

1. Congregational formation

The Bible does not teach us how to form a congregation, though various examples are given. Congregations will tend to form along the lines of the social organization model of its society. It is important that you understand how people in your UPG are inclined to organize themselves. You may want to introduce some new ideas and that has to be done in a manner that can be integrated in a logical way.

Strive to master how congregations form

2. Conversion vs. transfer and biological growth

Your congregation can grow in three ways. The most important is through the addition of new believers. However, it can also grow because of the transfer of members from other congregations. In our UPG, people tended to move frequently. This was not always a healthy sign. Until a few years ago, the main growth in our UPG had been biological. The majority of the believers were not doing evangelism so the church grew by reason of births in Christian families.

3. Discipleship

Christian nurture is about discipleship. When people come to faith they must be discipled in understanding the Christian faith and the nature of a biblical worldview. Most people do not understand this if they are not intentionally taught. This involves training believers to witness to their faith. In many UPG, most people come to faith because of a close relationship with a Christian. In some UPG, many of the converts need ministry concerning their experience with demonic forces. Even long time Christians may suffer from satan's bondage. We prayed with one seminary student who was suicidal and another who was disoriented and could not concentrate on his studies. Both had spiritual problems because of demonic influence in their families. Deliverance comes when people understand that Jesus is Lord and he can and will deliver them from all bondage.

Encourage converts to be led by the Holy Spirit

4. Baptism

Jesus commanded us to be baptized but he did not set any particular time frame. If there is a strong anti-Christian feeling in your UPG, it might be wise to delay baptism. In our UPG we delay baptism if the family is opposed. This gives the new convert time to make a strong testimony and appeal to his or her family to agree to baptism. The family will sometimes allow baptism even though they do not agree in principle. If there is no hope for an understanding, the new believer must decide. In our UPG, many believers usually want baptism before church leaders think it is wise. In those cases, they must negotiate the issue. We have seen new believers with a poor testimony or no testimony go to another church group because those who led them to faith were reluctant to baptize them.

Baptism of the faithful

5. Teaching

Since Jesus commissioned us to "make disciples…teaching them to observe all that I have commanded," we know that teaching is a serious obligation. As we saw in Phase 4 "Mentoring," every culture has teaching/

learning models that must be mastered. Catechism lessons should be constructed in view of the learning styles of the focus group. It may prove fruitless to just translate various confessions and catechisms without investigating whether their methodology will be understood.

Our primary responsibility is to describe biblical worldview and use Bible studies that relate to the spiritual questions of the culture. People mature in faith when they decide to leave an inadequate worldview and embrace the truth of the biblical worldview. As Paul expresses in Colossians 1:28, our goal is to "present everyone mature in Christ." This will mean that believers will not only have a deep fellowship with God but that they will also understand how to mentor others in faith.

6. Spiritual gifts

Paul tells the Corinthians that he does not want them to be uninformed about spiritual gifts (1 Corinthians 12:1). If this young congregation needed to develop and exercise spiritual gifts, then our UPG congregations also need to do so. Babying new believers is a major mistake being made in church planting today. Believers need spiritual gifts to mature in Christ, to resist the devil, to endure persecution, and to lead others to faith. A church will not grow spiritually if we are not nurturing the congregation in spiritual gifts.

spiritual gifts to resist evil

7. Fruit of the Spirit

Jesus emphasizes the fruit of the Spirit in many places but particularly in John 15. Fruit comes from abiding in the Son. The Father has made the Son the true vine that produces the fruit of the Spirit. If we do not abide in Jesus, we will not bear fruit. If we bear fruit, we show that we are disciples of Jesus. He describes this fruit in the context of love. Those who abide in this love obey the commandments or teachings of Jesus and bear fruit.

Continually seek the fruits of the Spirit

8. Ministry of love

The fruit of the Spirit relates to the ministry of love that Jesus describes in John 13:35. If we love one another, others see that we are true disciples of Jesus. In our UPG, many believers have difficulty loving those outside their families. Psychologically, there is a mistrust that runs through the culture. This is often a barrier even within families. We cannot change this kind of powerful cultural trait unless the love of God is poured out on believers.

9. Glorify the Father

Jesus teaches us that the purpose of the Son is to glorify the Father. When we lift up Jesus in word or in deed, we are pointing toward the Father. When one person told me that he did not understand how God could have a son, I replied, "Since you do not understand God as Father, it follows that you do not understand God as Son." He became pensive. However, when the Holy Spirit enlightens us, we can have faith that God is both Father and Son.

DANGER !! A new ministry will attract opportunists & malcontents from other churches and ministries. Usually, they bring many unresolved problems. Don't incorporate them before discipling them separately. If possible, communicate with the pastor at their former church.

CRUCIAL ISSUE: Remember- all direct evangelism and church planting work done by an expatriate or non-focus group person has disadvantages that may undermine your long-range goals (For example, in many countries the expatriate must overcome conventional wisdom that Christianity is a European or foreign religion).

EVALUATION of END RESULTS - CHECK LIST - PHASE SEVEN- PART TWO

- [ ] the Team has defined and agreed on a definition of church planting
- [ ] what was "Envisioned" is beginning to occur, i.e., measurable points, hand-off points, & deliverable ministry

[ ] name some of the measurable points that have been passed, some of the hand-off points, & some of the deliverable ministry, if any (See: Appendix 4)

[ ] faith building in the Team is deepening

[ ] Team members continue in language learning & in sharpening skills in the use of cultural models such as leadership

[ ] constant renewal of the Team's spiritual resources and vitality is carried out

[ ] conflict issues within the Team are handled immediately and according to Scriptural principles

[ ] the Team's focus on holiness and unity of spirit is not sidetracked by work goals

[ ] congregations are being developed holistically with concern for social as well as "spiritual" aspects

[ ] new believers are being discipled & taught to share their faith

[ ] evangelism is structured to answer questions people are asking

[ ] working through the implementation of contextual models of evangelism & Christian nurture with the new believers

Tips: **1. It is crucial to stick to your game plan (unless you are aware of a glaring error). Any change may confuse your Team. So make changes carefully. It is seldom productive to constantly tinker with your approach.**

2. You cannot do it alone- train leaders of all ages and social ranks.

3. You need wisdom in placing personnel.

Roger's Suggested Reading List
For Vacations

CHAPTER TWELVE

PHASE SEVEN - DEVELOPMENT-PART THREE

"According to the commission of God given to me, like a skilled master builder I laid a foundation, and another man is building upon it."
1 Corinthians 3:10

In addition to the evangelism and nurturing models discussed in the second part of Phase 7, it is critical to develop church theology that covers political and social factors as well as religious ones. As we saw in the theoretical section on theology of church planting, it must be based on a biblical model. However, this biblical model is more clearly understood by new believers if church structure and church order are contextualized to the culture. The chapter on contextualization gives examples of this. Converts from the focus group must work out agreement. When outsiders try to install contextualization models in the church, they can unknowingly reinforce mistaken theological concepts from the culture. An example of this is the way some expatriates have substituted the religious language in Muslim ritual prayers so that converts would continue to pray five times a day. This reinforces "works" theology. One convert in our UPG called it a "return to bondage."

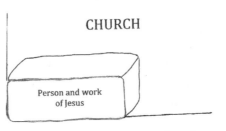

CHURCH

Person and work
of Jesus

The cornerstone of the Church
is Jesus, Son of God

When you have reached this level of the Development Phase of your church, you should be defining contextualization models in considerable detail. The effort to construct contextualization models will go on as long as you are in the focus group and will continue after you leave. It is a long process.

THEOLOGY FOR CHURCH PLANTING

Evangelistic Models

1. Christocentric

Exalt Jesus as the Son of God

The evangelistic model you use should be the beginning of your effort to define faith and the Church in terms of Christology (person and work of Christ). You will encounter many problems in this area. As a case in point, people in our UPG have difficulty understanding that the Son of God would die for them because their culture teaches them that the people die for the king, not the other way around. If they come to faith in Jesus without realizing that he died for their sins, they really have not grasped a central message of salvation by grace.

Some expatriates are teaching people that they can come to faith in Jesus without considering the truth that he is the Son of God. They base this on the theory that they can teach converts after they are baptized. This presentation establishes a theology of the church where people become children of God without receiving and believing in his name (John 1:12). In addition to that, it results in a church theology that forgives sins without the death of the Son of God. If converts do not understand that their sins are forgiven through the death of the Son of God, they are trapped in religious ritual for the forgiveness of sins. The implication remains that the forgiveness of sins is related to works and that sin is not serious enough to necessitate a holy and perfect Savior.

2. Biblical worldview

Evangelistic models must answer the spiritual questions of the people in light of a biblical worldview. When we sublet our house to a focus person, he asked that he officially take charge of the house a few days before the contract was signed. We were uneasy about this but he assured us that he would not move in before we left the house. When he came on that day, he brought his spiritual practitioner with him. Although he was a Muslim, he had a shaman pray around the house and he planted a bush in the yard. He did this because his formal religion is intertwined with a mystic belief system so that the two operate in conjunction with one another.

In Colossians chapter one, Paul clarifies the biblical message that "all things were created through him and for him" (v. 16). The magic bush, like everything else, is subject to Jesus Christ. It is important to understand the philosophical basis of the focus religion before we explain biblical orientation. The biblical message is clear but it is no small task to explain it to a person with a non-biblical worldview. The Holy Spirit must convict and convince the hearer.

3. Biblical models of theology

Perhaps the most difficult problem we faced in our UPG was focusing the evangelists and pastors on creating biblical models of theology that would interact with false theological systems and refute them. Although they had some success in doing this verbally, creating a model that could be written down has been illusive. In our UPG, there is both a formal and an informal belief system operating simultaneously. The evangelists and pastors have to weave their way through this labyrinth of thought and feeling to explain the gospel. The variety of the pattern is so complex that no one has yet written a comprehensive theology of evangelism for our UPG.

Looking for the head of the family!

4. Contextualize to cultural models

Evangelism is more easily understood if it is contextualized to comprehensive cultural models such as family systems or status/role models where religion is integrated. Jesus explained that faith is like coming through the door of the sheepfold or coming to the good shepherd (John 10:7, 11). He also speaks of the father who will not give his son a serpent instead of a fish (Matthew 7:10) and of the person who must first be reconciled to his brother (Matthew 5:24). An illustration in the status/role category is when Jesus teaches that "whoever would be great among you must be your servant and whoever would be first among you must be your slave" (Matthew 20:26-27). These are models that related to the people of his day either as an affirmation of culture or as an antithesis to cultural values. In either case, the evangelistic model reaches the heart of the hearers. This is the type of contextualization we need to consider in the area of evangelism.

Church Structure Models

1. Leadership model

Every culture has a leadership model and studies indicate that most of the UPG will follow the top down or Episcopal model. This is when a single person or a small group controls everything. Your indigenous (or contextual) church will tend to replicate the prevailing model of society because that is the model they know best. Introducing another model takes time, patience, and wisdom. As soon as the Southern Baptist missionaries in Indonesia allowed their mission church to make their own decisions, they chose to introduce a modified Reformed church structure that had similarities to the prevailing Dutch Reformed pattern that dominated Indonesian church life. Although it was contrary to what the missionaries had taught the converts about the Baptist tradition of independent congregations, the Indonesians wanted some type of interconnectivity between their churches. They created a type of synod.

2. Power structure

There has to be some logical system in every congregation that guides them in numerous administrative tasks such as approval of membership and financial accountability. This is the system that structures power. It will organize the way a congregation handles decisions and accountability for those decisions. It is this church government that will guide in receiving or removing members, auditing finances, addressing social problems, representing the church in the community, and handling other political issues.

A critical aspect of your church is its structure

In the beginning, the evangelist/pastor may do all this but the congregation should engage these issues as early as possible.

3. Pastoral models

As you can see from the discussion on power structures, much will depend on the pastoral model introduced by the evangelist/pastor who starts the congregation. Churches in Indonesia with denominational backgrounds reflect variations of the patterns of those denominations. Churches with Reformed, Lutheran, and Methodist beginnings have been remodeled to fit the Indonesian mindset. On one occasion a number of so-called reformed churches were run by pastors using the Episcopal model. Such models change the way church government, services, and ritual are conducted. Contextualization of some kind happens whether one person or a group instigates it.

4. Contextualization of worship and celebrations

In this section we are using contextualization to mean the biblical re-formulation of ceremonies to answer spiritual questions. For example, the sacraments of Baptism and Holy Communion should be interpreted for the focus people in order to shift their worldview to a biblical one. In our UPG, ritual bathing is common. A person who desires spiritual power bathes seven times in special water. This procedure is associated with spirits that impart power to the person. If Baptism and Holy Communion are not explained as a different worldview, the new believer is likely to understand these biblical ceremonies in terms of spirit power. Christian ceremonies can become part of the spiritist configuration.

5. Life cycle ceremonies

The use of life cycle ceremonies is common in every culture. Rites of marriage and death are universal but they are not performed in the same way nor do they necessarily mean the same thing. In our UPG, all these rites are related to spirit appeasement in order to avoid misfortune. Many relate directly to Dewi Sri, the goddess of the earth and rice. Every life cycle rite in your UPG will probably have to be reinterpreted in biblical terms. It is critical that we investigate focus group ceremonies for such occasions as birth, circumcision, coming of age, birthdays, marriage, and death in order to reframe them in a biblical worldview.

Strive to establish sound models of church life

6. Counseling models

Every culture has counseling models that are used by parents, teachers, and spiritual guides. These models deal with matters such as discipline, conflict, and reconciliation. Some workers may not consider that these aspects of spiritual guidance are important to the development of a congregation. But the church needs to be able to help people in these areas. Some "insider" workers in our UPG did not think anything was important besides evangelism and forms of worship. They did not study the local worldview and did not understand when problems were being solved by non-Christian principles. Finally, they asked friends in a more developed ministry to help them in counseling their members.

The importance of empathy

7. Social principles

No church will be able to speak to the social issues in its community if the members do not study the biblical worldview concerning society. The church's social principles should speak to all aspects of society from the perspective of biblical teachings. These might include poverty, labor, marriage, education, medical care, and the like. The focus people might cling to their unbiblical customs but the church must continue to interact with these cultural traits.

8. Places of worship

Most people revere certain places as especially sacred. This tendency includes the buildings they use for worship. It is characteristic of many cultures that religious affiliation grows more quickly when people have their own churches, temples, mosques, or other places of worship. In some groups, the building is considered the face of religion and, in some UPG Christians are not allowed to build places of worship. However, biblical worldview teaches us that God does not dwell in a specific place or building. Christians should mature spiritually without buildings but there is little doubt that many congregations grow faster when they are able to have their own place of worship. Buildings give people a sense of belonging and permanence. There are many types of church buildings in use and many symbols used in them but none of them are absolute or required by scripture.

Church polity & administration

1. Administrative structure

Churches have many different types of administrative structure and there are variations to each type. As mentioned several times in this manual, the three major models are Episcopal, Presbyterian, and Congregational. The Episcopal type church is a connection of congregations under the supervision of a bishop. The Presbyterian system uses councils called presbyteries under a synod and the Congregational system emphasizes the autonomy and independence of each congregation. In secular terms, they can be summarized as strong man leadership, government by council, or self-regulatory communities. If one of these systems is characteristic of the organizations in your focus culture, you will have a difficult time convincing them to use another system.

Most mission leaders agree that each church should be self-governing, self-propagating, and self-supporting though they define these principles in different ways. When you are working in a UPG that has a strong tradition of dependency, it will take time to teach them to be independent in any of these areas. It may take many years to foster a biblical model of dependence on God to bless the church members through what they can do on their own. The self-supporting trait includes financial responsibility through good bookkeeping and reporting procedures. Church members should be involved in instituting all these principles as soon as possible.

Insist on an indigenous church model

2. Constitution and by-laws

Every church should have a constitution and by-laws that agree with the philosophy of ministry set forth by the founders. This establishes and guides the formal organization of the church and the implementation of the spiritual ministry. In some cases, this is required in order to register the church with the government. When this is not done, members do not have a sense of identity or permanence. In our early experience in our UPG, many members moved from one church plant to another looking for clear and decisive leadership.

3. Theological agreement

Churches planted by different agencies or churches will have more cohesion if their theology is the same or similar. Churches with different theology on the same field tend to fracture more easily. In the 1970's period of evangelistic renewal in our UPG we tried to get all churches to agree to baptize by immersion because some church theologies were adamant on this point. However, not all the protestant churches would agree. This difference created insecurity in some believers who felt they were not properly baptized.

Promote the education of all children

4. Educational philosophy

Every church should consider the educational needs of its children and youth in order to enable the church to take a leadership position in the society of the future. Many evangelists and pastors in UPG work continue to be dependent on support from sponsoring churches because their UPG congregations are not financially able to support them. If the youth are not trained to do well-paying jobs, they will not be able to support the church of their future.

5. Other ministry areas

More will be discussed about the various ministry areas in the following sections. It is important to keep in view all the groups in the church. Adults, youth, and children all need attention and no one should be neglected. Many church planting efforts concentrate on adults only in order to gather a congregation. If the children and youth of converts are not evangelized and taught, they will become poor church members in their adult years. You will begin to see this problem develop within a decade.

A REMINDER: Be careful of improper evaluation and reporting of progress. Do not become discouraged by slow growth. The number of believers in your UPG may increase very slowly over several decades. The success of your church may be like that of a mustard seed. *"You never count your money, when you're sittin' at the table. There'll be*

Ask the Lord for praying donors

time enough for countin', when the dealin's done." ("The Gambler" by Don Schlitz)

CONTEXTUALIZING FELLOWSHIP (*Koinonia*)

Contextualization occurs when all of the areas of church life are grounded in biblical theology and have meaning for the believers. This will not happen overnight. It may take decades for your church leaders to experience comprehensive worldview change. There will be great pressure from the community for them to continue to follow some or all of the local customs. In our UPG, believers in one village were accused of bringing sickness to the village by not following spirit related practices. It will take time for believers to work through all of the multiple issues they face because of their faith in Jesus Christ. This requires much prayer for wisdom and direction from the Holy Spirit. God has solutions. He also has power.

In this section, we discuss some aspects of corporate religious life that involve change in worldview. When the believers join the fellowship (*Koinonia*), they begin to grapple with vast changes in categories such as worship, symbols, and rites. They should all be encouraged to engage in the process because contextualizing the meaning of words and practices to the focus culture is critical to understanding. Not all your members will be interested in doing this but you should involve the ones who are. Your personal opinion is only one element of the process. Ultimately, the focus people must internalize these new understandings.

> *Your goal is to change the local worldview and culture*

Contextualizing Worship
1. Function and meaning

Christian worship involves all the activities in a believer's life that are expressed to glorify God. Emile Durkheim used a biological analogy. He referenced "the contribution made by one organ, or part of an organism, to the life of the organism as a whole" (Seymour-Smith, 1986:125). If we apply this to the activities of worship, it would indicate the mutual dependence of all Christian activity as an integrated whole. However, for the purposes of this discussion, we are dividing worship and Christian education into two categories.

Missionaries often talk about function and meaning but definitions are not always clear. The entire congregation participates in the prayers, confessions, and hymnody of the Church but they do not necessarily understand them the same way. If the Muslim convert faces Mecca for his prayers and the Buddhist convert shakes his *mandala*, what does that mean in terms of biblical worldview? Do you integrate that custom into Christian worship and if so how do you do it? Seyyed Hossein Nasr (1988:61) writes, "the soul of a Muslim is like a mosaic made up of formulae of the Quran in which he breathes and lives." He goes on to describe the impact of formulae such as the *Shahadah, Bismillah, Alhamduli'-llah, Allahu akbar, insha Allah,* and *masha Allah.* In closing he says that "these phrases are means by which God is remembered in daily life, in regular conversation and speech…. The very existence of these formulae in every day life is a reminder of the continual presence of the Quran and its message in Muslim life" (Ibid., 65). The worldview of a Muslim is different from that of the Bible. The practices that reinforce non-biblical worldview have to be forsaken but this might take considerable time.

2. Process of contextualization

Professor Nasr's explanation warns us of the difficulty of separating forms of worship from their inherent meanings. A biblical worldview is an integrated whole and does not allow for the inclusion of non-biblical acts of worship. As new believers in the UPG begin to understand God's call to pure worship as stated in Romans 12:1-2, they should reflect on all their forms of worship and decide by biblical standards which is pleasing to God and which is not. Many believers in our UPG have not yet given up their magic charms though they have been taught that they should. They may understand the teaching with their minds but they have not yet internalized it in their spirits.

3. Spiritual gifts

Prayers for healing are commonly made by shamen but their orientation is not a biblical one. The Old Testament describes and forbids the use of diviners, fortunetellers, sorcerers, mediums and necromancers to heal and perform other supernatural acts such as contacting the dead. What some people describe as power encounters are understood in different ways by those observing them. Spiritual gifts are biblically based when they reflect the glory of God in the life of the individual. A shaman in

East Java could not understand missionary Detmar Scheunemann when he explained that he did not possess power. Scheunemann said that the power to pray for healing came from outside him but in the worldview of the shaman, power is an inner force.

4. Christian symbols

Christian symbols are also part of worship that reflect different meanings. The cross is a symbol that reminds us of God's grace in saving us through a great sacrifice. Raila Odinga, a candidate for president of Kenya in 2008, had a negative meaning when he calls Christians "worshippers of the cross." This opinion shows us that the same symbol can have different meanings depending on the worldview of the observer. True worship must locate symbols in their proper perspective so that they do not become fetishes.

A symbol of God's grace

5. Language

Worship is almost always more meaningful when a person uses his or her heart language. With few exceptions, evangelism, teaching, and worship should be conducted in the language of the focus people. While many people may understand a trade or national language, they respond better to the language their mother uses to speak with them. This might not be the case with young people who are educated in a national language. Their thinking language may no longer be their mother's language. Biblical worldview must be processed in the minds of people in order for it to reach their hearts. When an evangelist or pastor does not have command of the real language of the people, he cannot effectively help the congregation in processing biblical worldview.

6. Relevance to both cultures

The great challenge of contextualizing worship is that it must speak to both the Christian and the non-Christian cultures. The new believers will begin to move into a biblical worldview when they see the relevance of Christian worship to bring them into the presence of God. If biblical worship does not answer their spiritual questions, they will doubt its relevance. In our UPG, the newborn child must be presented to the goddess

Christian worship must speak to the entire culture

of the earth. This has meaning for the identity and prosperity of the child. If Christian ceremonies do not speak to the spiritual questions embedded in these kinds of practices, they will fail to attract them to a biblical worldview. Dr. I.W. Mastra explains the church architecture of Bali in this way. "We try to make the church building a sermon in stone so even if the spoken sermon does not attract them, the symbolism of the church structure and the carvings will help them understand the Lord" (Dixon, 2009a).

Contextualizing Christian Education

1. Biblical theology and worldview

Biblical theology determines the worldview of the Bible. Every culture has a theology underlying its worldview. Most people will not be able to describe what that theology is or how worldview reflects it but they have internalized it. Every aspect of Christian education must be based on the Bible if it is going to present a biblical worldview. If the believers understand and agree with biblical worldview, their cultural worldview will begin to change. When a believer from our UPG explained how he put a glass of water in the rice bin overnight so that he would accrue power to heal a sick person, he was demonstrating local worldview. We explained that healing does not rely on the water or on the water having been in the rice bin. Healing simply depends on the action of a loving Father responding to the faith of his children.

2. Education for all groups

Christian education must be inclusive of all age groups. Everyone needs to interact with Bible truth. Adults are the most strategic group in deciding the relevance of biblical teaching. However, children and youth must not be neglected because they will be adults within a few years and they will then be involved in the contextualization process. Many groups fail to recognize this and their youth become adults without sufficient worldview change. In many UPG, women are the guardians of the culture and yet they are often left out of important community decisions. This should change in the church where women should take an equal place in affecting worldview change.

3. Bible studies

Reading, studying, and grappling with the biblical text is the best way to experience worldview change. Churches that do not have a Bible or fail to use the Bible do not develop deep understanding of biblical worldview. In our UPG, there were and might still be congregations whose educational tool was primarily a catechism. We have visited churches that did not have Bibles and did not understand much about biblical worldview. Many of their youth think that salvation is essentially being baptized and confirmed as members of the church.

4. Prayer

We see in Luke 11:1 that the disciples had observed Jesus praying alone and in isolated places. They knew that there were ritual prayers in their religious worldview but they did not understand the theology and worldview that guided Jesus' prayers. So one day they asked him to teach them to pray the way he did. Practically every UPG will have a worldview and a tradition about prayer. But the worldview underlying that custom may be quite different from that of Jesus. In our UPG people pray primarily to spirit powers because they feel that God is far off while the spirits are all around them. They may know some formal prayers that are used in their formal religion but they believe that the shamen deliver the most effective prayers to the spirit powers.

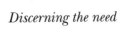

Discerning the need

5. Diaconal service

Diaconal ministry is essentially a model of service to the community. Probably every culture has some sort of tradition of helping neighbors though there is wide variety from one culture to another. In some UPG only those who are members of the clan are considered subjects of financial or material help. This worldview excludes everyone who is not related in some way. In the story of the Good Samaritan, Jesus describes biblical worldview as helping anyone who is in need.

Our entire life should be our worship

Churches in the country where we served were not focused on helping the poor and suffering. Some did help at times but there was little teaching and action in these areas. When biblical worldview is not taught, it will probably not be practiced. When the tsunami struck Indonesia in December 2004, churches responded to an amazing extent to help a province that was very hostile to Christians. Natural disasters have helped create a growing change in the worldview of the Church.

6. Frequency of Christian education

Ministering to the poor

The examples given above illustrate the need to be involved continually in relating UPG worldview to that of the Bible. We compare and contrast local worldview with biblical worldview through Christian education. The media of preaching and teaching are the two most frequent ways we do this. However, all of our activities as Christians should be geared to practicing biblical worldview. Our daily conversations are a powerful tool in this endeavor.

> **DANGER:** New congregations tend to isolate themselves & become introverted. An isolation model is counter-productive in the long term.

> **Tip: It is much easier to formulate and implement a ministry for new converts if you do not mix them with transfers and other long time Christians.**

MAJOR CHALLENGES IN CROSS-CULTURAL CHURCH PLANTING

Personnel problems

By the time you reach the Development Phase of your work, you will have learned what Andrew Murray meant when he said, "*The missionary problem is a personal one*" (see Phase 2). Your biggest challenge is keeping your team on point. There are many distractions that will divert your team from their mission. Here are a few.

Try to limit distractions though there are many

1. Poor preparatory training

By this phase of your work you will be aware of any lack of preparation by team members. This will be evident in language facility, ability to organize a project, communication skills, knowledge of the culture, and the like. Knowledge can be acquired at any time. It is still not too late for your team members to improve their usefulness through re-medial work to improve competence. Hopefully, the discipline of your team is such that this can be done. Review Appendix 1 for important competencies.

2. Concern with finances

Too many teams depend on foreign funds to promote and execute their mission. Frequently, members spend so much time in fund raising that the fieldwork suffers. Churches can be planted with little or no for-eign funds being used. The team must learn how to live on or as close as possible to the level of their colleagues among the focus people and to develop the ministry at the rate they can sustain. If the expatriate funds are withdrawn, the congregational ministry should continue without a hitch.

3. Change of personnel

One of the biggest problems that teams face is the loss of members and the addition of new members. Every change in team membership requires a reorientation of the entire team. The more changes you experi-ence in personnel, the more problems you will have. Some of the teams in our UPG experienced collapse due to personnel changes. The stress of adjusting to the work or to one another was so great, the team dissolved. Even when a team might assimilate the change, it consumes much valu-able time. Avoid as many personnel changes as possible and be attentive to reorient and refocus your team when it happens.

4. Breakdown of trust

One of the most important traits of your team is the bond of trust (see Phase 3). When this breaks down, the team can spin out of control. Discouragement, dissatisfaction, or petty jealousies due to a loss of calling or vision can erupt and embroil the team. Don't let busyness divert you from continual team building.

5. Multiple illnesses

One of the biggest problems we faced was keeping our workers in the field. Typhoid, typhus, diarrhea, cholera, and parasites were some of the major problems in our area. In addition, influenza and other illnesses af-flicted workers. Whenever people were sick, other team members had to care for them. The loss of work hours in a UPG due to health problems is enormous.

Keeping A Team On The Job
(Just keeping people on the job is a major effort, including yourself and your family- it consumes enormous time and requires a deep commitment)

6. Culture stress

National workers from non-UPG ethnic groups experience culture stress in the same way that expatriates do. They may have less but it is still significant. Our focus team members could not understand the stresses felt by expatriates or other ethnic team members. Because of that, they were often not sympathetic about the homesickness and loneliness felt by their national colleagues from other ethnic groups.

Prioritize encouragement

7. Crises of confidence

In the beginning of the work among the UPG it is common for all the team members to be bubbling with confidence that they will be victorious in planting a church. With some, this euphoria disappears in less than a year. With most, it will fade in time unless there is a remarkable turning among the focus people. After a few years of sowing the seed, the overwhelming challenge and perceived failure becomes a burden for most workers. It is important to maintain the perspective that there is no failure, unless it involves sin. The penetration of a UPG is culturally formidable. The team must depend on the Holy Spirit to open hearts to the gospel. This will happen in time if the team is faithful.

8. Rejection

Rejection is one of the hardest experiences for people to face and if it is repetitive, most people will become insecure. Jesus' advice to go two by two is sound psychologically as well as spiritually. We need to both dialogue and pray while we evangelize but we also need to have a comrade to give us moral support. Most of the people we meet in the UPG will be friendly unless they think we are going to witness to them. When we talk about Christ, many will reject us. They walk away, they give our literature back to us, they may throw it on the ground, they may insult us, and they may threaten us. Church planters have been ordered out of communities, beaten, arrested, jailed, and killed. Rejection creates a sense of insecurity in the team members that must be addressed. If not, they will quit.

9. Depression

There are many experiences that can cause church planters to become depressed. Sickness is probably the most common. Good health is critical for church planters. In the stress of work, many people do not keep this in mind and the team members should be aware of any drastic mood swings and any behavioral or personality changes. Failure in reaching work goals will also adversely affect some people more than others. Some of our focus team members had Bible school classmates working in other ethnic groups who gathered a congregation of 60 people in a year while our team members led only one family to the Lord. This caused a sense of failure that drove over half of our team to move to another ministry or area of the country. Expatriates give many reasons for leaving the field but we feel that depression due to a lack of self-fulfillment underlies most of them.

Depression shows up in many forms

10. Breakdowns

For lack of a better term, breakdowns describe various inappropriate behaviors of a church planter. Spiritual and physical breakdown can result in confused and aberrant thinking and emotion. Team members can become involved in immoral or unethical behavior apparently without recognizing what they are doing. Problems such as the improper use of funds or inappropriate relationships by team members should be quickly addressed. While these may not be frequent problems, they are common experiences for church planting teams.

11. Moral sins

Unfortunately, the best of teams can have a member who commits a moral sin. It is frequently difficult to address these problems because many factors are involved. A worker usually has family members and church leadership who become involved in the fallout. One of our UPG teams had a member who committed adultery. He was suspended from the team and his church also suspended him for a year until he could rectify his spiritual and family life. However, his wife did nothing and before long another church used him in various ministry. He did not accept the discipline of his team or his church but continued with the new church that accepted him as he was. Despite any kind of inconsistencies on the part of others, the team must act in the best way possible to maintain Christian witness and discipline in their ministry.

Syncretism as a major challenge

Syncretism has been defined as "the combination or blending of elements from different religious (or cultural) traditions.... The term is however particularly employed to refer to situations of culture contact which generate religious systems which are a mixture of Christian and native or traditional beliefs and practices" (Seymour-Smith, 1986:274). In this CC CP manual we describe syncretism as a blending of biblical worldview with non-biblical worldview.

Bong Rin Ro of the Asian School of Theology writes that this is a major issue. "The key issue in the whole argument of contextual theology is whether biblical and historical doctrines of the Christian church can be preserved without compromise in the process of contextualization" (Ro,1991:63). It is important to point out that the word of God does not condemn beliefs and practices that do not contradict biblical teaching. Therefore, many customs and beliefs of a UPG may be compatible with biblical teaching. Our primary concern is to portray the character of God the Father, the person and work of the Son, Jesus Christ, and the ministry of the Holy Spirit in the same way that the Bible portrays them. All our other beliefs flow from this.

You must know the Bible to overcome syncretism

1. Challenges

In Phase 7 Part One in the section on Contextualization, we stated that all those involved in the process of church planting are legitimate agents of contextualization. However, they all do not play the same role. The challenge to you as the church planter is to stay within the confines of your role. You will normally have the power to persuade the new believers in any direction you choose. You must resist this pressure. The challenge that new believers face is to be honest about their non-biblical beliefs and practices. It is critical that they can discuss these issues openly and without condemnation. This is the only way you will be able to identify and address the underlying worldviews.

2. Boundaries

There are theological and cultural boundaries that must be clarified. Usually, the church planter will know many of the theological boundaries but not the cultural ones. It is the opposite with the focus person. A friend of ours ministered to a focus group that had pig feasts in which they ate the cooked blood of the pig. His wife was a member of that focus group and she told him not to eat the blood because it was based on a non-biblical worldview and was associated with spirit beliefs. However, he liked the taste of the blood so he ignored her advice. In doing so, he sent a message that believers did not have to struggle with issues concerning the spirit world.

Heed the advice of nationals

3. Authority

For many religions, authority resides in a book. The Muslim has the Qur'an, the Confucian believer has teachings, and the Hindu has the Vedas. The Christian has the Bible but its interpretation is by the Holy Spirit. When this authority is operating in the Church, new believers will be able to work through all their cultural laws and traditions in light of Scripture.

4. Understanding worldview

It is very difficult to understand the worldview of other belief systems because they are based on different presuppositions and structures. One example is the comparison of *Yin Yang* with biblical worldview. *Yin Yang* is a philosophy which holds that the ideal situation is a balance of shadow and light. In principle, it is relative, inclusive, oriented to change, and has "a rotation of dominance" concept. The Bible teachings are absolute, exclusive, permanent, and

Converts need commitment to follow the BIBLE

have a 'this or that' dichotomy. You must study the worldview of your focus group in order to understand how they interpret the Bible.

5. Models of change

Every culture has its particular models of change. Darwin thought that change was based on natural selection. Marx proposed a conflict model. Your focus group will tend to follow its own model of change. Inherent in that model will be the elements of control and power. This subject is too complicated to discuss here but you must seek to include all believers as actors in the process of contextualization so that syncretism will be reduced. You are seeking to implement a catastrophic change in worldview. Seek to understand how the focus culture experiences change.

6. Rigid models

The models of isolation and/or dominance that are still practiced by many expatriate workers are not the answer to syncretism. The danger of subscribing to a rigid model is that the focus group may sublimate its desires or practice them in secrecy. When this happens, the non-biblical practices are no longer the subject of discussion. In Indonesia, there are many church leaders who are still practicing magic arts because the Church no longer discusses its spiritual dangers.

7. Role of coaching

When your church planting team begins to think about the scope of syncretism and a contextual church, the average church member will not be helpful unless they have been oriented to the task. Coaching them into this position is one of the top priorities of the expatriate and focus group church planting team. This is one of the hardest jobs the team will undertake.

FACTORS THAT HINDER GROWTH

In addition to the personnel problems listed above there are many ministry, community, and political challenges that hinder the establishment of a church. At the same time the team is learning all that it can in order to communicate the gospel to the focus people, it must also deal with these hindrances that are a continual challenge.

1. Weak foundation for conversion

Appendix 10 contains a list of reasons why some Sundanese people of West Java have an interest in becoming a Christian. Some of these reasons may be true of the focus group you are trying to reach. While a few of these reasons are not good spiritual reasons, they may be normal for a person in any culture. At any rate, you have to counsel with believers to make sure that they have a sound foundation for their faith.

2. Poor modeling of Christian life

The very fact that many people come out of a worldview and lifestyle that is materialistic, domineering, insecure, or immoral means that their lifestyle may not change in a short time. This affects the view other people have of faith in Jesus. Even leaders in the congregation may not have achieved the level of commitment that is necessary to attract others. Jesus gives an example in Luke 22:24-27 when he contrasts the model of the benefactor (or patron) with the model of the servant. In Phase 4 we discussed how common the patron-client model is in cultures. People are drawn to Jesus when we model his life to them.

3. If Jesus is not eminent

When a person models the Christian life in an inferior way, others do not see the eminence of Jesus. Living a life that glorifies Jesus is a continual challenge for everyone. Those who come out of a non-biblical worldview will undoubtedly have some shortcomings in their testimony. However, when unbelievers see that Jesus is eminent in some parts of their lives, they will be drawn to him. The important thing is to encourage converts to give Jesus eminence in their lives.

Teaching the Bible empowers believers to live holy lives

4. Weak basic teaching

Growth is hindered when core biblical worldview is poorly taught. For example, if new believers are not counseled about assurance of salvation, they will not have a strong testimony of faith. Assurance of salvation comes when people understand clearly why they accepted Jesus as Lord and what that means as a gift of God. Forgiveness of sin,

The word of God gives life

hope of the resurrection, the indwelling of the Holy Spirit, power to live a holy (set apart) life, and assurance of eternal life are all basic biblical teachings that are necessary for your congregation to grow. The Word of God is the basis of assurance. Flowers grow well when they are nurtured.

5. Unregistered churches

Many governments require religious organizations to be registered. In some cases governments will not register Christian churches or church buildings. If there are church buildings, they may not allow them to expand. If local, regional, or national leaders do not recognize a church, there are great difficulties in developing ministry to the congregation and to the community. This has led to an "underground" model practiced in many places. It is a hindrance and not a desirable model but church planting can still go on.

6. Problems overwhelm little faith

Growth is not necessarily hindered by excessive and difficult problems but it can be if the faith of the congregation is not strong. In our UPG, we have had church buildings damaged, burned and destroyed but the congregations continued to worship and testify about Jesus. They were not overwhelmed by vicious attacks. Other congregations were threatened with attacks and they closed down to prevent them. When faith is not sound, congregations can be overwhelmed.

Never slack in teaching the Bible

7. Out sourcing converts

Numerous para-church organizations have placed converts in local churches because they were interested in evangelism but not in pastoral responsibilities. When you can cooperate with a church of similar faith and practice, it is useful to partner in ministry. However, when you place a convert in a church that is not committed to spiritual growth, evangelism, and/or contextual approach to the focus people, there is a danger of losing that convert as a contact person. New converts tend to copy the Christianity they see practiced and if their congregations are not committed to reaching focus people, they are unlikely to reach out to their own focus group.

8. Exercise of gifts not encouraged

When leaders do not encourage the development of spiritual gifts, believers do not receive and employ the gifts that bring growth. In 1

Corinthians 12:1, Paul tells us that he does not want us to uninformed about spiritual gifts. Then he lists a number of gifts that God gives to believers for the "common good" (v.7). We should encourage all believers to prepare their hearts to receive and use whatever gifts God has for them.

9. Isolation

Identity with a larger community is a common desire of people in many UPG. You need to determine if that is the case with your focus group. When this desire is present, it is a mistake to isolate believers from other Christian communities. Isolation models in our UPG have not produced as the church planters hoped. Even though believers were told not to associate with other Christians, they secretly contacted them to find out what their lives were like. The desire for identity is a natural and "contextual" desire that should not be suppressed.

10. Inadequate accountability structures

Every team needs a manageable and integrated accountability system. One of our UPG teams operated under the auspices of a sponsoring church but it was a separate unit of missions in that church. As long as it functioned as a unified team, it maintained accountability both to the team and to the church. However, when its system of congregations "graduated" to become separate units under the authority of the sponsoring church, accountability broke down. The sponsoring church leadership did not know how to discipline the activities of the evangelists and they began to drift in their ministry. We had failed to build an accountability system that would incorporate the transfer of congregations to the direct guidance of a sponsoring church.

11. Insufficient local leadership

The lack of local leadership was a serious problem in our UPG home churches because our focus group had a culture of limited leadership. Since few of the converts had any experience in leadership, we needed to train congregational leaders. This was difficult because the people had the psychology of followers and few wanted the responsibility of being a leader. According to their understanding, leaders were socially, politically, and financially responsible for all decisions affecting the congregation.

Some examples of some hindrances you may encounter are summarized in Appendix 10: MAJOR PROBLEMS IN SUNDANESE EVANGELISM AND CHURCH PLANTING

Tips: 1. **It is easy to forget people & lapse into just expanding or maintaining the <u>program</u>.**

   CC CP should not be about the program but rather about the people.

2. **Your biggest problems will come from within yourself/ your Team.**

3. **The educational and social status of your Team members will determine where they can work and with whom.**

   Usually workers are most effective with those of their own level or below. Also, there are aspects of ministry that your Team members may not be trained to do; e.g.- literature, recordings, & other technical areas.

COMMUNITY AND POLITICAL PROBLEMS

In addition to the factors that hinder growth mentioned in the last section, community and political problems also eat up huge blocks of time. Try to eliminate or reduce these. **A good tip to remember**: slow development usually creates fewer problems than fast growth.

1. Unclear financial support structure

One of the first questions local community leaders will ask you concerns your financial support system. In other words, they will want to know how you make your living. In the same vein, they will ask where your congregation gets its money to present programs, celebrate religious festivals, and travel to meetings outside the community.

Engage & reconcile every problem

2. Jealousy among new believers due to perceptions of inequality

When one of our focus group evangelists distributed used clothing to his congregation, members were angered that some got better clothing than they did. This complaint was particularly distressing to the evangelist because some of the clothing they coveted was actually too small for them to wear. Loaning money also creates jealousy and the culture of borrowing should be investigated before you loan money. Social or financial inequality can disrupt a ministry.

Social jealousy can become a critical issue

3. Conflict with community leaders including political/religious leaders

This is almost impossible to avoid in a UPG village because the community is tightly organized and every resident is considered a constituent of the political and religious leaders. They will view gospel preaching as an attempt to lure away their supporters and they will take measures to block your activities.

4. Persecution

Practically every new believer is persecuted in some way and evangelists are also persecuted. Believers may be beaten, forced from the families, lose their jobs, and not receive any government subsidies. Their children may be expelled from school and even beaten. Congregations may not be officially registered by the government or recognized by the community. Establishing credibility in a new community is difficult.

5. Mistakes in evangelism strategy

When one of the tract distributors from Every Home Crusade passed out tracts near a mosque, people were angered and word went out to find and punish the offender. There were five members of the team and they returned to the local distribution post. Their local sponsor told them to go quickly to their home base which was in another city. People who were chasing them around the district were not able to find them before they fled the area. Mistakes in evangelism can cause an area to react against all evangelism for a very long time. Wisdom is needed so that passions will not be inflamed more than is absolutely necessary.

6. Social welfare needs

Evangelism is often more effective if it is correlated with attention to social needs. However, when evangelists get involved in social work, their evangelism usually suffers. When the Dutch mission in our UPG shifted their efforts to education and medical ministry in the early part of the 20th century, their evangelism almost stopped. Although evangelists may not have expertise in health, education, agriculture, or other basic concerns, they should be able to negotiate agreements with social service organizations that will assist the church planting effort. The cooperation of such groups will free the evangelists to witness and teach God's word.

Pastor your congregation

7. Sheep stealing

Many workers are disturbed by the actions of other ministries who entice their disciples away. This is often done with promises of more money, work opportunities, and the like. However, many times these promises are not fulfilled. For reasons unknown, some churches like to add members even though they are not faithful in pastoring them. As much as possible, create procedures to protect your ministry against outsiders and when sheep stealing does occur do not react in kind and lose your testimony.

Be watchful for those who entice your members

8. Any combination of the above can lead to collapse of work

Sometimes, one of the problems mentioned above can demoralize or collapse the work. In most cases, two of these problems will be devastating. It is impossible to avoid all hindrances but they can be minimized if a church planter is faithful in prayer to seek God's wisdom in approaching the society.

TOWARDS MATURITY (anticipating closure)

1. Be people oriented

Many church planters begin with a focus on evangelism and get diverted into promoting a program. Growth tends to wane when your evangelists and pastors are more concerned about having worship services and Bible studies than they are in reaching people with the gospel. One of the focus teams we coached was powerful in its early days and it was able to start several strong house churches. But some of the evangelists only went to the villages to conduct programs and before long, there were no new baptisms. We need to have ongoing evangelism. Congregations develop when we spend informal time with people to evangelize.

2. Emphasize the whole person

Most people in the UPG are oriented to a holistic life style. They focus on community and their religious worldview is integrated with all aspects of their lives. We need to emphasize this in the preaching of the gospel so that they see that the gospel is relevant for all areas of their lives.

3. Evangelism & pastoral models

As soon as possible, put your models of evangelism and pastoral care in place. As we said before, this is very difficult to do but the church will not be strong without them.

4. Infrastructure installed

The infrastructure of the church must be started as soon as you have converts. (See Phase 5 - First Steps In Engagement- "Start developing infrastructure for a focus group congregation" and Phase 7 Part 2, **The Congregations #8** Implement infrastructure for social welfare). In some cases, you can begin even sooner. Try to do it with volunteers using development models and not with paid workers. Don't be discouraged, as it is very hard to do.

5. Church Planting is not personal kingdom building

Many workers have a difficult time with personal kingdom building. Church planters are usually aggressive, ambitious people but this can be channeled in a healthy way. But if the church planter is sucked into the deception of building a personal kingdom for one's own reputation, it will be harmful to his or her empowering ministry. Expatriates or non-focus people who are not committed to empowering the focus people will ultimately fail to produce the church that scripture envisions (1 Corinthians 3:6).

Kingdom building is a common failing

6. Truthfulness/faithfulness

Truthfulness and faithfulness are the foundation blocks of trust (2 Corinthians 4:2). Because of the difficulties of cross-cultural work, it is likely that you will have failures in trust building. But God is faithful to override our errors if we are faithful to be honest and humble. Seek wisdom to never lose the trust of your co-workers because your team's success depends on continual trust.

7. Envision more than a house church (or cell) model

Most church planting begins with some form of cell. It is rare that a single convert can bring a large number of people into faith. When a spiritist group in our UPG was closed down by the government, over 5,000 of them joined the Roman Catholic Church. This kind of turning is extremely rare. Usually, you will start with one person or a family and slowly grow a congregation. However, your vision has got to go beyond the cell group if you want to impact a community.

SUMMARY OF SOME MAJOR NEGATIVE INFLUENCES IN CHURCH PLANTING

1. Fear

The section on fear in Phase 7, Part Two- "Continuum Of Misunderstanding To Understanding," illustrates the high probability that this is one of the problems you will face in drawing people to the Lord. In Indonesia, this fear is prevalent among people who are very committed to the majority faith. They hear all kinds of misinformation about Christianity that convinces them to avoid

Develop problem solving models

anyone who talks about Jesus. Others who are less indoctrinated are more open about spiritual discussions.

2. Inappropriate discipline

The effective church planter is one who knows how to administer discipline according to the style of the focus people. One of our national colleagues was ministering to new believers who had done some small thing that was unbiblical. Instead of talking to them privately, he broached the subject from the pulpit and even though others sympathized with those who were in error, the shame drove them from the church. A good focus group leader will not drive his followers away with inappropriate discipline.

3. Conflict

Conflict is sure to erupt in the congregation and the effective church planter will know how conflict is handled in the focus group. In recent interviews with elders of one focus group, we learned that there are several models that are followed in that focus group. The most common is the use of a mediator to arbitrate between the disagreeing parties. Some western expatriates interpret Matthew 18:15 to mean that one should personally confront one's antagonist. However, leaders from our focus group interpret that scripture to mean that a mediator can represent a person in confronting his opponent. The indigenous conflict model may have to be modified if it is not biblical but the church planter cannot do that effectively if that model is not defined.

4. Poor Spirituality

Spirituality is caught, not taught. Your congregation will not grow if they do not see an example in you and in their evangelists and pastors. Poor spirituality is the result of poor example and poor teaching. A seminary student testified that, despite some liberal teaching he received, his faith remained strong because of the example of youth leaders he witnessed in his home church. They demonstrated that the Bible was trustworthy.

5. Disunity

Sometimes unity in one's team and in one's congregations seems almost impossible to maintain. We must pray and work to foster unity as much as possible because disunity is one of the major reasons ministry collapses. The effective church planter continually strives to eliminate any intrusion of disunity.

EVALUATION of END RESULTS - CHECK LIST - PHASE SEVEN - PART THREE

[ ] all previous End Results in each Phase are reviewed to see if more work needs to be done

[ ] leaders are fashioning church theology that is biblical

[ ] all contextualization models are being held to the light of Scripture

[ ] all the spiritual aspects of congregational development are reviewed regularly

[ ] leaders are monitoring any syncretistic worldviews being demonstrated in the congregation

[ ] negotiating a contextual model that can be owned and utilized by converts and developed by the fledgling congregation

[ ] the adapted **Blake's Academic Administrator Grid** (Phase One) is reviewed with each Team member to see how they are doing on their church planting competencies

[ ] agree with a trained counselor who has missionary experience to guide your team members in evaluating family relationships

[ ] relationship issues of all kinds are resolved as soon as possible

[ ] am keeping the church planting vision in focus (see: Chapter 5, Phase 3)

[ ] am keeping track of passing measurable points, hand-off points, deliverable ministry

[ ] am dealing with Critical Issues & other issues surfacing (See: Appendix 3)

[ ] am making case studies of church planting work

[ ] am evaluating overall success/failure aspects (this is hard to do)

DANGER: Don't be misled by quick, shallow results due to the influx of marginal people, materialism & other novelty attractions. Be patient- church planting is a long-term process.

CHAPTER THIRTEEN

PHASE EIGHT - CLOSURE & ONGOING INVOLVEMENT

"...a time to embrace, and a time to refrain from embracing;..."
Ecclesiastes 3:5b

In 1980, very few cross-cultural church planters in underdeveloped countries had access to telephones. The situation with mail correspondence was also slow and unreliable. Since most UPG were in underdeveloped countries, this meant that many hours were spent traveling to meeting places where the workers discussed their plans. In today's world, communication via cell phones is possible at any given minute. Workers can quickly contact their mentors and coaches as well as their supervisors in the work. Cross-cultural church planters who once found it extremely difficult to maintain a distant relationship with their colleagues can now do so from anywhere in the world. Modern communications have changed the face of closure and connectivity.

The Former World

In most of our experience with church planting teams, communication was primitive. There were few telephones and therefore no electronic gadgets like there are today. From the outset, the focus group and national evangelists went into the field to find open people, evangelize them, and form cell groups. They took the lead in church planting. But they did not have the self-confidence to negotiate relationships with churches, develop infrastructure, struggle with leadership training, and all the other tasks of cross-cultural church planting. It was in these areas that coaches and mentors were necessary partners. Some of these were national workers and some were expatriate church planters.

Closure embedded at entry

In the model we have been describing in this manual, closure was anticipated from the very beginning of the work. If the cross-cultural church planter was an expatriate or a national who did not intend to stay in the focus group ministry, his or her boundaries were clarified from the beginning of the work. Considerable effort was made to remove any doubt in the minds of the evangelists and pastors that the work was theirs from the beginning. Slowly they assumed leadership roles. This took time because they recognized their need for a coach or mentor. We functioned in those roles with no intention of establishing a permanent leadership role. When the government threatened to end our visa permit, colleagues suggested we apply for citizenship. Our main argument against that was the perception that we would then become permanent leaders in church planting. If we were citizens, why would we not control church planting teams rather than train others to lead? Why would we turn over control to those with less experience? Our exit strategy was clear from the outset. But our ongoing connection, if any, was not clear at that time.

Church planting teams must assume ownership

Learn the elements of closure early

Closure cannot occur unless the church planting team assumes ownership of the ministry. Sometimes the evangelists and pastors do not comprehend when this has happened but the experienced church planter should. Even though the teams we coached and mentored did not realize it at first, the work was always theirs. Gradually, this understanding came to be a conviction. Workers who did not take ownership tended to drift away from CC CP. Those who took ownership were recognized and promoted by the sponsoring church from one status to another. Closure should be a continuous process from the first "handoff point" that your team makes to a church-planter.

The transfer of ownership is the secret to closure. This is true in the secular world as much as it is in missions. Chapter Five highlights several salient points made by David Kyle concerning the importance of envisioning and defining a project or, in our case, the church plant (Kyle, 1990). Project managers talk about "milestones," "deliverables," and "handoff points" and we need to consider them in our church planting process. Examples of "milestones" are found in the END RESULTS listed at the end of every chapter. A "deliverable" is a time when a certain aspect of the church plant is considered complete. A "handoff point" would then be when you turn over the leadership of an aspect of your church plant to a qualified national. Eventually, your goal is to have all aspects of leadership in the hands of the focus group.

Difficulty of closure

There is not a great amount of guidance concerning closure in mission literature. Moreover, few books on church planting or cross-cultural church planting have much to say about closure. Most do not even mention it. Yet, in the past, the failure to affect closure by many denominational and other types of mission agencies has resulted in intense conflict and broken relationships with the national churches they have birthed. This unfortunate situation has resulted from the inability of the church planters for one reason or another to create closure.

Difficult to exit for many people

From a personal viewpoint, no matter how careful you are about planning an exit strategy, in real life it is not easy to execute. Most people need the help of a mentor in this situation because letting go is hard to do.

> *You must have determination to exit*

    "'Tis hard to part when friends are dear,
    Perhaps 'twill cost a sigh, a tear"
        Life - Anna Letitia (Aikin) Barbauld

Closure for you in the particular work you are doing does not mean that your life's work is over. God has other plans for you. It may be another area of cross-cultural church planting or it may be a form of "retirement," but be assured that he is not through using you. You have matured in faith and learned new skills. As you did before, ask Him to show you your new areas for service and for glorifying Him.

Traditional departure strategies

In *Passing the Baton*, Tom Steffen writes, "Doubtless the time is ripe for a new look at our inherited departure strategies. We must correct and modify them if local believers are to receive and reproduce a church planting model that responsively empowers others" (1993:14). He goes on to say that key components of a responsible phase-out include many aspects. In this final chapter, we are not going to go over these factors because Steffen describes them in his book. Buy his book! It is essential. Our purpose here is to specify some other compatible factors in an effort to expand the reader's thinking about this critical aspect of church planting.

Some writers like David Garrison have agreed that closure is a critical element in the church planting process. For example, he has listed it as one of his Ten Commandments. It is number nine- "Model, Assist, Watch, and Leave" (2007:257). He also refers to "passing the torch." Despite highlighting the need for closure, he does not give guidelines as to how to do it. Every church-planting situation is different and it is not easy to give generic advice that will fit every situation.

Envisioning the end

Since we believe that closure is the final phase in the process, we are attempting to state some important factors to consider. If you envisioned the church plant as we suggested in Appendix 4, you would be impressed that you "must have a crystal clear picture of what the organization is trying to accomplish." Did you do that? If you did, were your goals accomplished? When you have a "crystal clear picture" of the end, it is not hard to tell when you get there. People have many ways of defining a church plant. One worker in our area was satisfied to gather a small group of traditional Christians from various churches and form a little congregation with some new believers. He then baptized a man and ordained him as pastor in the same day. He felt that had accomplished his goal. Another man gathered a group of Christians with some new converts and formed a congregation as a branch of his home church in Kansas City. That accomplished his goal. A third person led an evangelistic outreach to a village area and formed a congregation that was integrated into her denomination. That fulfilled her goal. Each had a "crystal clear picture" of what they wanted to see and they knew when that was achieved.

Your goal is to achieve the handoff points

Factor in the end from the beginning

The end must be factored in at the beginning. What do you want to see? Are you a church planter who is a mentor or a manager? Are you and your cadre training the indigenous believers as leaders or as followers? Are you selecting and mentoring/coaching candidates for ordination? Sometimes the church planter is the ordained leader. That is less desirable than having the indigenous person as the ordained leader. Your training model that produces lay leaders, teachers, evangelists, and pastors must contain the "milestones," "deliverables," and "handoff points" that we need to consider from the beginning of our church planting process.

Last step in the church planting process

Closure will vary depending on the type of organization you are working under and the type of church you are planting. If you are connected to an indigenous denomination, your church plant will be developed under their authority and at maturity it will be functioning as an element of their system. You will simply move on to another task. However, if you are working with a para-church organization, there are a variety of ways it might function with indigenous leadership. Many of the para-church agencies in our UPG tried to form new denominations. Some continued as discipleship groups.

If you are planting an independent church, your leadership should be in place and functioning independently of you when you withdraw. This is usually a process that takes place over a period of time. An accountability structure is more difficult to guarantee with this type of church plant because there will not be any denominational oversight or cooperation after you leave. A similar problem can arise if your church plant is integrated into a foreign mission structure. Many national churches formed by foreign missions tend to resent ongoing control or supervision even though they are financially dependent on the mission.

Importance of the Philosophy of Ministry

Your Philosophy of Ministry is critical (see: Appendix 8). If the church plant is founded on a philosophy of ministry to which leaders are committed, continuation is likely. If there is no philosophy of ministry, your church plant is likely to experience considerable drift. Joanie Yoder recounts a fable that is pertinent. "A man was browsing in a store when he made the shocking discovery that God was behind a sales counter. So the man walked over and asked, 'What are You selling?' God replied, 'What does your heart desire?' The man said, 'I want happiness, peace of mind, and freedom from fear ... for me and the whole world.' God smiled and said, 'I don't sell fruit here. Only seeds'" (*Our Daily Bread*- Nov. 4, 2009).

What kind of seeds have you sown in your church plant? Have they resulted in the maturity of the leaders you have trained?

Check off the phases as you progress

Indicators for closure

Are the key tasks accomplished? These are the deliverables. They are the signs of maturity in your church plant. Evangelism and nurturing models are functioning and bearing fruit and congregational life is deepening spiritually. The fellowship of which John speaks in his first epistle should be flourishing. Pastors and evangelists are growing in grace and in wisdom. They are exhibiting the competencies needed for mentoring individuals and congregations and they are showing gifts for negotiating community as well as congregational problems. They may not be perfect but they are manifesting the fruits of the Spirit. They are ready!

Roger still has a list!

Some check points for closure

Besides productive pastoral care, the leadership of the congregation should be in the hands of the focus people. New leaders will be ready if your church planting team has empowered them from the very beginning of their work. You set the pattern by empowering the church-planters. The converts become the elders and the deacons who guide their congregations. Culture has a tremendous influence in this respect because many cultures are oriented to top down leadership and the pastoral role tends to dominate. In Indonesia, we have some well known "reformed" churches that are ruled by the pastor rather than the elders. While you may not have the ideal leadership system you desire, it is important that it is stable and acceptable to your focus group.

Your leadership-training program should be in place and functioning to produce the next generation of leaders. You will need people to fill the role of teachers, administrators, counselors, and other workers in the church. The recruiting process for pastors and evangelists should be in place for the ongoing multiplication of house churches. When you are planting early churches in a UPG, you need people to develop Christian education that is biblically sound and relevant to your focus group. Some of these functions may not be in place but the vision should be.

Is your church plant self-governing, self-propagating, and self-supporting? This is pretty easy to determine. If the congregation is standing alone, these functions may be simple. If there is a connection with a larger church structure, other factors will have influence. A church plant following the congregational system will differ from one in a Presbyterian structure. The point is this. Your church plant should be oriented fully into the model that suits the members. Otherwise people will experience difficulties adjusting to the way the church is operating.

At this closure point, the members should be progressing in the fruits of the Spirit. If these biblical truths are being taught, you do not have to concerned about the continuing spiritual maturity of the members. This is critical for closure. Do not leave a congregation without a firm grasp of the work of the Holy Spirit in their lives and a demonstration of that work in their daily experience.

Hand-off points

Closure is where your list of hand-off points is proven. Some of these hand-off points may be as follows. Is your congregational outreach ready to reproduce itself in forming other congregations? When faith is growing, people share with others. Some may be sharing in their family web and this could lead them to other villages or communities in cities. You may be selecting a special area for prayer and visitation witnessing. A common result would be the establishment of house churches where families are open.

Are you having an impact on society? This may be negative or positive. Some of our congregations experienced community pressure all the time. However, at times the community leaders would admit that the ministry was benefiting the local people. For example, community development projects had a positive effect.

Even though your congregation is small, they should already be considering ways to contribute to social welfare in as many areas as possible. This may include such projects as tutoring for children, medical help, or literacy programs. These programs may not be large but they indicate that the congregation is a mature group. They are giving.

Is the congregation aware of the worldwide fellowship of believers and does it have a desire for involvement in ministry among the nations? These are areas that create excitement in a congregation even though they may not be personally ready to launch out. Churches in many places have found that their horizons were expanded when they were challenged with a vision for the nations. When the youth of the church are given this vision, they may seize the opportunities the Lord opens for them to serve in a UPG both within and outside their native country.

The New World of communication

Even though you move, you can be connected

One of my colleagues has reminded me of this important point. "Closure today does not mean being disconnected. I think it would be good to discuss the impact of modern technologies on the handover of the ministry. From my experience, closure means excising yourself from the day to day operational details but still be there to counsel and give input via the internet, etc." (email-Sept.9, 2010) He can write this because of the tremendous change in communications. As an example, practically every indigenous church planter in Indonesia now uses a cell phone and has access in some way to the Internet. Many are on Facebook via their Blackberries. Communications has evolved in amazing ways in the past 15 years.

If you have followed the guidelines in this manual and established indigenous leadership in your church planting program, you can continue to contribute in various ways no matter what your distance is from the UPG. Mentoring and coaching can continue via the phone or e-mail. However, leadership-training programs will usually require the presence of the trainers. Distance education via on-line courses is still in infancy in missions.

The Facilitator Era

Tom Steffen has tried to describe some aspects of this new condition in missions in *The Facilitator Era*. In particular, he tries to develop a rationale for the short-term missionary. It is a long book because of the inclusion of a series of Case Studies. These case studies reflect both trained and untrained teams in cross-cultural settings. As you read through the book, you will be aware of how many of the recorded experiences are able to happen because of modern transportation and other communication technologies.

Steffen has a character saying this: "It seems to me that a good practical communicator – one who communicates with simplicity but not oversimplification – you have to be a good listener. That's true of both pioneers and facilitators, whether in formal, non-formal, or informal settings. Communication skills are a must if either wants to see true transformation happen" (2011:64). It is precisely because of the new era in communications that we have to learn an entirely new way to engage, mentor, and negotiate through electronic media. This will be entirely different from face to face interaction. Whatever you may call the new era, it is certain that we are in a different time than we were 20 years ago.

Some final words

Take ownership of only the process

If your work has matured, you are ready for closure. Often the church plant is ready before the church planter is. If you take ownership of the church planting result yourself, you will tend to hold on to your little kingdom. <u>When you just take ownership of the process</u>, you will be ready to let go because the congregation is now implementing the process. Remember, you are just retiring from the process. You are not closing the church plant. It will always have a potential for problems as well as for growth. You cannot control all those variables.

The model one mentors will influence church leadership for strength or weakness. If you have been a manager, it may be hard for the congregation to adjust itself to your absence because you have created dependence on yourself. They look to you for direction. However, if you have been a mentor and a coach, you have done your job. You have created independence from yourself and dependence on the Lord. They will look to the Lord for direction. It is his congregation and he will enable. They will follow their elected leaders.

> *"See how the farmer waits for the precious fruit of the earth,*
> *being patient about it, until it receives the early and the late rains."*
> James 5:7

One of the hardest things we do is "Let Go." It is easier to hang on and control than it is to let go and trust the Holy Spirit.

"And only the Master shall praise us,
and only the Master shall blame;
And no one shall work for money, and
no one shall work for fame;
But each for the joy of the working,
and each, in his separate star,
Shall draw the Thing as he sees It for
the God of Things as They Are!"
Rudyard Kipling "When Earth's Last
Picture is Painted"

It was hard ... but ... oh, dear...
I'm going to miss them so much!

EVALUATION of END RESULTS - CHECK LIST - PHASE EIGHT (See: Appendix 4 - Envisioning the CP Project)

[ ] you have completed your major tasks

[ ] these tasks have been approved by the user

[ ] your measurable points have been achieved

[ ] you can look back and recount the milestones as they occurred

[ ] hand-off points have occurred and the ministry is in the hands of the focus group

[ ] your ministry has matured so that it can be considered a "deliverable" i.e., developed

[ ] you have achieved your goal of clarity, fit, and agreement among the project's community

[ ] your cp project is tied into the local, national, & world wide fellowship of believers

[ ] the UPG church (congregation and/or denomination) no longer needs the guidance of your CP Team

[ ] The Holy Spirit is leading you to another assignment

Tips: 1. **Secret to Closure: Mentor an independence model rather than one of dependence.**

2. **Every church should have at least <u>one</u> ordained minister for 3 congregations.**

3. **The leadership of each congregation should be congregational members from the focus group even though some of the pastors, evangelists, and lay leaders may not be from that focus group.**

4. **They are probably ready before you think they are. Trust the Holy Spirit to lead. This is His work.**

FINAL WORDS

Politics, illness, family needs or other factors may force you to closure before the church is ready. The work is far from over when you leave.

Remember, church planting is the work of the Holy Spirit. If you have mentored an integrated, biblical model with servanthood, independence, whole person, and communal characteristics, you can leave feeling you have done your best. You began with prayer; you end with prayer. Turn it over to God!

FINIS!

REFERENCES CITED

Appasamy, A.J. (1966). *Tamil Christian Poet: The Life and Writings of H.A. Krishna Pillai*. London: Lutterworth Press.

Benih Yang Tumbuh 7 : Gereja Kristen Jawi Wetan (1976). Malang: Gereja Kristen Jawi Wetan.

Bentley-Taylor, David (1967). *The Weather-cock's Reward: Christian Progress in Muslim Java*. London: Overseas Missionary Fellowship (Lutterworth Press).

Berry, John (1983). "Comparative Studies of Cognitive Styles and Their Implications for Education in Plural Societies." In R. Samuda and S. Woods (Eds) *Perspectives in Immigrant and Minority Education*. New York: University Press of America.

Biehl, Bobb (1996). *Mentoring: Confidence in Finding a Mentor and Becoming One*. Nashville: Broadman and Holman Publishers.

Blake, R.R., Mouton, J.S. and Williams, M.S. (1982). *The Academic Administrator Grid*. San Francisco: Jossey-Bass Publishers.

Brewster, E. Thomas & Elizabeth S. Brewster (1982). *Bonding and the Missionary Task: Establishing a Sense of Belonging*. Lingua House Press.

Brewster, E. Thomas & Elizabeth S. Brewster (1976). *Language Acquisition Made Practical: Field Methods for Language Learners*. Lingua House Press.

Chambers, Oswald (1975). *So Send I You*. Fort Washington, PA: Christian Literature Crusade. p.40.

Cohn, Elchanan and Richard A. Rossmiller (1987). "Research on Effective schools: Implications for Less Developed Countries." *Comparative Education Review*. August, 1987:377-399.

Condon, John C. & Fathi Yousef (1985). *An Introduction to Intercultural Communication*. New York: Macmillan Publishing Company.

Diaso, David A. (2010). "Preventing Discouragement and Keeping Church Planters Productive on the Field." *EMQ* January, Vol. 46 No.1, pp.82-89.

Dixon, Roger L. (1980). Interview with Kardi bin Karta- May 1, 1980. Dixon, Roger L. (2002). "The Major Model of Muslim Ministry." *Missiology: An International Review, Volume XXX, Number 4, October 2002*, pp. 443-454.

Dixon, Roger L. et.al. (2009a). Interview with I.W. Mastra (Feb.2), Christian Protestant Church in Bali.

Dixon, Roger L. et.al. (2009b). Interview with dr. Debora Murthey (Feb. 2).

Dissanayake, Wimal (Ed.) (1988). *Communication Theory: The Asian Perspective*. Singapore: The Asian Mass Communication Research and Information Centre.

Engel, James F. & H. Wilbert Norton (1975). *What's Gone Wrong with the Harvest?: A Communication Strategy for the Church and World Evangelism*. Grand Rapids: Zondervan.

Foster, George M. (1973). *Traditional Societies and Technological Change*. New York: Harper and Row.

Garrison, David (2007). *Church Planting Movements: How God is Redeeming a Lost World*. Arkadelphia: WIGTake Resources.

Hamilton, Reg (1993). *A Practical Guide to the Skills of Mentoring.* Petaling Jaya:Pelanduk Publications.

Hay, Alexander Rattray (1947). *The New Testament Order for Church and Missionary.* New Testament Missionary Union.

Hesselgrave, David J. & Edward Rommen (1989). *Contextualization: Meanings, Methods, and Models.* Grand Rapids: Baker Book House.

Hess, James (1985). *The Unexpergated Guide to Personality Theories: Everything You Ever Wanted To Know About Theories But Were Afraid to Ask.* Spearfish, SD: Mountain Plains Press.

Hiebert, Paul G. (1982). "The Flaw of the Excluded Middle." *Missiology: An International Review, Vol X/1* January: 35-47.

Hiebert, Paul G. (1976). *Cultural Anthropology.* Philadelphia: J.B. Lippincott Company.

Hunt, Robert (1996). *William Shellabear: A Biography 1862-1948.* Kuala Lumpur: University of Malaya Press.

Jeske, Christine (2010). *Into the Mud: Inspiration for Everyday Activists: True Stories of Africa.* Chicago: Moody Publishers.

Kraemer, Hendrik (1958). From Missionfield to Independent Church. The Hague: Boekencentrum.

Kolb, David A. (1983) *Experiential Learning: Experience as The Source of Learning and Development.* Upper Saddle River: Prentice Hall PTR.

Kraft, C. H. (1983). *Communication Theory for Christian Witness.* Nashville: Abingdon.

Kyle, David T. (1990). *Workshop on Managing A Project, The Success Factors.* Ontara Corporation, Human Performance Systems, USA. Unpublished Workbook.

Lencioni, Patrick (2002). *The FIVE Dysfunctions of a TEAM: A Leadership Fable.* San Francisco: Jossey-Bass.

Lewis, Jonathan & Robert Ferris (1995). "Developing an Outcomes Profile." IN Robert W. Ferris, (Ed). *Establishing Ministry Training: A Manual for Programme Developers.* Pasadena: William Carey Library. pp.23-41.

Lewis, A. Rodger (1999). *The Battle for Bali: The Story of Rodger and Leila Lewis.* Camp Hill, PA: Christian Publications.

Lingenfelter, S.G. (1985). Developing New Leadership, SIL Brazil Workshop 1985. Notes on Translation No. 116 (12-86):14-24.

Loss, Myron (1983). *Culture Shock: Dealing with Stress in Cross-Cultural Living.* Winona Lake, IN: Light and Life Press.

Mayers, Marvin K. (1987). *Christianity Confronts Culture.* Grand Rapids: Academie Books.

Minirth, Frank, Don Hawkins, Paul Meier & Richard Flournoy (1986) . *How to Beat Burn Out: Help for Men and Women.* Chicago: Moody Bible Institute.

Moreau, Scott (2006). "Contextualization That Is Comprehensive." *Missiology: An International Review. Vol. XXXIV, Number 3, July*:325-335.

Mulder, Niels (1983). *Mysticism & Everyday Life in Contemporary Java: Cultural Persistence and Change.* Singapore: Singapore University Press.

Müller-Krüger Th. (1966). *Sedjarah Geredja Di Indonesia.* Jakarta: BPK.

Müller, Roland (2006). *The Messenger The Message The Community: Three Critical Issues for the Cross-Cultural Church Planter.* CanBooks.

Murray, Andrew (1979). *Key to the Missionary Problem.* Fort Washington, PA: Christian Literature Crusade.

References Cited

Nasr, Seyyed Hossein (1988). *Ideals and Realities of Islam*. London: Unwin Hyman.

Partonadi, Sutarman S. (1988). *Sadrach's Community And Its Contextual Roots: A Nineteenth Century Javanese Expression of Christianity*. Amsterdam: Rodopi. A published doctoral dissertation from the Free University in Amsterdam.

Pirolo, Neal (1991). *Serving As Senders*. San Diego: Emmaus Road, International.

Ro, Bong Rin & Ruth Eshenaur (1991). *The Bible & Theology in Asian Contexts: An Evangelical Perspective on Asian Theology*. Seoul: Word of Life Press & Asia Theological Association.

Roembke, Lianne (2000). *Building Credible Multicultural Teams*. Pasadena: William Carey Library.

Schein, Edgar H. (1992). *Organizational Culture and Leadership*. San Francisco: Jossey-Bass Publishers.

Schreiter, Robert J. (1986). *Constructing Local Theologies*. Maryknoll: Orbis Books.

Seymour-Smith, Charlotte (1986). *Macmillan Dictionary of Anthropology*. London: The Macmillan Press Ltd.

Sinclair, Daniel (2006). *A Vision of the Possible: Pioneer Church Planting in Teams*. Waynesboro, GA: Authentic Media.

Steffen, Tom (1993). *Passing the Baton: Church Planting That Empowers*. LaHabra, CA: Center for Organizational & Ministry Development.

Steffen, Tom (2011). *The Facilitator Era: Beyond Pioneer Church Multiplication*. Eugene, OR: Wipf & Stock.

Sumartana, Th. (1993). *Mission At The Crossroads: Indigenous Churches, European Missionaries, Islamic Association and Socio-Religious Change in Java 1812-1936.* Jakarta: BPK Gunung Mulia.

Suyata (1986). "Educational Experiences Perceived by General Secondary School Students and their Cognitive Styles Among Three Indonesian Ethnic Groups in Bali and Yogyakarta: Balinese, Chinese, and Javanese." Los Angeles: University of California. Unpublished Dissertation.

Taylor, William D. (Ed.) (1997). *Too Valuable to Lose: Exploring the Causes and Cures of Missionary Attrition.* Pasadena: William Carey Library.

Travis, John (1998). "The C1 To C6 Spectrum: A Practical Tool for Defining Six Types of 'Christ-centered Communities' ('C') Found in the Muslim Context." *Evangelical Missions Quarterly,* 34, 4:407-408.

Travis, John (2000). "Messianic Muslim Followers of Isa." *International Journal of Frontier Missions, Volume 17 Number 1, 2000,* p. 53.

Turner, V.W. (1989). "Religious Specialists." In A.C. Lehmann & J.E. Myers, *Magic, Witchcraft, and Religion: An Anthropological Study of the Supernatural.* Mountain View, CA: Mayfield Publishing Company. (pp. 85-91).

Van Akkeren, Philip (1970). *Sri and Christ: A Study of the Indigenous Church in East Java.* Lutterworth Press.

Yoder, Lawrence McCulloh (1987). *The Introduction and Expression of Islam and Christianity in the Cultural Context of North Central Java.* An unpublished doctoral dissertation at Fuller Theological Seminary, Pasadena, CA.

Zamani, Asrul (2002). *The Malay Ideals.* Kuala Lumpur: Golden Books Centre.

APPENDICES

APPENDIX 1: MISSIONARIES' COMPETENCIES PROFILE: ARGENTINA

First Southern Cone Consultation of Mission Trainers
July 18-20, 1991, Córdoba, Argentina
In the following profile, training areas are listed in italics type, with competencies listed under each training area.

Church Relations
- _Is a committed member of a church
- _Maintains a good testimony
- _Knows how to subject self to church authorities
- _Knows how to inform the church on the missionary task
- _Understands the vision of the church
- _Has the support of the church to go as a missionary
- _Exercises an approved ministry in the church
- _Knows how to maintain communications with the church
- _Knows how to relate to other church bodies

Cultural Anthropology
- _Is able to analyze his own culture
- _Is conscious of his own ethno-centricity
- _Is informed on ethnic groups within the country
- _Respects other cultures
- _Knows biblical anthropology
- _Can contextualize biblical principles
- _Creates a kingdom culture
- _Has short-term missionary experience
- _Can see with anthropologist eyes
- _Can adapt to another culture

Interpersonal Relationships
- _Applies biblical principles to relationships
- _Knows how to manage interpersonal conflicts
- _Maintains good family relationships
- _Looks for relationships with others unlike self
- _Maintains a good attitude when criticized
- _Has a basic understanding of psychology
- _Knows how to listen to others and respond appropriately
- _Has experience in community-based living
- _Knows how to relate on intimate terms

Cross-Cultural Communication
- _Knows the host culture
- _Is willing to identify with host culture
- _Knows what communication is
- _Knows how to manage culture shock
- _Values all without racial prejudice
- _Is willing to incarnate self
- _Confronts communications problems
- _Interprets verbal and nonverbal messages
- _Distinguishes biblical principles and customs

- _Can detect cross-cultural bridges for evangelism

Linguistic Orientation
- _Is disciplined and persistent
- _Knows language acquisition techniques
- _Is willing to learn
- _Is humble and uninhibited
- _Can laugh at own errors
- _Knows the rules of phonetics
- _Can recognize idiomatic gestures and terms
- _Has experience with language learning

Biblical Knowledge
- _Is convinced that the Bible is the Word of God
- _Knows and loves the Bible
- _Knows how to conduct exegesis and interpretation
- _Knows geography, customs, history, canon, etc.
- _Understands that the Bible contains the solution to human problems
- _Knows how to teach the Bible using various methods
- _Applies biblical message to own daily life
- _Knows the biblical basis of mission
- _Has the habit of memorizing scriptures
- _Knows inductive Bible study methods

Appendix 1: Missionaries' Competencies Profile: Argentina

Theological Knowledge
- _Knows God, his person, and his work
- _Understands God's mission
- _Knows the doctrine and plan of salvation
- _Knows the function and mission of the church
- _Knows the concept and scope of the kingdom
- _Knows church growth principles
- _Knows systematic theology
- _Knows contemporary theological currents
- _Has knowledge of different religions
- _Knows how to defend the authenticity of the Bible

Leadership
- _Is sensitive to the voice of God
- _Knows how to work with a team
- _Knows how to delegate responsibility
- _Plans and establishes objectives
- _Encourages, motivates, and transmits vision
- _Knows own limitations
- _Has experience as a leader
- _Knows how to detect and use others' gifting
- _Serves with renouncement
- _Shows flexibility

Discipleship
- _Has been discipled
- _Shows sensitivity to the newly converted person
- _Is a model disciple and is worthy of being imitated
- _Transmits life as well as knowledge
- _Has knowledge of pastoral counseling and inner healing
- _Shows love for own disciples
- _Knows strategies and methods for discipleship
- _Is a mentor
- _Forms disciples who in turn disciple others

Evangelism
- _Evidences a strong spiritual life
- _Knows the message
- _Demonstrates a passion for souls
- _Knows how to communicate adequately
- _Practices personal evangelism
- _Knows how to prepare evangelistic sermons
- _Knows methods and techniques of evangelism
- _Knows how to identify with the person with whom sharing
- _Knows how to respond to problems and objections

Emotional Health
- _Has been approved for the field emotionally and psychologically
- _Has resolved significant emotional problems
- _Is open to receiving counsel for emotional health
- _Demonstrates an adequate self-image
- _Maintains emotional equilibrium
- _Is constant in motivation towards what he begins
- _Knows how to manage failure
- _Is approved physically to live on the field
- _Practices a hobby, pastime, or sport
- _Takes weekly and annual breaks

Spiritual Life
- _Is building an intimate relationship with God
- _Knows the power of prayer and fasting
- _Knows the principles of spiritual warfare
- _Studies the Bible systematically
- _Demonstrates the fruit of the Spirit
- _Uses his spiritual gifts
- _Shows an attitude of service
- _Demonstrates moral integrity

Christian Ethics
- _Knows biblical ethical principles
- _Analyses cultural norms in terms of biblical principles
- _Shows courage in conducting himself according to his values
- _Can facilitate the adoption of an indigenous biblical ethic
- _Is honest, just, and upright
- _Respects established laws and regulations
- _Knows the difference between ethics and doctrine

Practical Abilities
- _Knows how to take advantage of the situation
- _Knows how to "grow, raise, and repair"
- _Knows how to apply community help
- _Has working skills
- _Has knowledge of crafts and recreation
- _Knows how to perform household duties
- _Knows how to operate electronic equipment
- _Has knowledge of first aid medicine and hygiene
- _Has knowledge of preventive medicine
- _Has musical knowledge

[1] The original chart was published September 1991 in *Training for Cross-Cultural Ministry* 91(2):4-5 and April 1993 in *International Journal of Frontier Missions* 10(2):84.

APPENDIX 2 - NURTURING THE CENTRAL CORE

For those who are attempting to penetrate an unreached people group, the most important aspect is nurturing the central core. If we can define the core as the basic church planting team comprised of a number of families, the central core would be the nuclear CP family. This central core is formed by the husband (father), wife (mother), and any children they may have. The ministry stands or falls on the integrity of the central core.

Because an unreached people represents an alien environment, all spiritual thrust to this culture depends on the unity and stability of the key players. Although this seems so basic as to need no reiteration, in fact, many individuals and organizations involved in pioneer work tend to emphasize bureaucracy with its concomitant aspects more than they do the core. The further a person's focus moves away from the nuclear family and locks onto ministry goals, the more likely he or she is to disregard the absolute necessity of maintaining and nurturing the central core.

This divergence of focus can begin almost immediately with language study and intensify as real or imagined demands are made to develop strategy and/or implement programs. The emotional, mental, and physical needs of many people are such that they experience tremendous stress factors. These include expectations which have been inculcated by one's religious and secular culture and internalized by the individual. According to some experts, the need for self-worth is basic for every person. Men tend to get self worth through feeling significant and women find it because of a feeling of security, of caring for others and of being cared for.

Stress causes the individual to deviate from the basic responsibility of nurturing the family by concentrating on some hypothetical goal that may seem of utmost importance. In this way, one forgets that nothing is more critical than the central core. For example, the need for significance may be so great for some men that they become more concerned about their work than their families. The wife's need for security may be neglected and the breakdown of the central core begins. If this deterioration is allowed to continue, eventually the wife is no longer able to operate in an alien environment. This can also occur in reverse if the wife is diverted from her role as the key nurturer of the husband. However, observation indicates that the man is usually the one who is most often confused about the need for nurturing the central core.

The important point to remember is that few people deliberately do this. Culture shock and varying stresses create the situations in which people do not know what they are doing. Thus, it is important for everyone to listen to what their spouses and friends are telling them. When the situation is intolerable for one of the central core, the time for reassessment has come. Nurturing this core must take precedent.

There is a possibility that the cp family will not be able for various reasons to overcome the disparity within its unit. At such a time, the CP Team must act to reorient the cp family back to the central core. Experience shows us that this is a delicate and stressful process, that is frequently resented by one or more members of the cp family. However, when the central core is unable to sustain its unity, the CP Team must act to save them.

APPENDIX 3 - GUIDELINES FOR TENTMAKERS

PRELIMINARY

1. Pray and seek the Lord's will for a pilgrimage among your chosen unreached people group.
2. Seek an opening to live and work in your focus area, e.g., some basic options are:
   a. as a missionary
   b. as a student
   c. as a teacher
   d. as a company employee

STAGE ONE

Time Frame: 2 to 3 years, personal preparation and orientation

Develop a game plan -- keep your plans to yourself!

1. First priority:

   a. learn the national language and/or local language
   b. make friends

2. Simultaneously: learn culture - [possibly 3 cultures]

   1) national, 2) your unreached people group, & 3) church culture

3. Develop political awareness: the meaning and ramifications of nationalism in your country will affect your ministry broadly.

4. Your focus group language remains a fixed priority though its study may be delayed.

5. Develop a firm local church relationship.

6. You need to be involved in church ministry as much as possible both to learn and to be accepted as a spiritual leader.

7. Be in prayer and be alert as to whether the Lord is leading you to national co-workers.

STAGE TWO

Time Frame: third year

Continue to develop your game plan by evaluating it in terms of the contextual lessons you are learning. Adjust your game plan only when you have serious reasons for doing so. Keep your game plan to yourself unless you know you can trust the one with whom you share it!

1. Continue praying and seeking God's will for an in-depth ministry among your focus group (another ministry may be easier and you may get sidetracked to a different ethnic group).

2. Determine the approach, location, and lifestyle needed to reach your focus group.

3. Have a firm local church relationship with which you can associate your ministry.

4. By now you should have some definite national workers to minister with.

5. Continue to develop your game plan - keep it to yourself unless your national co- workers are mature and ready. You will have to envision it with them when they are ready.

STAGE THREE

Time Frame: unspecified

You should be sharing your game plan with your national co-workers and it should evolve into a unified game plan which produces a contextual cp model.

1. Constant forward movement toward goal, re-evaluations, learning, refining approach, etc.

2. All development should be slowly but continually integrated into local church context so that it blooms in place. (Ministry cannot be fully developed, then transferred into a local church without extreme stress on structure & process).

3. The game plan should be unified between national and expat. Do not be constantly changing your unified game plan. Begin to impart your long range vision with your ministry team. Conceptual thinking is difficult for many people.

   This should take you to the time of your first home leave and beyond. If you are with a secular company that allows you home leave every year, you can better use that time in intensive ministry.

APPENDIX 4 - ENVISIONING
THE CP PROJECT

A summary of guidelines, views, and statements from
Kyle, David T. (1990).
Workshop on Managing A Project, The Success Factors,
as they would apply to a church planting project

***THE FIRST STEP IN PLANNING IS THE ORGANIZATION
OF THE PROJECT***

A. ENVISIONING THE ORGANIZATION OF THE PROJECT means defining the project in detail.
  1. "go slow to go fast"
  2. "the seeds of any project's success or failure are found at its very beginning"
  3. a number of sub areas of the project are possibly preferable to one large project
  4. "we must have a crystal clear picture of what the project is trying to accomplish"
  5. there are many effective ways to develop the project
  6. "cost, features, schedule- if one varies, the other two must change"

B. THE EXPAT TEAM MUST ENVISION THE CP PROJECT IN DETAIL
in order to achieve a goal (These points will also apply later to a combined expat/national ministry team)
  1. **Purpose of this period:**
     a. To <u>appraise</u> the environment in which the ministry is to be developed

1) Have you satisfactorily set up housekeeping, got your family settled, got involved in your secular job, & begun language study?

2) Are you understanding the interrelationships among the project community [ministry leaders, people who will be benefited, & the members] that might affect the project?

3) Are you making planned efforts to get every project member directed toward a common objective?

b. To <u>define</u> the critical aspects before implementation

1) Have you identified the job tasks necessary to complete the project and to "fit" those tasks with the project teams' skills and interests?

2) Have you clearly defined your purpose?

3) Have you appraised the environment in which the project is to be developed?

4) Have you defined the magnitude of effort before implementation?

c. "To <u>develop</u> an organization strategy, i.e. tasks which need to be done"

1) Have you developed a team strategy, i.e., a coherent set of tasks? What are they?

2) The following sections on End Results and Critical Issues will help develop an initial set of tasks. This will likely be adjusted as the cp progresses.

2. **Preliminary Assignment Negotiation:**

a. Do you know the personal and professional objectives as well as the experiences and skills of your project team & community so as to structure the project to fit?

b. "Are you trying to surface people's personal goals and include these in your negotiations with them?"

c. Are you making sure commitments are firm and sign-ups are made explicit?

d. Are you getting out and making alliances with every one of the people who will impact your project?

e. Before you see and plan the project with your team, are you making sure "you have the visible, active support of key management persons?"

f. When activating the team, are you remembering to describe in detail the "big picture" (project vision) or are you focusing solely or largely on project goals? [*vision motivates; goals and objectives give direction*]

g. Are you encouraging creativity by avoiding "idea killers" or any other activity that inhibits the entrepreneurship or initiatives of team members?

h. Do you encourage enthusiasm, act as a cheerleader, & expedite initiatives? [Back the team 110%; let them know you will do whatever you can to make them successful]

3. **Defining End Results:**

a. Have you identified the end results you desire?

b. What progress is the team making in language proficiency?

c. How has the project team understood the need for effective communication & contextual leadership style? What have you done to achieve it?

d. Does the project leader (in this case, the ministry team) know how to create a clear vision of what the intended project must accomplish? Has this been written down?

e. Does the project leader know how to design and manage a strategy to accomplish the vision?

f. Have the characteristics of both the project and the environment been identified and evaluated so that there is a clear picture of the factors that will have an impact on the project?

g. In what ways has the project team learned how to get cooperation and involvement from the members of the project community & their other ministry leaders (such as pastors, etc.)?

h. How would you rate your success in the process of energizing team members (getting the right people involved in the right jobs) at the beginning of your project?

i. Has the team done a good job of clearly defining each member's role and responsibility? Have you begun integrating nationals?

j. To what degree has the team learned how to foster team and individual commitment to achieve peak and sustainable performance?

4. **Dealing with Critical Issues:**

a. Have you delineated the critical issues?

b. In what ways does the project meet the specific needs of the ministry, i.e. churches, para-churches, etc.?

c. Have you defined the project while involving the critical members of the project community? If not, why not?

d. Is the ministry team capable of creating and communicating a personal and organizational vision to which it is wholeheartedly committed?

e. Has the team worked out together the shared values, such as philosophy of ministry & non-negotiables, that go beyond project goals? If not, why not?

[*These "determine, to a significant degree, team alignment and project commitment."*]

f. Have you incorporated symbols, such as mutual prayer & spiritual pilgrimage, as a means of creating energy and commitment among team members?

g. Have you made extensive personnel changes on the project team(s)?

[*This is correlated with project atrophy*]

h. Would you consider that your project team(s) are experienced?

[*"The more experienced the project team, the greater the odds of success"*]

i. Do you consider every team member is important in the entire project, and are you recognizing individuals as well as the team for their contributions to the project?

j. Does each functional group on the team see every other functional group as equal participants in the vision and implementation of the project or do they perceive each other as competitive or adversarial?k. From the very beginning, have you been developing an accountability structure which will apply to each member of the project?

l. Has the job been defined on paper (goals, scope, objectives, tasks)?

m. Has the ministry team identified key milestones in the detailed project plan?

n. Is the criteria for project success measurable and objective?

o. Have validation and verification procedures been established that assure planning is complete and accurate and will produce what the users, i.e., churches and para-churches want?

p. Is there a process of constantly defining and redefining the critical success factors facing the project?

q. Does the project have the visible active support as well as a plan to inform and receive feedback from seniors during the operation of the project?

r. As the initiator of this cp vision, is your expat team perceived by project personnel as emphasizing control as an influence method, or as emphasizing call, the challenge of ministry, and the purpose of God for the team member? What makes you think this perception is what it is?

The right approach flows from what the project does rather than from what the organization is theoretically ("form follows function")

5. **The Four Areas that give Energy**
The first three are built around the fourth area which is commitment.
a. "Sympathy"   - concern for another's situation
b. "Compliance" - yielding to the will of another
c. "Cooperation" - working toward a common purpose
d. "Commitment" - being bound emotionally or intellectually to an idea or course of action

C. EVALUATION LIST FOR COMMITMENT
1. "Have you identified all the relevant relationships" within your project's community? (e.g., the expat & national teams as well as the miscellaneous cultural groups which will impact your project?)
2. "Where will your leadership challenges be?" Have you assessed who among these people may resist cooperating with you, why they resist, and how strongly?
3. "Have you developed wherever possible a good relationship with these people?"
4. "Are you actively communicating, educating or negotiating with these people to reduce or overcome their resistance?"
5. As you are meeting with people to obtain commitment, are you communicating the vision of the project and not just miscellaneous jobs you want them to do?
6. In your project community, are you understanding when you need to obtain compliance or cooperation or commitment?
7. Are you monitoring your project's ebbs and flows to maintain continuity? Are you checking to make sure the project community is still "signed up" and re- establishing commitments where necessary?

D. COMMUNICATION

"Effective communication means obtaining... CLARITY

FIT

AGREEMENT

make the implicit, explicit"

DEFINING THE ORGANIZATION OF THE PROJECT

A. TO DEFINE THE PROJECT means to obtain clarity, fit, and agreement of the following six elements

"1. vision

2. critical success factors

3. scope

4. phases

5. milestones

6. key tasks"

These six areas function as a focusing tool, not a blueprint.

1. Vision Statement

a. "What is the project going to produce? expressed as an END RESULT"

b. Why are we creating this project?

How well will it serve the customer? <u>express in terms of MINISTRY</u>

c. "How will you know if your project succeeds?

<u>express as OBSERVABLE and MEASURABLE CRITERIA</u>"

"Write your vision statement in a style that activates, that is an attention-getter, that distinguishes your project from just one more job to be done A VISION STATEMENT IS A FOCUSING TOOL, NOT A BLUEPRINT"

2. Critical Success Factors

a. Where to look

1) ministries of churches, para-churches, missions, evangelism programs, etc.

2) people

3) technical help

4) "the whole environment that surrounds the context of the project"

314

b. "Carefully look at
   1) size
   2) structure
   3) complexity"
c. "What to do about critical success issues
   1) resolve them now
   2) factor them into your plan
   3) change the vision"

3. Scope

("The scope of the project is a bundle of five negotiated constraints that must pass the 3rd party test"; i.e., will stand under the scrutiny of an unrelated 3rd party who challenges them)
   a. Quantity - How do you describe the overall breadth and depth of this project?
   b. Resources - How much will this project cost in resources of people & money and how many resources do you have?
   c. Product or service- What service/product are you capable of delivering?
   d. Delivery date - What is your delivery date?
   e. Quality - To what extent will your service/product match the quality you hope for?

   "The first rule of project management is change one of the five constraints and the other four must also change"

4. Phases

   a. Assessment - Have you defined, analyzed, identified (from the user's point of view) the features and functions to be included?
   b. Planning - Have you evaluated, prepared, defined what must be done to create the project?
   c. Building - Have you established or developed a prototype that works (or are following something similar already done)?
   d. Testing - Have you tested the feature functions under realistic conditions with user participation?
   e. Using - Have you set in motion or produced some part of the service of the project?

f. Evaluating - Are you examining & appraising so as to validate the product/service in the eyes of the user?

5. Milestones   How many have you defined? How many have you passed? [a milestone can be either "official" or "unofficial"]

a. Name a major task of the project which requires approval of the user.

b. Give one "significant measurable point within a phase."

c. What is one of your hand-off points (i.e., a part of the ministry that can be given over to a national worker)?

d. What is one of your deliverables (i.e., a ministry that is sufficiently mature and proven so it can be considered "developed")?

6. Key Tasks (Define the tasks in detail)

a. Have you obtained extensive input from marketing and production?

b. Have you made explicit milestones? What are they?

c. Have you made an effort to "surface critical issues before developing a detailed plan?"

d. Did you have a simple diagram or model (visual) of the final end result as early as possible? Do you have one now?

e. Have you written on paper a description of how the project is tied to the overall cp strategy?

f. Have you been thinking "strategically, not only tactically" so that everyone involved is able to understand what the end goal is?

* Remember that the ultimate criteria for your road map are" clarity, fit, and agreement among the project's community"

B. GUIDELINES TO ENERGIZING THE PROJECT:

1. "Projects don't fail, people do.

2. No one is apathetic except in the pursuit of someone else's goals.

3. When you really get to know the team, they show you how to inspire them.

4. 'Golden Rule' - Get the person who will do the work to plan the work.

5. Find out the team's strengths and play on them."

6. Flexibility is one of a team's strengths- you can only be flexible if you trust each other.

7. Things seem to go a lot better when you treat people on the project like they were truly called of God instead of just doing a church job.

APPENDIX 5 - A MODEL OF LEADERSHIP FOR THE SUNDANESE

INTRODUCTION

Using a political activity model (Lingenfelter, 1985), this paper investigates leadership patterns among the Sundanese. As one of the peoples of Java, the Sundanese show many characteristics similar to those of the Javanese. Thus, material on concepts of spiritual power and social relationships apply significantly to both groups.

Research on the model is recorded largely in tables. The model is applied to the case histories of four Sundanese Christian leaders in order to isolate and analyze leadership characteristics and evaluate the effectiveness of these leaders in the Sundanese community. The broader research question concerns the way these leadership patterns may be applied to the training of future leaders among the Sundanese Christians. The final section of the paper will suggest how the research findings apply to leadership training.

THE SUNDANESE COMMUNITY

The Sundanese are the second largest ethnic group in Indonesia after the Javanese. Their number is now about 30 million and nearly all of these live in the western third of the island of Java. Over a period of many centuries the Sundanese have been influenced by the great Javanese empires, the Muslim religion and the Dutch colonial government. Table 1 provides some major characteristics related to leadership.

TABLE 1 - SUNDANESE COMMUNITY

1) The **widest sphere** in which Sundanese are found is in West Java. There are very few elsewhere.

2) There are 4 major **groups** of Sundanese located in 4 regions. The Sundanese language differs in each of the areas of Priangan, Banten, Bogor, and Cirebon. There are some differences among the experts as to how the people should be divided socially. Koentjaraningrat (1967, p.245) divides them into what he calls "little people" and the *priyayi* (nobility). Geertz proposes that there are divisions along religious lines. *Abangan* are the nominal Muslims, *santri*, the serious Muslims and *priyayi*, the nobility (1960, p.126-127). Some other kinds of divisions used by sociologists or anthropologists can be listed as: a. urban/rural, b. educated/uneducated, and c. poor/average.

3) When **group relations** are defined, consanguineal is stronger than affinal. This leads to frequent divorce. Descent is counted bilaterally and the extended family takes precedence over the nuclear family. Sundanese are peasant producers who have only a small group of administrators. They stress negotiation/mediation to resolve differences and tend to a holistic orientation with community officials, military, and police all involved in the process.

4) The **action arenas** are the houses of the village heads- (*Lurah*), the village meeting house (*balai desa*), the mosque, the schools in both rural and urban areas and, in the cities, the offices of officials.

TABLE 2 -REGIME- The Structure Underlying Government

At this time, the Sundanese administrative system is similar to that used throughout Java and indeed throughout Indonesia. The national government has implemented various changes since independence in 1945 that duplicates the top-down control exercised by the Dutch and also by the former indigenous empires which flourished on Java. Table 2 illustrates the characteristics of regime among the Sundanese.

1) **Status hierarchy** is represented by the following Administrative Units and Leaders. The province, led by a governor, has 20 districts

(regencies). Each regency has a head (*bupati*). Under the district are several kinds of sub-districts including the *kecamatan* with the *camat* as head and the village that is directed by a *lurah*. Miscellaneous village officials are supervised by the *lurah*. The most important are the irrigation supervisor, the secretary, the ward head (R.W.), and the sub-ward head (R.T.).

2) **Authority** functions top to bottom with the governor appointed by the nation's president. The governor then appoints or supervises the election of the heads of regencies (*bupati*), the sub districts (*camat*) and the villages (*lurah*). All of these key officials are usually military men. While the ward and sub-ward heads are elected by the people, they are subject to the *camat*. In theory, the village assembly delegates authority to the *lurah* but in reality, the *lurah* has more spiritual power because he is part of the top down authority. The *lurah* has a general security unit (*hansip*) and, in addition, he can call on help from area police and military who also play a role in area politics and security.

3) **Mutual constraints** among the Sundanese are illustrated by the way appointed officials balance the police and military. The village assembly balances the village head. This process occurs through a consensus model assembly (*musyawarah*). In this process, general agreement, unanimous decision and integration of opposing views are emphasized. Palmer (1987, p.191) says the *musyawarah* has been functioning sporadically for some decades. There are also civil courts but they are not effective. Usually, resolution is achieved by appeal up a chain of authority.

4) **Value priorities** include matters such as rights of family (theoretical equality). These rights are seen as age over youth, male over female, rich over poor, and local over outsider. The priority of the local person is epitomized by *gotong royong* (community spirit) which involves cooperation, non-confrontative attitudes and an effort to avoid emotional conflict.

5) **Standards of legality** are illustrated by the centrality of spiritual power (see: Table 3), by government approval, the regard of customary rights and traditions, and by service to the people.

6) **Decision** is made theoretically through consensus (*musyawarah*). In the village, it supposed to be made by council, and in the city by the *lurah*. In fact, often policies are made and enforced by the central government.

7) **Communication** is conducted primarily through the use of mediation up and down hierarchy, and through *musyawarah* and personal relations.

SUNDANESE LEADERSHIP

Leadership among the Sundanese is perceived and functions in ways quite different from western views of leadership. Perhaps the most arresting difference is seen in the followers' concern for who the leader is rather than for what he can do (Jackson, 1978, p.125). While the Sundanese have many characteristics they enjoy seeing in their leaders, it most important that the leader be someone who has *sakti* (spiritual power). The Sundanese concept of spiritual power is radically different from that of the western mind. These two concepts are compared in Table 3. Adams (1975, pp. 9,10,31) represents the Western view while the Javanese/Sundanese concept is illustrated by Anderson (1972, pp.7-8).

TABLE 3 - CONCEPTS OF POWER

1) The **existence of power** to the Western mind is abstract and derives from controlling another's interest. It is a socio-psychological phenomenon. However, it is concrete to the Sundanese. Power exists. It has properties.

2) The **sources** of power are heterogeneous in western thought. They arise out of various sources of control that can be classified in such areas as environment, energy, and social relations. Jackson agrees with Adams in this (1978, p.345). The Sundanese, on the other hand, believe the sources of power cannot be classified or analyzed.

3) The Western view sees the **limits** of power as changing quantitatively according to the amount and variety of control exercised. This is opposed by the Sundanese concept of limits which sees power as constant in quantity although its distribution in the universe may vary.

4) **Legitimacy**, in the Western concept, is morally ambiguous. It depends on the agreement of society as to correct and proper acquirement and use. Swartz, et al (1966) gives an argument similar to that of Adams.

Quite contrary to this view, the Sundanese believe that power is. It pre-exists a basis of moral judgment on how it is acquired. There may be some question as to how it is used. (See also Samson, 1978, pp.200-201).

AN EXAMPLE OF SPIRITUAL POWER (*SAKTI*)

One of the army officers who was involved in the attack on the presidential palace in 1957 told how he was captured and brought to President Soekarno. Since the purpose of the attack was to assassinate Soekarno, this army captain did not hope for any mercy. However, he was shocked and awed by the jauntiness of the president in interrogating him as to the purpose and execution of their plan as though they were young boys doing a prank. Laughingly, Soekarno said that there was no chance of their assassination attempt succeeding, because he could not be killed. He was not even concerned with their attempt but since they had bombed the palace and injured other people, he would have to imprison the perpetrators for a few years so they would have time to think over their foolishness (Dixon, 1972).

Laksono emphasizes that legitimacy depends not on wealth or the ability to use force but on "qualities of spiritual greatness" (1986, p.xiii). *Sakti* or spiritual power forms the heart of what the Sundanese look for in a leader. As Table 4 shows, there are other traits that are important but *sakti* dominates.

TABLE 4   -   SUNDANESE LEADERS

1) Sundanese leaders are generally **recruited** through educational facilities, by family ties and because friends promote their choices.

2) The **selection process** is conducted through the recognition of mystical authority or divine anointing (*sakti*). Research by Anderson (1972) and Laksono (1986, p. xiii) support this understanding. The backing of a patron is a must for succession or as a new leader.

3) As indicated above, the major **criteria** for leadership is mystical spiritual power (see: Table 3). A leader replaces the old center of spiritual power with a new one. Spiritual power, in this sense, means control over blessing. This spiritual power creates awe (*segan*) of the leader. Thus

the leader manifests respect (*hormat*) among his followers as well as social unity/harmony (*rukun*).

In addition to this, the leader must display gifts and abilities along with interpersonal skills. In the city, education is particularly important. Throughout the leadership hierarchy being married and having children is a crucial criteria. Also, the leader should be *halus*, i.e., he respects culture and rules as well as exhibiting proper behavior. He has principles, is honest, consistent and experienced.

4) Sundanese leaders establish **esteem** by satisfying the demands of followers. This results in *hormat* (respect). Esteem is gained through success in a program or prosperity of some kind for the followers. This relates to the functioning of the leader as a patron for his followers. All this results from spiritual power. Persuasion, which is another form of spiritual power, is also important in gaining esteem (Jackson, 1978, p.345). Criticism, which results in the loss of esteem, is given when the leader evidences *pamrih* (personal aggrandizement or self indulgence), selfishness, uncultured behavior, or any actions not considered *halus*.

5) **Organization** is characterized by government hierarchy with operating units on federal, provincial, district, sub-district, village, and *kampung* (ward, sub ward) levels.

6) **Factions** affecting leadership are mainly political. Examples are *Golkar* (called a functional group but in essence a national political party run by the government) and PPP (the Islamic political party).

CASE HISTORY 1 - A VILLAGE LEADER- *Naria*

In 1964, a recently converted Sundanese traveling salesman shared the gospel with an acquaintance in Citepus. After six months this man, Naria, accepted the Lord. At the time of his conversion, Naria was a 40-year-old rice farmer. However, he had previously been the village head in the area of Citepus. Although he did not originate from that area, his wife did and in accordance with Sundanese custom Naria had moved to the house of his wife's parents. By way of this social custom, Naria became a member of the Citepus community.

Naria had the reputation of being a severe man. It was thought that sometime in the past he had killed a man over a disagreement and people were in awe of him ("reluctant" as the Sundanese use the term). In addition, with many others, Naria had supported the Communist reform movement in his area. After the abortive Communist coup in 1965, he fell into some disrepute in the community.

The traveling salesman who evangelized Naria had known him for some years previously. He witnessed to him over a period of several months. On one of his trips to Naria's area, he gave him a Bible. Later, when Naria saw the salesman again, he tried to give the Bible back saying it was like the words of the devil. The salesman asked him how much land he owned, how many houses he owned and how much money he controlled. When Naria answered each of these questions by saying he was poor, the salesman told him to read the Bible one more time.

On the salesman's next trip to the area, Naria accepted the Lord. Part of the reason, according to the salesman was Naria's desire for material blessing. Naria, himself, would not say this as it would be indicative of *pamrih* (selfish aggrandizement) and he credited his conversion to the desire for forgiveness of his past sins. Both reasons seem to have played a part.

Immediately, Naria began to share his new found faith with others. At first the people did not respond but he kept witnessing with the help of his salesman friend. Naria was able to reach some people in adjoining villages and, in 1968, fifteen people were baptized. Like Naria, they were baptized outside the village by a pastor from the city and they returned to their villages to win others. In 1969, thirty-four more were added, including Naria's wife. An additional fifteen were baptized in 1970. In three years, the number of baptized Christians had gone from one to sixty-five.

1970 was also the year some local reaction set in towards the ministry in the village. The city church responsible for the work made some serious errors in their approach and evangelism was curtailed. Before these problems could be overcome, Naria died in 1972. The salesman who first brought the gospel became inactive due to a hernia operation and the work ceased to expand.

After his conversion and baptism, Naria became a leader of a movement to Christ. Some of the reasons that he could influence people to consider Christ as Savior were probably characteristic of his previous leadership experience. One follower reports that people were "reluctant" (*segan*) or in awe of him because of his reputation for violence. In addition, when he became a Christian, he stopped farming yet continued to have an income. People were impressed that he could live without working. Of course, the reason was because city Christians were giving him monthly gifts.

A follower whom Naria made his assistant said the people looked to Naria as a source of blessing or as a possible patron for them if they became Christians. This relates to the importance in the minds of the people for a leader to be able to confer material as well as spiritual blessing to his followers. Naria gained spiritual power because he controlled access to material elements in the city which were desired by many in his village. But he also manifested spiritual power simply in the ability to attract followers to a new world view.

Besides this, Naria's respect for traditional village rules (*hormat* and *rukun*- respect and harmony) enabled him to work within the village system in such a way people were allowed to be baptized. After he died, there was no one to take his place and the village leaders had considerable success in almost erasing the Christian presence.

CASE HISTORY 2 - *Rahmat* (not his real name)

Rahmat, at 35 years old, was the treasurer of both his local church (which was not Sundanese), and the national publishing house of his denomination. This gave him the opportunity to juggle books so he could "borrow" the money. When his debts mounted so that he could not repay the books, he confessed his faults to the church. Because of this open confession, Rahmat gained prestige as a person who admitted his faults and humbled himself.

Two years later when he began to evangelize among the Sundanese, he was quickly recognized by his denomination because he began by faith and did not ask for a salary. Non-Sundanese Christians also acknowledged him as a viable potential leader for the difficult Sundanese ministry and he got much material support. The financial part of this support Rahmat used to fund his evangelistic travels and the development of a Sundanese ministry in his denomination. Rahmat had grown up in a Muslim family and understood how to approach Muslims with the gospel. Over a period of 5 years, Rahmat led about 200 people to the Lord and a good number of them were baptized in his church. On the weekends, many of these would come to Rahmat's house in the city for spiritual teaching and worship. With his wife, he also supplied food and other material benefits such as clothing.

At the end of five years in evangelism, Rahmat fell into adultery and dropped out of the ministry. Because he did not live in the village or have strong ties in any village, Rahmat was never able to be accepted as a leader in the villages. He was a leader only in his city home and church. In addition, he was not able to train any of his converts to be leaders in their villages and none of the ministries he started continued beyond his own activity. When he dropped out, all his groups dissipated. However, many of his converts moved into other churches and continued active.

CASE HISTORY 3 - *Masri*

Masri was converted at 18 after growing up in the home of his Christian grandparents in a Sundanese village. His own parents were Muslim. After a few years helping in a Chinese church, Masri went to a two year Bible school and returned to Bandung to work on a church planting team among Sundanese. A Chinese church that sponsored this team allowed it to function in an indigenous way in evangelism and church planting. There was also an understanding that the church would ordain the team members when they had planted a church of about 20 adult members.

When Masri came to this work, he impressed the Chinese church leaders with his abilities in music and in speaking. Also, his attitude toward his elders was respectful and he never asked for or hinted for money or material goods. In addition, he came out of a Pentecostal background similar to that of the Chinese church. Thus, he held beliefs similar to theirs concerning spiritual ministry.

In 1982, when this team began their ministry, Masri was 25 years old. Like the other members of the team, he was unmarried and knew very little about starting a church or working among Sundanese. Because he had never been an adult in a Sundanese community, he did not understand much about the structure and function of a Sundanese neighborhood. Progress was made in this area through experience and through association with an older man and wife who were recent converts and who came to live with the evangelists to study the gospel.

When Masri married at the end of 1985, he was able to move to a town and begin a ministry there. Because he had learned some of the Sundanese traditional music arts and owned a set of Sundanese *gamelan*, he was quickly accepted in the new community as a leader of music for the youth. This gave him experience in community leadership. After a year, he moved to a new neighborhood in Bandung and was able to use these skills to win acceptance there.

Beginning in 1983, preaching posts were opened in a number of Sundanese villages and three of them developed into small congregations. One survived as a solid congregation though it had only 8 baptized adults. Masri received credit for much of this progress because he emerged as the most outstanding of the team members. On Nov. 2, 1986, Masri was given responsibility for starting a Sundanese language service at the Chinese church in the city. By this time, his wife had had their first child. When this ministry developed steadily, the church leaders decided to give Masri the church's first ordination as "Young Minister."

When this ordination was offered, the official board talked about Masri's potential contribution to the Indonesian language congregation. To their amazement, Masri refused ordination if it meant he would have to sacrifice his Sundanese ministry time. Since it is virtually unheard of for a young man to dictate terms of ordination, this act of rejecting personal aggrandizement (*pamrih*) greatly impressed the church leaders and he was ordained on his terms. This took place in a public ceremony in April 1988.

CASE HISTORY 4 - *Arifin* (not his real name)

In 1970, Arifin was evangelized by a para-church worker. At that time, he had dropped out of college but could not find work to support himself and his wife. Through contact with the para-church organization, Arifin was not only discipled but also given a job as a manual laborer. Since educated people will not usually take jobs like this, he impressed the para-church group who then hired him part time to work in their office. Arifin proved industrious and talented in many aspects of office work. By 1973, it was apparent to the para-church agency that Arifin would not work out as a staff person so they sought to establish him in another Christian ministry. The opportunity opened for him to help in a Sundanese ministry and he worked there for 4 years. His background as a Muslim equipped him to understand many things involved in Sundanese becoming Christians. After two years, Arifin was recommended to be a part time regional coordinator of a national para-church organization involved in tract distribution. Eventually, he became full time in tract distribution. During this time, he also helped his original para-church sponsor in miscellaneous jobs.

In the tract distribution job, Arifin was able to encourage evangelists working in villages to plant churches. By 1980, several of these ministries had been started. Only one developed into a congregation. While Arifin frequently went to the villages, he never lived there or took direct leadership of the congregation there. However, the Christian converts perceived him as the person who had control of material benefits such as jobs in the city, borrowing money and getting other financial help.

Though Arifin functioned in a team ministry, he did not direct it on social unity principles but rather in the usual autocratic style of para-church organizations. He was answerable to his leaders in Jakarta but not to the team members. By 1982, there were many complaints about the way Arifin handled money. These came mainly from the tract distributors who received their honorariums from him. He was accused of banking their money for interest and paying them late. The feeling spread that he was primarily interested in personal gain. He also was able to build a house for which he incurred debts that he did not repay. In addition, he alienated some other leaders in Sundanese work by his arrogance. Finally, in 1986, he was found to be stealing postal money orders from the para-church sponsor's office and lost much credibility among other leaders in the area.

The tract distribution organization kept him on as their regional coordinator but no one in his own city trusted him anymore. He was no longer asked to participate in leadership training in the larger fellowship of Sundanese workers. It was felt among many Sundanese that he had failed in the area of mutual respect and solidarity in the community of believers.

TABLE 5 - APPLICATION OF RESEARCH

A. <u>NARIA</u>

How recruited - not consciously recruited
                background: little education,
                        family ties, wife and children
                        leadership experience in village-
           - patrons- evangelist/ church

Selection
Process
    - over 3 yrs. period, i.e., until converts won
    - church/patron recognized him as leader
    - became a patron mediating for converts

Criteria
    - *sakti* (spiritual power) demonstrated in conversions, prayer, etc.
    - *halus* (politeness) fits in with cultural process, etc.
    - *hormat* (respect) & *rukun* (social unity) shown in ability to operate in village system
    - *segan*- (reluctant) awe because of former life
    - married with children

Esteem
    - without *pamrih* (no self enrichment)- i.e., blessing (material and spiritual) from church and city patrons to new believers
    - continuing conversions, rising interest of outsiders (e.g. city church)
    - ministering to material & spiritual needs creates *hormat* (respect) among believers

Organization - understood village rules- after his death many mistakes were made by city church

    Note: Naria's spiritual power and authority were not transferable to a follower in equivalent intensity.

B. <u>RAHMAT</u>

How recruited - not consciously recruited
- background: education
family ties, wife a Christian
children
church leadership experience

Selection
Process
- over a 4 yr. period, i.e., until recognized as a Sundanese evangelist
- church/other patrons supported him
- indication of humility, confession of faults, (i.e., a Christian trait)
- became a patron to new believers

Criteria
- *Sakti* (spiritual power) shown in leaving job/getting new support; also testimonies of conversions & healings
- *halus* (politeness) -from a Muslim family- understood approach to village people
- *hormat* (respect) & *rukun_*(social unity)- established relations with other evangelists,
- cooperated with other churches
- married with children

Esteem
- without *pamrih* (self-enrichment) material goods which came to him channeled to others (even immediate family deprived for others)
- successful- new converts gave *hormat* (respect)
- *sakti* (spiritual power) shown in ability to be a major patron

Criticism
- adultery caused loss of esteem both among converts and patrons

Organization
- understood how to operate within village administrative system despite persecution

Note: Rahmat's spiritual power was not delegated. Thus he had no successor.

C. <u>MASRI</u>

How recruited - 2 yrs experience in city church
- sent to Bible school by patron
- background: Christian home influence educated
  not married, no children

Selection - a 6 yr. process from time he finished Bible School
Process - church and para-church group supported him
- he rose as leader within a team concept

Criteria - not married/no children until 1985-86 when he was rec
  ognized as a leader
- musical gifts and speaking abilities
- *sakti* (spiritual power) developed after marriage &
  development of new Sundanese work
- esteem rose when he put condition on ordination
- *hormat* (respect) & *rukun_*(social unity)- shown in success
  in urban community
- *halus* (politeness)- respected cultural rules, behavior, patterns even when they were not Christian
- deference to age, learned from others

Esteem - without *pamrih* (no self enrichment)- especially clear to
  Chinese church when condition put on ordination

Organization - learned to be *halus* (polite) even when opposed
- *hormat* (respect) to village & urban leaders-

D. <u>ARIFIN</u>

How recruited - recruited by para-church who transferred him to
  Sundanese ministry;
- seconded to para-church literature distribution
  organization
- background: married with children
  educated no previous
  leadership
- patrons- 3 groups mentioned above

Selection Process	- over a 5 yr. period gradually moved to higher responsibility
	- eventually two organizations recommended him for leadership
	- through cooperation with other leaders, he became a patron for new converts and young evangelists
Criteria	- *hormat* (respect) & *rukun_*(social unity)- worked well with other Christians & various organizations
	- patron- developed backing and shared material benefits with others
	- had other gifts and abilities such as consistency and courage
	- *sakti* (spiritual power) shown mostly in ability to move up in leadership and be a patron
	- married with children
Esteem	- *hormat*- result of supervising village work as well as tract distribution
	- willingness to defend those under persecution
Criticism	- *pamrih*- shown in dishonesty, misuse of money
Organization	- hailed from a small city and was able to understand the way in which regime operated
Note:	Arifin's spiritual power and authority was not delegated as he gained it from his place in the para-church group.

SUMMARY OF KEY VALUES IN LEADERSHIP DEVELOPMENT

The political activity model clearly shows certain recurring traits in each of the life histories developed in this paper. Even though these life histories represent men from both educated/ uneducated, middle age/ young, rural/urban, new converts/Christian family, as well as miscellaneous other differences, leadership characteristics of the Sundanese society as a whole appear in each.

It is crucial, then, for the Church to be involved in the training of leaders who will demonstrate these traits in their lives and ministries. What emerges from this profile is a strong indication that prospective leaders in the Church will not be able to lead anyone if they do not fulfill the expectations of society.

This can be seen in the following list of the key values as summarized from the study:

1. Recruitment-
    a. Group ties seem to be the most important trait here. Someone needs to promote the new leader.
    b. While not necessary in the village, education plays a large role as to who is chosen in the city.

These may seem to be automatic in the training of new leaders but, in fact, many young people are being trained in Bible schools without the sponsorship of a group or church. When they finish their training, they have nowhere to go. They have education but no "Sundanese society" in which to operate.

2. Selection-
    a. The selection of leaders is made over a period of time <u>after</u> they have finished their schooling; the younger the person, the longer the time.
    b. They need to be married with children.
    c. Not only do they need a patron but they must demonstrate the capability of <u>being</u> a patron to those they seek to lead. This means they must have some financial and morale backing since they would not have the means to be a patron otherwise.

If one considers these requirements from the paradigm of a Bible school, it becomes apparent that a school cannot train a leader for the Sundanese. It can only give a person the important Bible knowledge and cultural understanding necessary to minister to the community. The potential leader must have an organization within which he/she is trained on-the-job by a recognized leader who will transfer legitimacy to the candidate until he/she is recognized independently.

3. Criteria-
    a. *Sakti* or spiritual power seems to be the foremost characteristic of a leader. It means being a patron as well as having spiritual authority. Without this, the other traits seem inadequate.

b. *Hormat* and *rukun* (respect & social unity spirit) also are mentioned in every life history. This is necessary for success within the Sundanese culture.

c. The feature of *halus* (politeness) is also important for most of the leaders studied.

From the features mentioned above, it is apparent that Sundanese leadership does not depend on gifts and abilities as much as it does on certain perceptions of the society. *Sakti* is not something that can be taught in a Bible school or transferred from teacher to student. Thus, it is difficult to predict whether the persons being trained for leadership will, in fact, be accepted as leaders. Since this is the case, it makes sense to seek out the potential leaders among those who have already gained some recognition as a leader before they undergo intensive preparation for a future ministry.

Hormat and *rukun* (respect & social unity), as well as the trait of *halus* (politeness), all develop within the milieu of Sundanese society. Without exposure to the indigenous community, a potential leader has little opportunity to develop or display these characteristics. In a Bible school or training program, the theoretical implications of these traits can be taught but it takes practical experience in applying them that enables one to know if a potential leader is going to be successful. Those who do not succeed in these areas are not going to be perceived as leaders.

4. Esteem-
   a. The major quality that emerges in this category is that of "without *pamrih*" (not seeking personal aggrandizement). The opposite of this trait, that is *pamrih*, is the primary cause of criticism. Of all the leadership attributes mentioned above, *pamrih* or, more properly, the exclusion of it is a lesson that can be learned in Bible school. The lack of *pamrih* is a major fruit of the Christian life. It is also a peculiarity of the patron.
   b. Success in what one attempts to do does not give as much esteem as the absence of *pamrih*. However, the accumulation of followers raises esteem because it indicates that the leader is able to provide for their interests.
   c. Other behaviors that elicit criticism are things like adultery. However, this concern is more characteristic of Christians than it is

of Sundanese. In Rahmat's case, his adultery brought the loss of his patrons in his church and in the Christian community. This meant he was unable to continue to fulfill the interests of his followers.

5. Organization-

    a. The ability to understand regime and work within the boundaries of Sundanese community politics must be mastered by each leader. If the young people who are being trained to lead do not understand this, they must seek the experiences necessary to learn it. Although he was quite young, Masri showed wisdom in learning a skill that was in demand in the society. In his case, it was music. When the offer came, he was prepared for an important role in his community.

    b. It is also interesting to note how only Masri of the afore mentioned leaders worked within a structured organization where the transfer of leadership is integral. He rose from no position to a place of leadership within a single organization. Leadership was delegated to him by the church.

CONCLUSION

The political activity model used in this paper has provided the framework for investigating leadership patterns among the Sundanese. By applying the research to four life histories of Christian leaders among the Sundanese, indications arise that their attributes reflect those of society at large. Since this seems true, it is important to realize that these leadership patterns must be taught to future prospects for the Church. Most of these leadership traits are such that they cannot be taught in Bible schools. Therefore, the major result of this study is to show the necessity of training new leaders outside of the Bible schools in the context of the society.   R. Dixon - 1989

BIBLIOGRAPHY

Adams, R. N. (1975). *Energy and Structure: A Theory of Social Spiritual Power.* Austin: University of Texas Press.

Anderson, B. (1972). "The Idea of Spiritual Power in Javanese Culture." In C. Holt (Ed.), *Culture and Politics in Indonesia.* (pp. 1-69). Ithaca: Cornell University Press.

Burger, D.H. (1956). *Structural Changes in Javanese Society: The Supra-village Sphere.* Translation Series Modern Indonesia Project, South East Asia Program, Department of Far Eastern Studies. Ithaca: Cornell University Press.

Dixon, R. L. (1972). [Unpublished interview with Soebroto].

Emmerson, D.K. (1976). *Indonesia's Elite: Political Culture and Cultural Politics.* Ithaca: Cornell University Press.

Geertz, C. (1960). *The Religion of Java.* London: The Free Press of Glencoe, Collier-MacMillan.

Glicken, J. (1987). "Sundanese Islam and the Value of Hormat: Control, Obedience, and Social Location in West Java." In R.S. Kipp & S. Rodgers (Eds.), *Indonesian Religions in Transition* (pp. 238-252). Tucson: The University of Arizona Press.

Hardjono, J. (1987). *Land, Labour and Livelihood in a West Java Village.* Jogjakarta: Gadjah Mada University Press.

Heidhues, M.F.S. (1985). "Review of Indonesian Chinese in Crisis." *Journal of Asian Studies, 45,* 191-192.

Hoadley, M. C. (1988). "Javanese, Peranakan, and Chinese Elites in Cirebon: Changing Ethnic Boundaries." *The Journal of Asian Studies, 47,* 503-517.

Jackson, K.D. (1978). "The Political Implications of Structure and Culture in Indonesia." In K.D. Jackson & L.W. Pye (Eds.), *Political Spiritual Power and Communications in Indonesia* (pp.23-42). Berkeley: University of California Press.

Jackson, K. D. (1978). "Urbanization and the Rise of Patron-Client Relations: The Changing Quality of Interpersonal Communications in the Neighborhoods of Bandung and the Villages of West Java." In K.D. Jackson & L.W. Pye (Eds.), *Political Spiritual Power and Communications in Indonesia* (pp. 343-392). Berkeley: University of California Press.

Jay, R. R. (1969). *Javanese Villagers: Social Relations in Rural Modjokuto.* Cambridge: The MIT Press.

Koentjaraningrat, R. M. (1957). *A Preliminary Description of the Javanese Kinship System.* Yale University, Southeast Asia Studies, Cultural Report Series.

Laksono, P. M. (1986). *Tradition in Javanese Social Structure Kingdom and Countryside: Changes in the Javanese Conceptual Model.* (E.G. Koentjoro, Trans.). Jogjakarta: Gadjah Mada University Press.

Lingenfelter, S.G. (1985). "Developing new leadership, SIL Brazil Workshop" 1985. Notes on Translation No. 116 (12-86):14-24.

Madge, C. (1974). "The Relevance of Family Patterns to the Process of Modernization in East Asia." In R.J. Smith (Ed.), *Social Organization and the Application of Anthropology* (pp.161-195). Ithaca: Cornell University Press.

Palmer, A.W. (1967). "Situraja: A Village in Highland Priangan." In Koentjaraningrat (Ed.), *Villages in Indonesia* (pp.299-325). Ithaca: Cornell University Press.

Palmer, I. (1987). [Review of S.M.P. Tjondronegoro. "Social Organization and Planned Development in Rural Java."] *Modern Asian Studies, 21*(1), 191-194.

Palmier, L.H. (1960). *Social Status and Spiritual Power in Java.* London School of Economics, Monographs on Social Anthropology No. 20. New York: Humanities

Press Inc. Samson, A. A. (1978). "Conceptions of Politics, Spiritual Power, and Ideology in Contemporary Indonesian Islam." In K.D. Jackson & L.W. Pye (Eds.), *Political*

Spiritual Power and Communications in Indonesia (pp.196-226). Berkeley: University of California Press.

Soemardjan, S. (1963). *The Dynamics of Community Development in Rural Central and West Java: A Comparative Report.* Monograph Series, Modern Indonesia Project,

South East Asian Studies. Ithaca: Cornell University Press.

Swartz, M.J. & Turner, V.W. & Tuden, A. (1966). "Introduction." In M.J. Swartz, V.W. Turner, & A. Tuden (Eds.), *Political Anthropology* (pp.1-41). New York: Aldine Publishing Company.

Ten Dam, H. (1961). "Cooperation and Social Structure in the Village of Chibodas." In W. F. Wertheim et al (Eds.), *Indonesian Economics: The Concept of Dualism in Theory and Policy* (349-382). The Hague: W. van Hoeve Publishers Ltd.

APPENDIX 6 : URBANIZATION AND CHANGE IN PATRON-CLIENT RELATIONS

INTRODUCTION

The importance of the patronage system in Indonesia can be seen in the way it forms a model by which social change is evaluated. K.D. Jackson (1978) hypothesizes that changes in patronage indicate the metamorphosis of personal relationships in contexts such as urbanization.

Based on research conducted among high school juniors and seniors in Bandung (Dixon, 1988), this author seeks to extend Jackson's hypothesis to show how in some cases the conduct of relationships of power among urban youth have moved beyond patron-client relations as he describes it. Empirical evidence drawn from the Basic Values Model indicates that change among educated youth has traits not hypothesized by Jackson. Thus, this evidence strengthens the theory that patronage change is indicative of social change.

PATRONAGE IN CONTEXT

Redfield's folk-urban continuum developed a framework "for studying the role of cities in cultural change..." (Singer, 1972, p.6). Jackson (1980, pp.289-305) builds on this theory and elaborates it through a continuum of five types of power relationships that focus on patronage. However, Jackson alters the model somewhat by hypothesizing that all types along the continuum actually exist to some degree in every society. Different societies give varied emphasis to specific types of patronage (1980, p.289).

The two types most frequent in rural society are physical force and traditional authority whereas reward/ deprivation, persuasion and changing basic values dominate patterns of power in urban society. Patronage is a term he seems to restrict to traditional authority and patron-client relations. The latter falls between the two types of power he labels traditional authority and reward/deprivation (Jackson, 1980, p.294). It is not clear why Jackson does not make patron-client relations a model of power also. He believes the styles of traditional authority and patron-client relations is the context through which relationships of power among urban people (including high school youth) can be understood.

Of the two types of power relationships most frequent in the rural area, traditional authority is the most common. The other, which Jackson calls physical force, is typified by such strategies as martial law, military occupation and other draconian measures. Jackson's (1980, p.186f) description of traditional authority in Sundanese villages would be characteristic of rural Java in particular and also of other areas of Indonesia in general. Patronage is based on a type of power where "one actor (the influencer, R) changes the behavior of a second actor (the influencee, E)" (1980, p.186).

TRADITIONAL AUTHORITY AND PATRONAGE

"Traditional authority is the exercise of personalistic power accumulated through the past and present role of the influencer as provider, protector, educator, source of values, and status superior of those who have an established dependency relationship with him" (1980, p.186). Jackson's understanding of traditional authority reflects R.R. Jay's description (1969, p.185). Jackson defines traditional authority in terms of decades rather than years. These bonds establish continuity for an individual in the ongoing community from past to present. Secondly, traditional authority means that leadership has an ascriptive nature. Status comes from inheritance or some other traditional pattern. It is not conferred on someone because of personal accomplishments or other qualities located outside the community.

Jackson follows James C. Scott (1972, pp. 92-95) in outlining the similarities between traditional authority and patronage (patron-client relationships) in two groups of characteristics. The first includes vertical, dyatic and asymmetric traits (Jackson, 1980, p.188). These can be described as typical of a face-to-face relationship. The hierarchical nature of vertical social relationships is characteristic of the rural areas but Jackson says it is also normal in the urban society. Asymmetry in relationship means the patron practically always gives more than he gets. While the relationships are geared to maintaining the client and insuring help in times of crises, the client gives mostly prestige value to the patron in the city.

Other similarities of traditional authority and patron-client relations are noncontractual, diffuse and whole-person. Here we see the holistic nature of the relationships. In fact, most of the traditional authority bonds are those of kinship. Multiple kinds of services are rendered in these systems. Even in the city, it is difficult to obligate the client to a contract.

The differences between traditional authority and patron-client relations are seen as qualitative. "Patronage is primarily instrumental, responsive to changing opportunities, and more attuned to material facets of life. As such, these relationships have a shorter duration and entail less extensive feelings of binding, affect laden reciprocity" (Jackson, 1980, p.190; Jackson, 1978, p.348). Kahane agrees with Jackson that the Indonesian patronage configuration was transformed by the mixing of market and family systems into a "more instrumental framework based on an ad hoc balance of power" (1984, p.20).

Jackson lists five areas in which a patron and client delineate their relationship.
"1. The client clearly acknowledges the patron as the superior partner in the dyadic relationship.
2. The patron and client must have sustained a mutually rewarding, respect-filled relationship over at least a few years.
3. The patron and client must have sufficient trust in the reciprocal nature of their relationship to enable it to transcend exchanges disproportionately benefiting only one of them.
4. The patron and client, while not sharing identical interests, knowledge, skill, and power, must possess a general complementarity of interests, especially within the economic realm.
5. The patron's requests must be moderate, rather than unlimited, and tailored in magnitude to relatively recent services performed by the patron" (1980, p.190-191).

Instrumental and material aspects are more important to the patron-client relationship than they are to traditional authority patterns. Traditional authority exhibits more affective quality. Once the relationship is established, the client will seldom fail to obey the patron. However, the patron-client connection depends more on prestige achieved and the client looks for continued evidence of that.

THE TRANSITIONAL LINK

An understanding of this patronage framework is necessary to appreciate how Jackson connects the rural society to the urban through patronage and uses this connection to illustrate culture change. He does this by interpreting the *Bapak-Anak buah* pattern as characteristic of both traditional authority and patron-client systems thus linking the rural and urban societies. Kahane seems to misunderstand Jackson here or disagrees with him because he overemphasizes the narrowness of the *Bapak-Anak buah* system to make it a type of 'bossism' (1984, p.18). He fails to understand that holism and person-centered relationships never are completely eliminated in the Indonesian context. Research shows that, even among the high school students where cultural change is greatest, holism dominates as a basic value and person orientation scores significantly also even though it is not dominant. (Dixon, 1988).

For Jackson, the trend away from traditional authority is one that moves through a stage of patron-client relationships and eventually arrives at reward/deprivation. This latter stage is described as "explicit, impersonal, and completely opportunistic interactions" (1980, p.192). Patronage is the style of power that facilitates the transition from rural to urban. "The importance of patronage as a power type in the analysis of migration and urbanization is that it forms a particularly attractive way station for those who have abandoned traditional authority but as yet show no sign of entering horizontal interest groups based on homogeneity of economic and social interests" (1978, p.350).

RELATING THE BASIC VALUES MODEL TO JACKSON'S THEORY

The reason Jackson's theory has been outlined here is to observe some of the values he places on patronage at its different stages. In terms of the

Basic Values Model (Mayers, 1974), the only distinction Jackson makes between traditional authority and patron-client relations is in the area of status. The rural form is seen as status ascribed whereas in the city it is characterized by status achieved. Theories, such as A.F.C. Wallace's (1966, pp.158-163), indicate much greater distortion in changing societies.

When compared to other areas of the Basic Values Model, Jackson's traditional authority and patron-client relations are described as having holistic thinking, noncrisis orientation, person orientation, and vulnerability seen as weakness. (Mayers' category of time/event orientation is not considered in this paper.) In testing these categories, the Basic Values Model agrees with Jackson's thesis that status ascribed focus changes to status achieved and holism and noncrisis orientation continue as values in both areas of patronage. But the Basic Values Model also comes up with divergence answers in two areas, i.e., in task orientation and vulnerability as strength.

In order to appreciate how the Basic Values Model can be used to understand values in Indonesian society, contributions by anthropologists such as H. Geertz and J. Glicken give us further insight in regards to Jackson's theory. Geertz's description of the Javanese family (1961) can also be applied in many ways to Sundanese. She notes that "the most important dimension of grouping of relatives is their nearness to Ego..." (1961, p.19). These relationships have 'hierarchical elements' (p.148). From this, Geertz hypothesizes that the two most important values for the Javanese are "the proper expression of 'respect'" (*urmat* or feeling *sungkan*) and "the determination to 'maintain harmonious social appearances'"(*rukun*) (1961, p.147).

Jackson's concept of traditional authority and patron-client relations can be viewed as extensions of what Geertz sees in the hierarchical relationship of kin to Ego. If compared to the Basic Values Model, the value of 'respect' relates to the orientations of person and also to status ascribed and also to vulnerability as weakness in the Basic Values Model. The latter value is seen because "respect in itself is also an expression of distance..." (1961, p.19). The Javanese or Sundanese never wants to admit fault or failure in completing their responsibilities in relation to either superiors or inferiors. The second Javanese value of *rukun* which relates to maintaining "harmonious social appearances" can be compared to holistic thinking in the Basic Values Model.

In writing about Sundanese religious instruction, Glicken (1987) describes the word *hormat* (which corresponds to Geertz's use of *urmat*) as transmitting and reinforcing the values of obedience and respect (p.239). These Sundanese values reflect both status and person orientation and also vulnerability as weakness. "*Hormat* should be glossed as knowing one's social location and acting in accordance with its attendant rights and obligations. One demonstrates *hormat* by correctly using the formalized level of politeness of the Sundanese language..." (Glicken, 1987, p.240). This also relates to social distance and vulnerability as weakness.

The contributions of Geertz and Glicken, appear to agree with Jackson's understanding of the values of traditional authority societies. However, when Jackson hypothesizes the change to a patron-client society, he does not project a significant variation in values. It is helpful to evaluate Jackson's five areas of the patron-client relationship (1980, p.190-191) [see page 2-3 of this paper] as they relate to the Basic Values Model: Number one indicates status (which Jackson describes as achieved rather than ascribed as it is in traditional society). The second relates to both person orientation and vulnerability as weakness (which is seen in not revealing faults for fear of losing a patron). This latter value is dominant in Jackson's third point. Number four illustrates a holistic value and the final point is characteristic of noncrisis orientation. This would be seen in the client's dependency on the assurance of patron help in time of need which relieves one of the necessity of planning ahead.

Thus, in terms of the Basic Values Model, Jackson can be understood as proposing that traditional authority is oriented to holism, noncrisis, person, status ascribed, and vulnerability as weakness. In the area of patron-client relations, the only significant difference (in relation to Basic Values Model) is in status focus. Status changes from ascribed to <u>achieved</u> with patron-client relationships.

BASIC VALUES MODEL RESEARCH

Mayers' Model of Basic Values (Mayers, 1974) is "an approximate representation of priorities" (Lingenfelter & Mayers, 1986, p.28) that has proven helpful in American society because it indicates major basic values. Its results among Indonesian high school students show some correlation with points in the hypotheses of Jackson and others.

The Basic Values Model research was carried out in the same region where Jackson did his study. The area is in the western end of the island of Java. Java, with a hundred million people, is twice the density of Japan (Bonner, 1988, p.50). Java has the top three cities in Indonesia with Bandung, in West Java, being the third latrgest. There are 400,000 university students in Indonesia (Johnstone, 1986, p.232) and most of them are in Java which, with only nine per cent of Indonesia's land mass, is the center of everything. As Clifford Geertz wrote, "Any discussion of culture and change in Indonesia that did not have the past, present, and future of Javanese demography constantly before it would hardly be worth much" (1984, p.513).

The Basic Values Model research was based on Lingenfelter & Mayers, <u>Questionnaire for Ministering Cross-Culturally: A Personal Profile of Basic Values, 1988</u>. The 48 questions were translated by the principal of a senior high school in Cimahi, a suburb of Bandung in West Java, Indonesia. The principal attempted to make the translations culturally appropriate and they were discussed with the researcher (Dixon, 1988) in an effort to ascertain as correct a translation as possible.

In August,1988, the instrument was administered by the principal to some of the juniors and seniors in her own school. This was done without the presence of any outside people. The completed questionnaires were returned to the United States where this author entered them into a computer program in April, 1989.

The results of this research is based on a sampling of 66 female and 87 male junior and senior students in high school. Their ages run between 16 and 19. Since Indonesia has no senior high schools in rural areas, this sampling is of urban youth. Some of the students originated in rural areas but they are presently incorporated into the life of the city. Cimahi is a suburb of Bandung which is the third largest city in Indonesia with a population of over 2 million. Bandung is also one of the major university towns in Indonesia. Other than sex, age, and high school class, the only information we have on the sampling is that over half of them are Sundanese and about one-half of these students are children of military personnel.

A SUMMARY OF FINDINGS

	Male	Female	Average
Time/	5.38	5.52	5.45
event orientation	3.63	3.99	3.81
Dichotomistic/	4.18	3.99	4.09
holistic thinking	4.78	4.65	4.71
Crisis/	4.65	4.67	4.66
noncrisis orientation	5.26	4.28	4.77
Task/	5.70	5.61	5.66
person orientation	4.42	4.24	4.33
Status/	3.38	3.26	3.32
achievement focus	4.95	5.42	5.19
Concealment of vulnerability/	3.60	3.39	3.50
willingness to expose	4.67	4.38	4.52
vulnerability			

INTERPRETATION OF FINDINGS

Scores for males and females do not indicate great differences between them. Males trend significantly higher only on noncrisis orientation. Females show strength vis-a-vis the males in the achievement focus. Other than achievement focus, females score higher in time/event orientation and in crisis orientation. But these scores are not much greater than that of males. Correspondingly, the scores of males do not show much variation from that of females in the other areas.

In light of Jackson's hypothesis on patron-client relations, the major surprise of this research was the strength of the trends number four and six, i.e., task over person, and willingness to expose vulnerability over concealment of vulnerability. This counters Jackson's prediction of person orientation and vulnerability as weakness. On the other hand, the research supports Jackson's theory of urban (patron-client) relationships being oriented to holism, noncrisis and achievement focus.

EXPLANATION OF THE DEVIATIONS FROM JACKSON'S HYPOTHESIS

The students deviated from Jackson's hypothesis in two categories. In the areas of holistic thinking, noncrisis orientation, and status achieved focus, students scored as Jackson predicted the urban population would. In addition, the deviation of the scores in the two areas of task orientation and willingness to expose vulnerability indicate a trend toward the center of the continuum. Thus, they are not extreme deviations from what was expected. The consistency of the scores between males and females indicate reliability. Also, in the two areas in which the students scored differently than expected, both males and females were strongly trending together. Thus, this writer sought reasons why the students scored as they did.

REASONS FOR NEW BASIC VALUES

First of all, urbanization has been taking place at a rapid rate and expanding the number of youth in secondary education in the Indonesian society. Secondly, education exerts pressure toward rapid change in basic values. Another interesting element is the change in approach to status in modern Indonesia.

In 1930, urbanization was at 7.5% (Nitisastro, 1970, p.177). But the Dutch colonial government restricted secondary education to a small number of youth. Only 240 Indonesians graduated from high school in 1940 (Legge, 1964, p.105). By 1961, the urban population had doubled to 15% (Nitisastro, 1970, p. 177) and hundreds of thousands of youth were in schools. The 1980 census showed 22.3% urbanization in Indonesia (World Almanac, 1982, p.569).

The development of high schools brought youth into the cities from the villages as there have never been secondary schools in the villages. This meant that high school youth were experiencing the values of the urban areas rather than those of their local villages. Over recent years, this influence has continued to increase. An additional influence on youth in Bandung has been the large number of university students living in close proximity. By 1970, there were 38,814 university students in Bandung alone (Surjadi, 1985, p.92).

Sociologists like Surjadi say that education, along with nation building and the mass media, are the prime factors in changes taking place in Indonesia today. Innovations in society are affecting changes both in the villages and in the cities (Surjadi, 1985, p.177). This agrees with Palmier's study on social status and power in Java. Palmier and Surjadi would agree with Wertheim that "tradition, too, determined each person's status within the social hierarchy" (1959, p.6). Palmier argues that, under the Dutch colonial government, education was a principal mechanism of changing tradition and orienting people to the same values (1960, p.161). In a study on migration into Surabaya, the second largest city on Java, McCutcheon showed that, even among the rural population, education is the most important factor in affecting attitudes. "The other variables appear to affect educational opportunities, and only indirectly affect attitudes" (1983, p.129).

Karl Jackson supports this premise in his evaluation. "In changing basic values, the time span is long, the mode is usually education, and the attitude is usually a fundamental one..." (1980, p.294). However, the case of Indonesia would seem to indicate that the time span is not necessarily long. Over the past 30 years, drastic changes in basic values appear to have taken place. It is interesting to note that Geertz (1961) completed her research 30 years ago and Jackson's (1978) was done in 1968-69.

A third element that might be affecting the results of this research (especially in Status/Achievement, Task/Person) is the transition that has taken place in the way Indonesian youth view status. Wertheim (1956, p.118) points out the character of the rigid status system applied by the Dutch before World War II. The Dutch were on top with those of Dutch culture ranked close to them. After that came other Orientals like Chinese and Arabs while on the bottom were the Indonesian masses. With the Japanese occupation, this hierarchy was turned upside down. After the war, the new status system continued to dominate in the development of independent Indonesia.

However, an Indonesian student at Biola University points out that American influence has begun to dominate in Indonesian education over the past 30 years. Since the American system is much more achievement focused, Indonesian youth are being programmed in a new way in task vs. person orientation as well as in achievement vs. status focus (Dixon, 1989). Besides this, about half of the youth in this research were from military families and this could also account for basic values being more time/dichotomistic/ task/ and achievement oriented. If these theories are correct, it would appear that education was a major force in creating a colonial status before World War II and it is also powerful in creating a different status today.

A COMPOSITE PROFILE OF THE PATTERNS OF BEHAVIOR

Because the findings do not indicate significant differences between male and female, profiles for each group are similar. Therefore, for the purpose of this evaluation, a single profile is presented in outline form to indicate some of the implications of the trending toward task and exposing vulnerability.

1. Task Orientation
   a. Trending task over person was quite strongly indicated in the findings. This means the students feel objects are more important as goals than is relating to people.
   b. The nature of school life may be an intensifier of concern for definite goals and the achievement of those goals.
   c. Friendships are secondary to goals (see question # 17 in Questionnaire).
   d. What a person has as his goal may justify a variety of actions geared to achieving it. This could affect ethical decisions.

2. Willingness to Expose Vulnerability
   a. This is also referred to as "vulnerability as strength" (Mayers, 1987, p.160). It means the students are not afraid to expose their weaknesses.
   b. They are not overly concerned with making errors in their work because they realize that everyone makes mistakes.
   c. Telling jokes on oneself or accepting the kidding of others indicates a willingness to reveal weakness.
   d. This trait also indicates a probability of getting involved in new experiments and activities in life.

MINISTRY APPLICATIONS

1. Urbanization as environment

The change in values from the traditional authority model to the urban patron-client relations is affecting about 25% of the population. In regards to youth who are getting at least a high school education, 100% are being conditioned by the values of the city. Since practically all of the future leadership in both city and country will come from these educated youth, we can project a change in values that will permeate the entire society in a few years. Not only is this happening to those in the urban orbit, but also many more are being pulled into this circle of influence each year.

Up to this time, a large part of the Church in West Java has not thought of a strategy to address these changing values. The shock of the speed with which this is happening has left the Church in an eddy of the mainstream. Very few churches sponsor serious programs to reach youth and only a few para-church organizations are targeting high school or university youth. In addition, most of those who do are ministering to them in the same way they approach adults. This means that the evangelistic and teaching ministries are geared to people with the old values.

This research points up the fact that values have not only changed in the cities but they are moving toward what Jackson calls reward/deprivation which is more opportunistic than what is presently practiced by the urban people. The Basic Values Model research supports this hypothesis. All of this means the Church must anticipate the change that is occurring in values and develop evangelists, pastors and teachers who understand it. Research would help accomplish this by supplying information to enable the Church to properly evaluate what materials were most suited for training workers and educating the laity.

In order for the Church to anticipate the change and relate to it, the Church must have an awareness of its present orientation to the traditional authority mentality. If the Church understands this, it can anticipate the urban context in the future. The Church can then develop strategies of evangelism and church growth to meet the present and future situations. As part of the Church, the para-church organizations need to have this same concern. Seminaries and Bible schools also must comprehend the need to give new direction to their training programs.

2. Education as method

All youth who go to high school and college move to the city. This means that the influence of education on the potential future leaders is 100%. Some of them may return to the rural areas as leaders and readjust to some degree to traditional values but the vast majority will affect others more than they are affected. Since values have been shown to change faster with education, it is clear that most of the future leaders in the country will have either patron-client values or something more extreme.

The challenge of Christian ministry is to reach these youth in their formative years. It is clear they are going to change. Their values will not be the same after they finish their education as they were before they started. Thus, the Church must intervene in these formative years and not wait until the youth are out of school. Action now can be considered preventative and positive whereas waiting with the idea of only reaching adults will result in the need to develop a remedial program of evangelism and Christian education.

It is important to develop a theology of evangelism and of the Church that has a strong biblical moral base. The values of the urban area will result in an ethical system antagonistic to the gospel. In order to counter the influence of changing values, the Church needs to get into the schools. Fortunately, this is possible in Indonesia because of the government's policy of universal religious education. Salary is a problem for Christians as the pay of a religious teacher is very low and the prestige is not much better. The Church must create a new high level status related to religious teaching to draw good teachers into this field. Also, government teacher salaries can be supplemented so that the teachers do not feel the monetary sacrifice is too great. In short, the Church must insure that Christian teachers get into the schools to teach as many students as possible in Christian values.

The universities are a more formidable challenge because religious training is optional and it only requires a few teachers to handle the

classes. Informal training outside the classroom is more difficult because the Muslim pressure against Christian groups on many campuses
is strong. Christian students are a large percent of the student bodies
in many colleges and there are also many Christian teachers. But the
Christian teachers do not give time to the students' spiritual needs and
the lack of student chaplains and other full time Christian workers is
crucial.

In Indonesia, there are only a few student para-church organizations
such as Navigators and Intervarsity. Many more are needed. In addition,
churches near the colleges could open their campuses to student meetings and even initiate special student ministries. At present, few churches
serve students who have not originated from their own church family.

3. Status as key to acceptance
One of the major problems for the Christian is the struggle with
pride. Because of this, the church teaches humility and the serious believer subdues all inclination to elevate him/herself above others. This
is done even to the point of not letting others know of one's accomplishments or awards. However, in a status achieved society as research shows
the Indonesian educational community to be, this is tantamount to cutting oneself off from any effective ministry. It is important to the urban
ministry and to youth especially to have a prestigious teacher model of
evangelism and Christian teaching.

An example of this need was revealed to us in a strategy to reach a
new community in Bandung where most of the youth were high school
students or graduates. My wife drew them into a friendly relationship by
sponsoring English lessons. Several times a week the students would come
to our house to practice their English. Our plan was to have the evangelists who were living with us share Christ with the students. But they never
did. After a period of time, we realized what the problem was. The evangelists were from a lower educational level and did not have the courage
to approach the students about spiritual matters.

Language is another area of concern when it comes to a status conscious
society. All of the Sundanese youth are being educated in Indonesian,
which is the national language. Thus, there is no status involved in

learning good Sundanese. As Glicken points out, the Sundanese language indicates social distance. Indonesian youth today do not want to recognize social distance. They are more interested in egalitarian relationships. Sundanese is being lost as the urban youth fail to learn the levels used in this traditional language.

With the loss of social distance, students become more frank in their relationships. The fear of being exposed that is characteristic of the rural mentality is being replaced by vulnerability as strength. Youth are being taught how to try new things even if they fail. Their willingness to admit mistakes and risk humiliation is changing their attitudes towards authority, even at the highest levels. The gospel message must relate to this kind of attitude.

The Church needs not only a prestigious teacher model but also Christian education that relates to the desire of youth to achieve something. This will probably be a plus in Christian teaching. Up to now, rural Christians have been syncretizing the gospel with their own religious beliefs. With the advent of a willingness to expose vulnerability, there is a possibility of the new converts standing more firmly against the rejection of their communities. This will, in turn, allow the Holy Spirit to work in the hearts of many to listen to the gospel.

CONCLUSION

In this paper, Jackson's hypothesis of changing values from traditional authority to patron-client relations have been examined in light of empirical research with the Basic Values Model. The research indicates that the hypothesis of change is accurate to some degree. Change may even be occurring faster than Jackson believes.

With the corroboration of the Basic Values Model, the hypothesis of change in societal values, especially those of youth, spurs the Church to look for new ways to approach urban youth with the gospel and also to train them after they believe. Changing values represents a great challenge to the mission of the Church in Indonesia today.

R. Dixon, 1989

REFERENCES CITED

Bonner, R. (1988, June). "A Reporter at Large: The New Order- I." *The New Yorker*, pp.45-79.

Dixon, J. B. (1988). [Scores of the Basic Values Model in a Cimahi High School]. Unpublished raw data.

Dixon, R. L. (1989, 13 May). [Interview with Iwan Marantika]. Unpublished.

Geertz, C. (1984). "Culture and Social Change: The Indonesian Case." *Man, 19*(4), 511-532.

Geertz, H. (1961). *The Javanese Family: A Study of Kinship and Socialization.* The Free Press of Glencoe, Inc. A Division of Crowell-Collier Publishing Company.

Glicken, J. (1987). "Sundanese Islam and the Value of Hormat: Control, Obedience and Social Location in West Java." In R.S. Kipp & S. Rodgers (Eds.), *Indonesian Religions in Transition* (pp.238-252). Tucson: The University of Arizona Press.

Jackson, K. D. (1978). "Urbanization and the Rise of Patron-Client Relations: The Changing Quality of Interpersonal Communications in the Neighborhoods of Bandung and the Villages of West Java." In K.D. Jackson & L.W. Pye (Eds.), *Political Power and Communications in Indonesia* (pp.343-392). Berkeley: University of California Press.

Jackson, K.D. (1980). *Traditional Authority, Islam, and Rebellion: A Study of Indonesian Political Behavior.* Berkeley: University of California Press.

Jay, R.R. (1969). *Javanese Villagers: Social Relations in Rural Modjokerto.* Cambridge, MA: MIT Press.

Johnstone, P. (1986). *Operation World: A Day-to-Day Guide to Praying for the World.* Pasadena, CA: William Carey Library. Kahane, R. (1984). "Hypotheses on Patronage and Social Change: A Comparative Perspective." *Ethnology, 23*(1), 13-24.

Legge, J.D. (1964). *Indonesia*. Englewood Cliffs, NJ: Prentice-Hall, Inc.

Lingenfelter, S. G. & Mayers, M. K. (1986). *Ministering Cross-Culturally: An Incarnational Model for Personal Relationships*. Grand Rapids: Baker Book House.

Lingenfelter, S. G. & Mayers, M. K. (1988). "Questionnaire for Ministering Cross-Culturally: A Personal Profile of Basic Values." Grand Rapids: Baker Book House.

Mayers, M. K. (1974). *Christianity Confronts Culture*. Grand Rapids: Zondervan.

Mayers, M. K. (1987). *Christianity Confronts Culture: A Strategy for Cross Cultural Evangelism*. Grand Rapids: Academie Books.

McCutcheon, L. (1983). "The Adjustment of Migrants to Surabaya, Indonesia." In C. Goldscheider (Ed.), *Urban Migrants in Developing Nations: Patterns and Problems of Adjustment* (pp.91-136). Boulder, CO: Westview Press.

Nitisastro, W. (1970). *Population Trends in Indonesia*. Ithaca: Cornell University Press.

Palmier, L. H. (1960). *Social Status and Power in Java*. University of London: The Athlone Press.

Scott, J. C. (1972). "Patron-Client Politics and Political Change in Southeast Asia." *The American Political Science Review, 66*(1), 91-113.

Singer, M. (1972). *When a Great Tradition Modernizes: An Anthropological Approach to Indian Civilization*. New York: Praeger Publishers.

Surjadi, A. (1974). *Masyarakat Sunda Budaya dan Problema* [The Sundanese Community's Culture and Problem]. Bandung: Penerbit Alumni.

Wallace, A.F.C. (1966). *Religion: An Anthropological View*. New York: Random House.

Wertheim, W.F. (1956). *Indonesian Society in Transition.* Bandung: Sumur Bandung.

World Almanac and Book of Facts. (1982). New York: Newspaper Enterprise Association.

APPENDIX 7 - THE CENTRALITY OF THE SHAMAN IN SUNDANESE SOCIAL ORGANIZATION

INTRODUCTION

W. H. Rikin (1973) has shown the centrality of customary law and traditions (*adat*) to the Sundanese social system through his exposition of the *tali paranti*. Literally, *tali paranti* means a "string of traditions, the image of a string implying both binding and measuring" (p.168) (referred to hereafter as 'model of life'). From early times the people have felt it was obligatory to observe these traditions handed down by their ancestors. There are many punishments associated with the failure to complete the 'model of life', the most fearful one being the loss of soul rest.

The practitioner who contributes the most energy in seeing that the people practice these traditions is the shaman (in Sundanese society this person is called a *dukun*). In this paper, the *dukun* will be referred to as shaman. In doing this, I follow Turner's definition of shaman as one who "enacts his roles in small scale, multifunctional communities whose religious life incorporates beliefs in a multitude of deities, daemons, nature spirits, or ancestral shades..." (1989, p.88). This distinguishes them from priests. As Von Furer-Haimendorf describes the priest category, it would be more like the Muslim religious leader among the Sundanese; that is, they "influence the gods through prayer and ritual performances..." (1989, p.95).

If we follow Firth's model for describing social organization as "the way things get done over time in the community" (Redfield, 1969, p.42), we see how the Sundanese shaman plays the central role. In this paper we will examine how the shaman gets things done by gaining and maintaining power in guiding the community in fulfilling their obligations. The framework of this study will be oriented around two case studies. In each of these case studies, it will be apparent how the shaman demonstrates his/her control of spiritual power and conveys it to his followers.

CASE STUDY 1 - OOM'S STILLBORN CHILD

Oom was a young Christian mother in a village on the outskirts of Bandung, West Java. When she was in labor with her third child, her family sent word to her husband at his job in the city and also to the evangelist who pastored the congregation. The evangelist arrived in the village before the father and found that the baby was stillborn. He then sent word to his co-workers and to the local Christian community to gather for a funeral service. While he was at another house awaiting arrival of these friends, the shaman who helped the mother in childbirth pressured the distraught mother to bury the child quickly without waiting for others. On returning to the house and finding the child already buried, the evangelist then sent word to the people not to come and he, himself, returned home.

The young mother, with her husband, and several other families in the village had been Christians about three years. It was the general understanding that the leaders of each person's religion took responsibility for the various important activities surrounding life and death as well as the other rites involved in the 'model of life.' But this shaman 'usurped' those rights apparently because she believed that it was detrimental to the community to leave the child unburied for more than a short time. Also, in this case, she was able to pressure the mother into allowing her to bury the child even though they were supposed to be awaiting the arrival of the Christian 'practitioner.' In addition, she was able to elude any repercussions for doing so.

BACKGROUND

The Sundanese are the second largest ethnic group in Indonesian after the Javanese. Their number is now about 30 million and nearly all of these live in the western third of the island of Java in Indonesia. While their language and customs are considerably different from that of the Javanese, these two groups have more similar cultural traditions with one another than they do with other Indonesian ethnic peoples. Over a period of many centuries the Sundanese have been influenced by the great Javanese empires, the Muslim religion, and the Dutch colonial government.

Rikin (1973) has argued cogently that the strongest belief system of the Sundanese is what is called the 'model of life.' The 'model of life' rites begin while the soul is still in the womb and continue until one thousand days after physical death. There are sixteen rites observed: three before birth, ten during life (including death) and three after death. Of these, the most crucial to the community life are circumcision and marriage, circumcision being the most important for men and marriage for women. The purpose of the 'model of life' is to insure the Sundanese will return to his/her origin.

To aid the people in their spiritual needs, there are practitioners of the magic arts called shaman. These shaman are active in healing or in mystic practices like numerology. They claim contact with supernatural forces that do their bidding. Some of these shaman will exercise black magic but most are considered beneficial to the Sundanese. From the cradle to the grave few important decisions are made without recourse to the shaman. Most of their activity lies in an area outside Islam and which is in opposition to Islam (Koentjaraningrat, 1979, p.315). But they are still counted as Muslims. Most people carry charms on their bodies and keep them in propitious places on their property. Some even practice magic spells independently of the shaman.

In describing Javanese society, Rienks and Iskandar list the shaman as the largest category of indigenous healers or 'capable' persons (1988, p.80). As advisors and healers, the shaman may "become mainly associated with one field of problems or sphere of activities..." (p.80). Thus, among the Sundanese, we also have *dukun bayi* (birthing expert), *dukun sunat* (circumcision expert) and many other types of shaman.

SHAMAN AS COMMUNITY LEADER

From the point of view of a political activity model (Lingenfelter, 1985), the Sundanese administrative system, both in regime and government, is similar to that used throughout Java and indeed throughout Indonesia. The national government has implemented various changes since independence in 1945 which duplicates the top-down control exercised by the

Dutch and also by the former indigenous empires which flourished on Java. While the shaman does not 'fit' in this hierarchy of government officials, he plays a central role because of what he can do. Both the folktales and the ancient as well as recent literature indicate that the shaman has, since memory, functioned in the Javanese/ Sundanese worldview. He was believed to possess the magic power needed to overcome problems of one's daily life (Guillot, 1985, p.193).

Laksono emphasizes that legitimacy depends not on wealth or the ability to use force but on "qualities of spiritual greatness" (1986, p.xiii). *Sakti* or spiritual power forms the heart of what the Sundanese look for in a leader. As Rienks and Iskandar point out, "no one can become a healer without explicit popular support" (1988, p.75). The recent introduction of medical cadres into the village health system resulted frequently in the insecurity of the cadre themselves. Not only did they not get popular support, but they felt themselves impostors (p.75).

If Redfield is right in defining social organization as 'the way things get done' (1969, p.42), then the actions of the shaman as well as the reactions of the mother in our case study begin to make sense. By leaving the shaman out of the Christian model of social organization, the evangelist ignored her integral role in everything important that happened in relation to the baby. Redfield's description of the practitioner of the supernatural and his/her relationship with others in the social organization is helpful in understanding how religion is part of the 'state of mind' of the society. "One does not move from social structure to religious system" (1969, p.50) in a holistic society.

In Sundanese society, the shaman is part of the social structure and thus part of "the central organizing idea in terms of which everything else in the life of the community, as far as proves possible, is seen" (Redfield, 1969, pp.49-50). The evangelist failed to explain to the shaman (and to the mother) how the Christian faith was an expression of the social structure to the degree that the shaman no longer had a role in the burial of the baby. Because the congregation in Oom's village was less than three years old and the evangelist was inexperienced, no one had ever thought about how a Christian should act toward a 'birthing expert.' The shaman was allowed to help birth the baby, but it was expected that she would not proceed further with any of her religious functions. However, this was obviously not clear to the shaman.

The following case study will further illustrate how the roles of Christian evangelist and shaman overlap during the transition period when a person becomes a believer but is not yet clear how the functions of the different spiritual leaders relate.

CASE STUDY 2 - ROAT'S BROKEN BACK

Roat was about 24 and a laborer in house construction when he broke his back. In a closed van, his boss was moving 3-foot square ceiling board made out of asbestos. The load was quite heavy and fragile and Roat was assigned to sit in the back of the van. The thin squares were stacked on edge and Roat was supposed to keep them from tipping over and breaking. However, he was careless and sat with his back against the load. Due to the van lurching on a bad road, the load tipped toward the back of the van like dominoes and crushed Roat beneath it.

Roat's boss took him to the hospital where he spent a few weeks. Although the doctors gave him good care, Roat was paralyzed as a result of the accident. The doctors felt he would not improve as there was no way they could correct his condition through an operation. During this time, Roat's boss witnessed to him about faith in Christ and also brought evangelists to talk to him. Roat gained some encouragement because of this. He also felt their prayers resulted in some feeling returning to his lower body.

When he returned home, his family urged him to visit a shaman who was well known for fixing people's backs. The shaman assured him that his back was not broken (despite the x-rays) and gave him physical therapy by walking on his back. This immediately caused him excruciating pain that did not subside for many days. In addition to the pain, he lost what little feeling there was in his lower body. Although the shaman urged him to return for more treatments, he refused to go as he realized his back was really broken and the actions of the shaman compounded the injury.

THE SHAMAN AS A PURVEYOR OF POWER

Adams defines power as being derived from the "relative control by each actor or unit over elements of the environment of concern to the participants" (1975, p.10). In the case of the shaman, this involves the interplay of supernatural forces as they relate to the health and well being of the Sundanese. The goal of the shaman is to maintain or (if broken) re-establish the condition of *selamat*. *Selamat* is derived from the Arabic *salam* and is equivalent to shalom and involves order from chaos, harmony among all parts of the created universe, mutual care, trust, and understanding, and movement toward and reconciliation with God, neighbor, and nature.

The role of the shaman grows out of society's needs. Thus, there is a social contract created between them and their clients. A Durkheimian model is illustrated in the exchange between these practitioners of the 'model of life' and their clients, i.e., "something goes on between the two to make new." The actions of the shaman create changes in the clients and conversely, their actions cause change in the shaman. The success of the shaman in bringing *selamat* to the people is determined by how the people themselves evaluate the helpfulness of his actions. Out of their separate contributions something new is created.

In another Indonesian context, Jane Atkinson describes the *Wana* shaman of Sulawesi as being primarily concerned with his audience rather than his patient. The healing performance of the shaman is 'effective' when the position of the shaman is reified by the interrelationship of the shaman, his patient, and the audience. Atkinson believes the healing work of the shaman is secondary to this identification of the shaman as protector and protagonist (1987, p.345).

As was shown in the two case studies, power is exercised by the shaman in ways that exceed what might be expected. For example, a wife does not await her husband before burying their child and a man can be talked into having his back walked on when he knows it is broken. The type of power illustrated by these two case studies transcends simple control. As Adams points out, this power is "a psychological facet of a social relationship...it is social in that it exists by virtue of the complementarity of social concern of each actor with respect to the other" (1975, p.21).

Appendix 7 - The Centrality Of The Shaman

We saw earlier that *sakti* was spiritual power. It is that divine anointing or mystical authority needed by all who would become leaders. In the holistic Sundanese society, *sakti* exists in a concrete way. It has properties and it is constant in quantity. When the shaman demonstrates that he has cornered a significant distribution of power, it means he has control over blessing. His *sakti* replaces the old center of power and his authority is established in satisfying the demands of his followers. He gains influence through success and loses it when he cannot selflessly provide *selamat* for those who trust in him.

LEGITIMACY

It can be shown by these case studies and many others that most shaman do not force their patients but rather their control over the supernatural environment is such that it exerts pressure or control over those affected by the environment. The mother whose baby died feared either the malevolence of the spirit world or the displeasure of her neighbors. As a Christian, she may not have feared the spirit world but she knew the community would be upset with her if she did not heed the advice of the expert. Thus, we see how the shaman can be legitimized. Adams writes that "a thing is legitimate, then, when people agree that it is in some manner correct, proper, or the way it should be" (1975, p.31).

When we ask why the shaman is doing what he does and why the people allow him to practice his arts, the answer lies in the reciprocity of power relations between the shaman and the people. It is here the shaman gets his legitimacy. C. Bailey describes the Malaysian *penghulu* (sub district headman) in much the same terms. He says his powers are invested in him by virtue of the sanctity of the past. His quote from Max Weber relates well to the Sundanese shaman. "The person or persons exercising authority are designated according to traditionally transmitted rules. The object of obedience is the personal authority of the individual which he enjoys by virtue of his traditional status" (Bailey, 1976, p.11).

Spiritual power (or *sakti*) is crucial for the Sundanese. It is there; it exists. Anderson describes the way the Sundanese conceptualize power in the world around them (1972, p.7-8). Unlike Western views of power, it does not arise out of various sources of control that can be classified in areas of environment or energy and the like. Rather, it is homogeneous and cannot be classified and analyzed. If the Sundanese do not control power or get it controlled for their benefit, it might be used to their detriment. The job of the shaman is to insure that this mystical power is controlled and in doing so they exercise a goodly portion of social power.

THE SHAMAN AS A MODEL OF SOCIAL ORGANIZATION

When the function of the shaman is seen in the context of modeling social reality, one can see how the activities of the shaman reifies the way people perceive the ordering of their world with the natural under the supernatural dominance of spirit activities/powers. As Rikin (1973) points out, there are sixteen major rites of the 'model of life' in which the shaman acts to control the supernatural influence in the lives of natural people. Besides this, practically every event of importance to people such as planting, harvesting, moving house, building a house and other activities too long to list are guided by the shamen as they determine the will of the spirits and appease the spirits on behalf of the people. It has been frequently reported that the shamen advise all political leaders. Even the president of the country has these advisors.

Redfield paraphrases Firth as proposing that the "social structure is that important system of elements which lasts and which everybody takes account of" (1969, p.42). Palmer (1967) and Jackson (1978) describe the secular leaders of the established system of administration used among the Sundanese. While the shamen do not have a spot in this political structure, it is obvious from the central role they play that the shamen are part of the "system of elements which lasts." The existence of the shamen emphasizes the subservience of society to the unseen spirit world. This enhances a feeling of solidarity, a sense of belonging that, in turn, brings an experience of *selamat* to the people.

SUMMARY

In this section we have considered the way in which the shaman of Sundanese society illustrates Firth's theory of the organizing principle of society. The shaman is one of the figures who 'gets things done' and thus plays a central role. He does this by gaining and maintaining power in the interplay of the natural and supernatural world as he guides people in fulfilling their obligations to the spirit world. The reciprocity between the shaman and the people is the key to how he is able to 'get things done.' This reciprocity is seen in their mutual desire for supernatural control, blessing (*selamat*) and spiritual power (*sakti*). In the following section, we will look at a few aspects of this relationship that can be applied to the life of a Christian worker.

APPLICATION

There are a few aspects of the relationship between the shaman and the people that give clues as to how a Christian worker might relate to the Sundanese. These ideas are based on an analogical view of the shaman's role in relation to the function of a Christian worker. It is important to see how biblical models direct our attention to this way of seeing relationships. The Bible gives many examples of the attitude of the early believers toward relating to people through analogical relationships. These examples will help us see how a Christian worker can relate to the Sundanese.

BIBLICAL ANALOGIES

When Paul, through the inspiration of the Holy Spirit, enjoins us to "become all things to all men..." (1 Cor. 9:22), we know he does not mean for us to fall back into the sin from which we have been saved. When he talks of becoming "as one under the law," we understand that he did not consider himself as bound by the law (1 Cor. 9:20). Paul is speaking of the analogy of those ways of life which are meaningful to people. An analogy in this sense is the understanding that if two or more things agree in one way, they are likely to agree in others.

An example of this can be seen in the blinding of the magician Elymas in Acts 13. When this occurred, spiritual power was ascribed to Paul by the proconsul and the other people. Paul was seen as greater than the magician in control over supernatural power and blessing. Again, when the man at Lystra was healed, the people gathered to worship Paul and Barnabas as embodiments of their gods. They saw the control the apostles seemingly had over the supernatural world and they ascribed status to them because of it. The honor given in Cyprus Paul accepted but that which occurred in Lystra he and Barnabas rejected.

The Bible clearly teaches that honor and glory is the Lord's. But there are times when God, himself, accords glory to his servant so that through the social organization his witness can find a place. Another example of this is Paul's approach in Athens. The well-known strategy of presenting an "unknown god" was Paul's utilization of an analogy with which the Athenians were all familiar. At the same time, he was at the Areopagus as a 'philosopher' for it was a place where philosophers gathered. Apparently, not everyone thought Paul was a philosopher (Acts 17:18, 32), but this was an analogy they understood. Many such analogies can be seen in the lives of the early disciples as they attempted to identify with the people they were seeking to reach with the gospel.

SHAMAN AS AN ANALOGY FOR THE CHRISTIAN WORKER

When we speak of the shaman as an analogy for the Christian worker, the biblical pattern must be kept in mind. The Holy Spirit must guide in finding one's status and role in society. It is obvious that the Christian worker should not be perceived as a purveyor of spirit powers like the shaman. But, it is permissible for the Christian worker to be seen as one who is superior to the shaman in having direct contact with the supernatural, blessing, and spiritual power.

In the case study of Oom, the shaman as midwife guided the woman through delivery of her baby. In this ministration, the shaman acts to allay the natural fear of the unknown that is common to most people. The transition of a new life in childbirth is very crucial for the Sundanese. They believe, particularly, that every time one crosses a boundary, one needs special help with the supernatural. The shaman is perceived as having this kind of power. For many Christians, the evangelist or pastor also has this contact with the supernatural.

The key to serving the people is to establish God's priority and sovereignty as beneficial to the community. The Christian leader must become a functional substitute for the shaman. The Christian religious offices of pastor or evangelist approximately relate to the Muslim religious leader.

But the shaman performs a function different from both of those and that also needs to be filled. Although the shaman may have a secular role, it is not of primary importance to their role as shaman. Like the shaman, the Christian must gain recognition for what he can do for the people in the supernatural realm while guiding them to understand that 'his' power is actually Christ in him.

SHAMAN AS AN ANALOGY FOR THE TENTMAKER

Of particular importance to the expatriate Christian who serves in an incarnational role as a layman in other lands, the shaman is an analogy for life. The 'tentmaker' does not work in the way that a religious leader or missionary does. Thus, he (or she, because the shaman can be either a man or a woman) has no status or role that is clearly defined in the society, either in the church or in the community. If the expatriate Christian seeks to be perceived and accepted as a messenger of God, he or she needs to establish an identity in the community.

The primary relationship between the expatriate Christian and the community depends on the exchange that takes place between them. As we saw in the discussion on the shaman, the key to what he does is the reciprocity of power relations between the shaman and the people. In the same way the expatriate Christian will receive legitimacy through the exchange that takes place. If he is primarily an English teacher, the exchange will center around that. If being a student or a businessman is the primary relationship, that will structure the way people respond.

On the other hand, if the critical aspect of the 'tentmaker' is perceived as having a social significance in the area of spiritual matters, the people will relate to him in an entirely different way. The key is the reciprocity between the "tentmaker" and the people in the area of spiritual power (*sakti*). In a way similar to the shaman, the 'tentmaker' may work at some secular job. But in his relations to the people, he must convey an attitude that takes into account the people's need of someone who has a relationship with the supernatural, with blessing, and with spiritual power.

This relationship may take the form of the midwife (only suitable to women) who brings the woman through childbirth in a way that maintains balance in nature and in the unseen world. Or he may be a healer who helps people answer the problem of illness and death. Some role like this is necessary if the "tentmaker" is to establish himself in the eyes of the people. Whatever this role is, it must deal with the supernatural, with blessing and with spiritual power and he must relate this power back to God in a biblical worldview.

A STRATEGY FOR RECIPROCITY

This study has shown that the shaman has an ascribed status because of the reciprocity of power relations between the shaman and the people. In a strategy for the 'tentmaker' among the Sundanese, three things are critical. He must exhibit influence with the supernatural, convey some kind of blessing (*selamat*), and manifest evidence of spiritual power (*sakti*). Without these, one can hardly expect to be accepted as a spiritual leader.

The first thing one can say about such a strategy is that it cannot be embarked on lightly. In order to begin the investigation that will lead to some particular role analogous to the shaman, the 'tentmaker' must have extensive knowledge and understanding of the Sundanese culture. Minimally, this means sufficient language skills and cultural adaptation.

When a person has an idea of how to perform what he feels God will have him do in the society, he needs to begin to promote himself as available to those who would like to relate to him. Like the shaman, legitimacy comes when the people perceive that one has the spiritual power to help them. Thus, one is cast fully on the power of the Holy Spirit to undertake in supernatural ways. As people are 'blessed' by the activities of the 'tentmaker', they will respond more and more to his ministry.

Specific areas of ministry may include those of the healer, of midwifery, and of the exorcism of demonic spirits. It may cover the conveying of blessing at child naming ceremonies, at weddings, at funerals, and at other propitious times such as plantings, housewarmings and the like. At these times the 'tentmaker' can share Christ as the One who ushers in the Kingdom of God into the life of everyone who receives him. Through his function, the 'tentmaker' is acknowledged as a spiritual leader. Through his testimony, Jesus is seen as the "power of God for salvation to every one who has faith..." (Rom. 1:16).

As one is establishing what one's ministry is in regards to the supernatural, another basic question concerns where one got the training to perform in this arena. Study at a Christian institution is what religious leaders do. Spiritual guides, on the other hand, are trained by personal teachers. It may be one's father or mother. It may be a good friend. In the case of the expatriate, the people will not know the teacher. But it is important to describe this person in ways analogous to the teachers of the shaman. Spiritual knowledge is of value when it is passed from a person who has been proved to another who has been chosen.

CONCLUSION

This study of the shaman's role in the social organization of the Sundanese world illustrates the importance of spiritual leaders who are not part of a formal religious structure. As a unique spiritual guide, the shaman is an important model for the Christian who is not a formal institutionalized leader. By utilizing the analogy of the shaman, it may be possible for many 'laymen', including some expatriate Christians, to be acknowledged as people who can 'get things done' in the Sundanese spiritual world. It is an analogy that needs to be pursued.

R. Dixon, 1989

REFERENCES CITED

Adams, R.N. (1975). *Energy and Structure: A Theory of Social Power.* Austin: University of Texas Press.

Anderson, B. (1972). "The Idea of Power in Javanese Culture." In C. Holt (Ed.), *Culture and Politics in Indonesia.* (pp.1-69). Ithaca: Cornell University Press.

Atkinson, J. M. (1987). "The Effectiveness of Shamans in an Indonesian Ritual." *American Anthropologist, 89*(2), 342-355.

Bailey, C. (1976). *Broker, Mediator, Patron, and Kinsman: An Historical Analysis of Key Leadership Roles in a Rural Malaysian District.* Papers in International Studies, Southeast Asia Series No. 38. Athens, OH: Ohio University Center for International Studies, Southeast Asia Program.

Guillot, C. (1985). *Kiai Sadrach: Riwayat Kristenisasi di Jawa* [Kiai Sadrach: The Story of the Christianization of Java]. Jakarta: PT Grafiti Press.

Jackson, K.D. (1978). "The Political Implications of Structure and Culture in Indonesia." In K.D. Jackson & L. W. Pye (Eds.), *Political Power and Communications in Indonesia* (pp.23-42). Berkeley: University of California Press.

Koentjaraningrat, R. M. (1957). *A Preliminary Description of the Javanese Kinship System.* Yale University, Southeast Asia Studies, Cultural Report Series.

Laksono, P.M. (1986). *Tradition in Javanese Social Structure Kingdom and Countryside: Changes in the Javanese Conceptual Model* (E. G. Koentjoro, Trans.). Jogjakarta: Gadjah Mada University Press.

Lingenfelter, S.G. (1975). *Yap: Political Leadership and Cultural Change in an Island Society.* Honolulu: University Press of Hawaii.

Palmer, A.W. (1967). "Situraja: A Village in Highland Priangan." In Koentjaraningrat (Ed.), *Villages in Indonesia* (pp. 299-325). Ithaca: Cornell University Press.

Redfield, R. (1969). *The Little Community and Peasant Society and Culture.* Chicago: The University of Chicago Press.

Rienks, A.S. & Iskandar, P. (1988). "Shamans and Cadres in Rural Java." In Dove, M.R. (Ed.), *The Real and Imagined Role of Culture in Development: Case Studies from Indonesia* (pp.62-86). Honolulu: University of Hawaii Press.

Rikin, W. M. (1983). *Ngabersihan Peranan Pola Hidup Masyarakat Sunda* [Circumcision, the model of life for the Sundanese people]. Unpublished manuscript rewritten from Rikin, W. M. (1973). *Ngabersihan als Knoop in de Tali Paranti.* Meppel: Ramco Offset.

Turner, V.W. (1989). "Religious Specialists." In A.C. Lehmann & J.E. Myers, *Magic, Witchcraft, and Religion: An Anthropological Study of the Supernatural* (pp.85-91). Mountain View, CA: Mayfield Publishing Company.

Von Furer-Haimendorf, C. (1989). "Priests." In A.C. Lehmann & J.E. Myers, *Magic, Witchcraft, and Religion: An Anthropological Study of the Supernatural* (pp.93-97). Mountain View, CA: Mayfield Publishing Company.

APPENDIX 8 - AN EXAMPLE OF A BIBLICALLY BASED PHILOSOPHY OF MINISTRY

A Process-Relational approach to ministry among a UPG

Introduction: This philosophy of ministry is developed for an unreached people whose social organization is oriented to a communal (holistic) model in contrast to a normal western individualistic model.

Each principle of a philosophy of ministry has 3 parts:
1) Biblical presupposition - these relate both to the Bible and the culture
2) Biblical basis   - Scriptural foundation for action
3) Biblical practices   - examples given here: these should be spelled out in detail

1. Presupposition : Salvation is through Jesus Christ
   Basis   : Acts 4:12
   Practices   : Teaching and preaching Jesus as Lord, Savior, Son of God, a person of unity in trinity; (all are foreign concepts to UPGs)
                    Catechism, evangelism, & all teaching give a biblical worldview

2. Presupposition : Bible is basis for authority & practice
   Basis   : 2 Tim. 3:16
   Practices   : goal is to shift local world view to biblical WV through teaching, preaching, Bible studies, training programs,

etc. that deal with theological issues such as: who is God?; what does he say in his word?; what does that mean for us?; ethical issues: lying, cheating, stealing, & other specific cultural sins & faults

3. Presupposition : Dependence on the Holy Spirit
   Basis   : John 14: 13-14
   Practices   : teaching/preaching/modeling fellowship with God, personal holiness, commitment to family prayer, Family Altar, family time, daily Bible reading, Quiet Time, etc.

4. Presupposition : Proclamation of a biblical gospel (not a western/ American gospel)
   Basis   : Acts 2:38-39
   Practices   : develop biblical content for teaching & preaching, use teaching/ learning models of focus group

5. Presupposition : Church related
   Basis   : Col. 1:24-27
   Practices   : expats supervised by national Christian leaders, ministry integrated into national & international Christian community; Corporate discipling & nurturing cell group model, lay training, interdenominational retreats, Bible Schools

6. Presupposition : Spiritual gifts and fruit are in the Church
   Basis   : 1 Corinthians 12
   Practices   : discipling of all believers, everyone nurtured in a cell group, all are given lay training for evangelism and other ministry

7. Presupposition : Planting contextual churches
   Basis   : Acts 20:17-35
   Practices   : understanding patronage model, corporate, whole person; discernment in use of spiritual life belief systems, & Islamic models, local language & cultural forms

8. Presupposition : Focusing on unreached people group

Basis   : John 10:16

Practices   : learn evangelism/cp models from non-focus group as well as focus group, individual preparation to penetrate culture, language, customs, leadership models, spiritual questions & biblical answers

9. Presupposition : Training focus group leadership

Basis   : 2 Tim. 2:2

Practices   : mentoring not managing, expats should not dominate, comprehensive training system for leadership: lay leaders, evangelism/pastoral seminars, Bible school, Cross-Cultural Training, consultant services

10. Presupposition : Use of indigenous methods

Basis   : 1 Cor. 9:19-23

Practices   : biblical models of evangelism/cp, non-confrontational but aggressive, servant, whole person, integrative, answering spiritual questions of focus group, concern for felt needs

11. Presupposition : Cultural transformation under authority of Scripture

Basis   : Acts 17:30-31

Practices   : whole person oriented, corporate evangelism/cp, nurturing family & community as well as individual, affirming God given cultural forms Community development. includes: job training, social services, education, health, etc.

12. Presupposition : Partnership/servant relationships

Basis   : Luke 22:25-27

Practices   : short term agreements, turn-over points, work with evangelism/cp teams under church leadership, encouraging, training, facilitating indigenous workers, live simple life style

13. Presupposition : Finances channeled through responsible churches & organizations

Basis   : 2 Cor. 8:16-24

Practices   : make financial agreements with accountability structures, designated & non-designated funds, -indigenous churches & organizations pay nationals, -expat organization does not hire evangelists or give money to individuals

14. Presupposition : Impart vision for UPG ministry to non-UPG churches
    Basis   : Mat. 28:19-20
    Practices   : UPG Awareness Seminars, recruiting multi-ethnic teams, developing prayer & financial support, empower believers to evangelize through cultural forms (e.g., the ritual meal common to so many religions)

Conclusion: 1. The Presuppositions should apply to all ministries
2. Scriptural bases should be consistent with one another
3. Need more detail on Practices (vary with each ministry). They should be recorded on paper in as much detail as possible.

APPENDIX 9 - BECOMING INVOLVED IN A LOCAL CHURCH IN INDONESIA

1. Basically most churches are doctrinally orthodox but not necessarily following their doctrine spiritually.
2. Pray for leading to the right church where you can learn and which may sponsor your focus group ministry; have faith the Lord will guide.
3. Someone has suggested a rotating attendance to 3-4 churches to see if one is indicated; if not, create another rotation. Attendance may need to be 8-10 times.
4. When you decide on a church, attend all kinds of functions they hold and try to fit in with the church's culture. The most difficult part is going often enough to become known.
5. The only effective way to influence the church is to be recognized as a spiritual leader. Thus, it is imperative to dress and conduct yourself as their spiritual leaders do (e.g., carry Bible, come on time, be able to pray, etc.)
6. Draw close to the pastor and members of the Church Board. Remember that relationships are the key to all leadership. The pastor is key in the Pentecostal church & the church board is equal to the pastor in the Protestant church.
7. Don't come in as a know-it-all. Let them discover your gifts. The church will <u>assign</u> you a status and role. You may not be able to <u>achieve</u> any status with them because they will <u>assign</u> it. But you may negotiate the one they <u>assign</u> you.
8. Do not get involved in doctrinal or cultural controversies until you are a recognized authority by that church. Even then you must understand why it has arisen; usually it is personality problems. Factions will try to enlist your support for their position.

9. Avoid all gossip and church controversies as they are always about personalities and power and you will be used as a pawn by one or both sides. You would be amazed if you realized how little you know about what is going on.

10. Slowly begin to advocate the work of your focus group. It is not good to tip your hand too soon. When the leadership is favorable, you might begin a prayer meeting, or other ministry.

11. It is best if your spiritual partners in your focus group are members of the church that you are attending (which you are praying will sponsor your focus group ministry). People are suspicious of members of other churches coming in, particularly when cp is being done.

OTHER SUGGESTIONS (from a missionary colleague)

1. It is probably not as effective to try to revive nominal Christians for your focus group work as it is to go into an evangelical church where people are evangelistic.

2. Be aware of the church's demographics ethnically, socially, and economically. Note if the church leadership is local or from another geographical area (or another ethnic group). Also, note where the center of the denomination's administrative authority is located. Ascertain how much autonomy the local leadership has.

3. Check on the local reputation of the church.

4. The word "charismatic" has a different meaning in many churches.

5. Do not expect to be spiritually fed by the church.

APPENDIX 10 - MAJOR PROBLEMS IN SUNDANESE EVANGELISM AND CHURCH PLANTING

Purpose : This report seeks to outline some aspects of the major problems of interest to the foreign (expatriate) worker who comes to Sundanese ministry from another country.

Many of these problems may be typical of UPG work in other countries.

1. **Lack of Workers** (including the problem of Integration of Foreign Personnel) Romans 10:14- *How are they to believe in him of whom they have never heard?*

    a. Historically, never more than 15 missionaries (couples) were in West Java even when the Dutch mission was strong in the early 20th century. At times there were 40-50 Indonesians working with them.

    b. 1940-1985- There were not more than 8-10 Indonesians and 2-3 missionaries (couples) in full time Sundanese evangelism; 20-30 (?) other Indonesians were involved part time.

    c. 1988- About 15 Indonesian couples and a few single people are active in full time Sundanese work. About 10 expatriate couples are committed though most are new, studying language and doing some secular job as well. (see g.)

    d. There is a lack of mission concern among the churches for Sundanese evangelism compounded with the problem of resentment of Muslims by Christians. It is difficult for a Sundanese worker to gain spiritual or financial support from the non-Sundanese churches because of the prejudice of Christians towards Muslims.

e. Foreign missions have also traditionally avoided Sundanese work. From WWII until 1980 no organized mission made a lasting commitment to evangelism and church planting among Sundanese.

f. Poor local/foreign organizational ties- The lack of both local and foreign missions has resulted in a paucity of organizational ties. It is difficult for both local and foreign groups who want to do Sundanese work to know who one another is.

g. Besides the lack of communication, the new category of foreign worker causes problems in integration. The Indonesian Church is used to the "missionary" category but not the lay worker (of whom we sometimes refer as "tentmaker"). Understanding must be developed as to what this category is and how it will be integrated into the church.

h. This lack of integration is compounded by the small number of Indonesian evangelists who are ready to team with foreigners. The local Sundanese worker is critical to the success of a foreign "tentmaker." The proliferation of foreign personnel without teaming them with indigenous Sundanese or other Indonesian workers is not going to establish Sundanese churches.

2. **No Contextualized Model** Sundanese Church-
1 Corinthians 9:22 - *I have become all things to all people, that by all means I might save some.*

a. The West Java Protestant Church which is heir of Dutch mission policy is a traditional Dutch Reformed Church. This church has few forms or meanings which are Sundanese. In only 4 congregations (out of 40) is any Sundanese language used in worship.

b. Because of this, there is not a clear understanding of a theology of evangelism or a theology of the church for the Sundanese. Few Christian ceremonies have been developed which have form or meaning that is characteristically Sundanese.

c. There have been recent developments of rudiments of a contextualized Sundanese church. Only in the last few years have 4-5 beginnings of congregations evolved which struggle with the meaning of a church for the Sundanese using methods of evangelism and church planting which are in the context of the Sundanese culture.

d. The purpose of these initiatives is to model genuine Sundanese ministries and a Sundanese church. They include the use of Sundanese language, music and other arts. Forms of worship, preaching, and teaching are being oriented to the Sundanese context. Other positive Sundanese cultural patterns of leadership, community organization (church government and discipline) and religious and philosophical thought need to be utilized.

e. There must be a theology of evangelism and a theology of the church which is Sundanese in context.

f. Most of the leading proponents of a contextualized Sundanese church are westerners. The national church leaders are just beginning to get excited about this.

3. **Lack of Identity** of Sundanese Christianity-
1 John 3:2 - Beloved, we are God's children now,....

a. Because the Sundanese, like all people, seek to maintain their identity, becoming a Christian means giving up a basic psychological need.

b. Besides having only a few contextualized Sundanese churches, West Java also does not have any church with a basic Sundanese character that is well known. There are a few isolated congregations with the majority of members speaking Sundanese but these are not sufficiently known to project an "identity" to the Sundanese.

c. There is no significant congregation with a national identity ministering to Sundanese. A few non-Sundanese churches have begun to struggle with this problem to create some profile.

d. Besides not having any national identity, Sundanese work has only a few Sundanese leaders who have regional secular recognition.

e. There are very few church buildings for Sundanese Christians which results in a poor image in the eyes of mosque-minded Muslims. It is perceived as a lack of identity (thus a lack of blessing).

f. There are few Sundanese Christians from the middle and upper leadership levels of Sundanese society.

g. There are practically no Sundanese university students who are active believers.

h. Most Muslim converts to Christ are from the lower economic levels.

i. Muslim Sundanese commonly reiterate that no true Sundanese becomes a Christian.

4. **Leaving One's People** to Become Christian-

Hebrews 11:8 - By faith Abraham obeyed when he was called to go out to a place that he was to receive as an inheritance. And he went out, not knowing where he was going.

    a. As a result of the Dutch mission practices, Sundanese were forced to leave the cultural patterns of their own people in order to become Christian.

    b. These converts were called "black Dutch" and Christianity was known as the "Dutch religion."

    c. Even today, in most cases, Sundanese who become Christian are physically as well as psychologically ostracized from their communities through social, emotional, economic and other forms of pressure (persecution).

    d. The Muslim/animist Sundanese culture forces them out and the Christian non-Sundanese cultures draw them out. Thus there is a two-fold pressure on converts.

    e. A true Sundanese church (Sundanese Christianity) and an understanding of Sundanese society is necessary to find the keys by which a Sundanese can be leaven in his family and community.

5. **Leadership-**

Ephesians 4:11 - And he gave the apostles, the prophets, the evangelists, the pastors and teachers, to equip the saints....

The difficulty of the call and preparation of church leadership among the Sundanese is probably the central problem of all present (1988) ministry. Even when workers are available it is difficult to train them in leadership.

    a. Sundanese converts have rarely come from leadership levels of society.

    b. Because they are feudal in mentality, there has been limited success in cultivating leadership potential in mature converts.

    c. Younger converts, by virtue of their age and lack of standing in the community, have difficulty being accepted as leaders.

    d. Sundanese who have had the strength of character to become leaders usually have not been willing to endure the persecution of the community. Instead, they have moved to the city and integrated into other ethic congregations where they have lost their Sundanese characteristics.

e. Other converts who have been trained as leaders in their localities have not survived various temptations which have destroyed their moral credibility.

f. Some converts who have been trained as leaders have been enticed away by other churches who offer them money and security if they will transfer.

6. **Sheep Stealing**/Transfer & Shepherd Stealing/Transfer-

Acts 20:28 - *Pay careful attention to yourselves and to all the flock, in which the Holy Spirit has made you overseers,....*

By virtue of the fact most Sundanese converts are poor, there is a tendency for them to be unstable in their Christian communities.

a. It is very common for members to transfer from one congregation to another depending on where they can get the greatest material benefits. An estimated 75% (author's estimate) of those won in the past twenty years have been in more than one congregation or in a congregation that has been under more than one organization.

b. Because most non-Sundanese congregations and pastors do not understand Sundanese people or Sundanese church ministry, many of them are deceived into interfering in other's ministries. Sometimes they are not aware that the Sundanese they are receiving have an official connection with another church.

c. Many non-Sundanese church leaders do not value the work of para-church organizations and will knowingly receive Sundanese who are under a ministry, thus disrupting the original church planting strategy.

d. Sundanese who experience real or imagined slights or insults will frequently switch congregations. Also, Sundanese who are disciplined by a church will frequently move to another congregation which will not be concerned with those disciplinary measures.

e. Because Sundanese ministry is so difficult, there are churches who will bribe gifted Sundanese away from other churches and organizations. This is true of the leadership level also and can be termed "shepherd stealing."

f. There are few leaders in Sundanese work who have not been in more than one church or organization. This illustrates the difficulty of continuity in the Sundanese church planting strategy.

7. Lack of Bible and Christian Literature-

1 Thessalonians 1:8 - *For not only has the word of the Lord sounded forth from you in Macedonia and Achaia, but your faith in God has gone forth everywhere,....* The importance of the written Word of God to a literate society like the Sundanese can hardly be overestimated. The fact that there is no complete Bible in print simply reinforces for them the belief (from Islamic propaganda) that the gospel is not for them nor are Christians interested in having them follow Jesus in a meaningful way.

a. The entire Bible was first printed in 1891. A new translation was published in January, 1991.

b. The New Testament was revised in 1978 and is in print.

c. There are very few tracts and books in Sundanese- Estimate: 30 tracts (few in print); 10 booklets (5 in print); 3 books available.

d. A hymnbook of translations in print (West Java Protestant Church). In 2010, there are many original Christian Sundanese songs circulating but only a few small hymnbooks containing them.

e. No Christian newspapers, but two Christian magazines in Sundanese.

f. No Pen Pal clubs, newspaper evangelism, theater evangelism or the like being done.

8. Lack of Multi-Media Programming-

2 Corinthians 8:15 - As it is written, *Whoever gathered much had nothing left over, and whoever gathered little had no lack.*
In a society where the country has a nation wide satellite and microwave system so that television is available in every village area, the lack of Christian mass media in the Sundanese language speaks of a lack of concern on the part of Christians to share the gospel.

a. In the 1980s, there were 400 one-half hour Sundanese broadcasts by FEBC via short wave from Saipan.

b. 4-5 local stations also played these programs on medium wave (AM frequency).

c. Other Sundanese radio programs were produced in Jakarta.

d. Besides the radio programs on cassette, many other cassettes of Sundanese Christian programs have been produced since then by various organizations.

e. In the 1970s, two Christian films were processed with a Sundanese sound track. Not until the 1990s was the Jesus film recorded in Sundanese.

f. 30 filmstrip stories of Jesus have been recorded in Sundanese language.

g. Slide programs were never done in Sundanese.

h. 5 flashcard Bible stories have been recorded in Sundanese.

i. Since the 1990s Christian video programs have been produced for television.

j. Some e-mail and other types of electronic communication is being conducted using computer technology.

9. **Lack of Economic Security** for Converts-

Philippians 4:19 - *And my God will supply every need of yours according to his riches in glory in Christ Jesus.*

a. Traditionally, Sundanese economic relationships have been based on a patron/client model. This means that those of lower economic levels look to family or acquaintances in higher income levels to make up their lack.

b. New believers are often persecuted by the threat of job or land loss and thus need to seek new patrons among the Christians. This usually means they ask the evangelist or nearest Christian acquaintance for help. They frequently go the rounds of all their new "brothers and sisters" in Christ looking for financial aid.

c. In West Java, the problem of jobs for new converts has never been adequately solved. For example, there has never been a job agency especially organized for Sundanese and very few businessmen have ever been enlisted to create opportunities for Sundanese.

d. A holistic approach, i.e., being concerned with the total spiritual, social and physical man and woman, while existing in Sundanese ministry, is poorly developed.

R. Dixon, 1988 (revised in 2010)

GENERAL INDEX